I'M HERE!

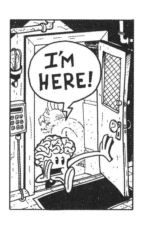

optical allusions

Jay Hosler

Active Synapse Comics
Columbus, OH

Also by Jay Hosler

Clan Apis
The Sandwalk Adventures

Optical Allusions

First Printing

Cover color and design by Troy Cummings

Printed in the United States

ISBN: 978-0-9677255-2-9

Active Synapse
5336 Park Lane Drive
Columbus OH, 43231-4072
FAX: (614) 882-8470
www.activesynapse.com
info@activesynapse.com

For my best friend,
Lisa.
This is the book she has
been waiting for.

To the reader

Optical Allusions is a hybrid of comics and traditional text created to inspire wonder about our amazing eyes. My vision for this book was to use comic book stories to introduce complex biological concepts and then use the text immediately following the story to address those ideas in greater detail. The National Science Foundation funded this work and comments about *Optical Allusions* from students, instructors and general readers can be sent to activesynapse@hotmail.com.

Contents

Chapter One: Toil and Trouble

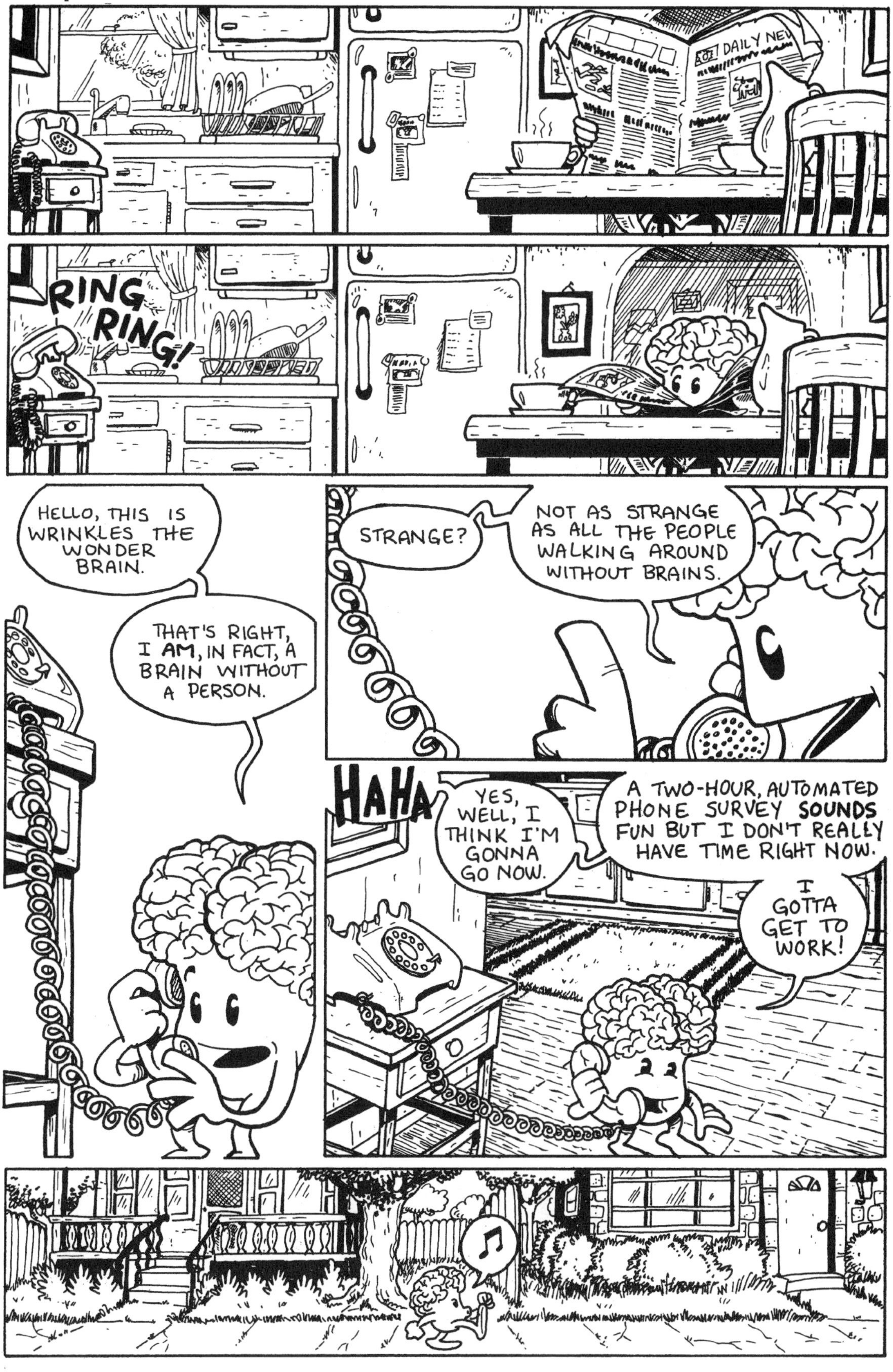
DAILY NEW
RING RING!
HELLO, THIS IS WRINKLES THE WONDER BRAIN.
THAT'S RIGHT, I AM, IN FACT, A BRAIN WITHOUT A PERSON.
STRANGE?
NOT AS STRANGE AS ALL THE PEOPLE WALKING AROUND WITHOUT BRAINS.
HAHA
YES, WELL, I THINK I'M GONNA GO NOW.
A TWO-HOUR, AUTOMATED PHONE SURVEY SOUNDS FUN BUT I DON'T REALLY HAVE TIME RIGHT NOW.
I GOTTA GET TO WORK!
♪

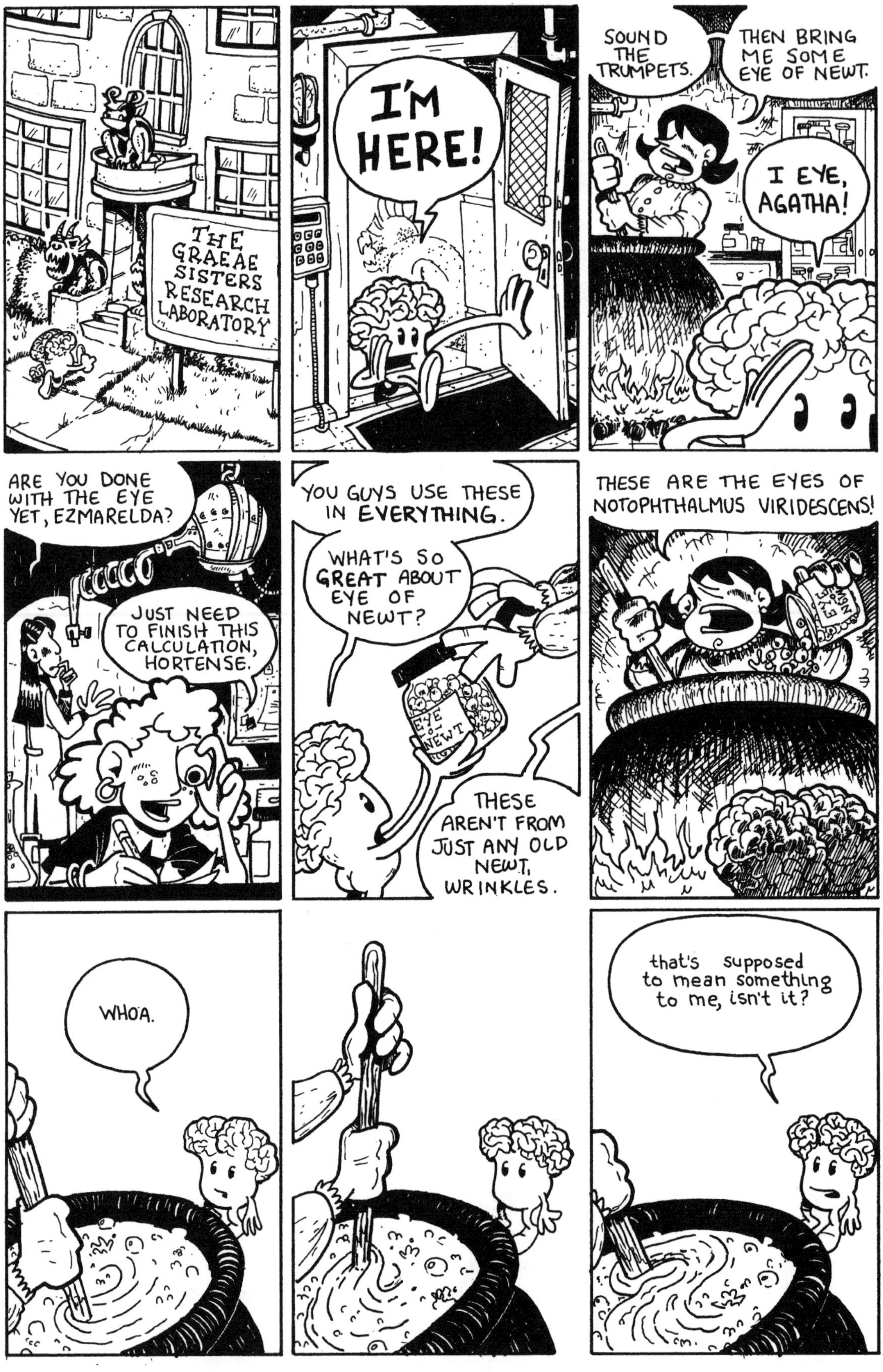
THE GRAEAE SISTERS RESEARCH LABORATORY
I'M HERE!
SOUND THE TRUMPETS.
THEN BRING ME SOME EYE OF NEWT.
I EYE, AGATHA!
ARE YOU DONE WITH THE EYE YET, EZMARELDA?
JUST NEED TO FINISH THIS CALCULATION, HORTENSE.
YOU GUYS USE THESE IN EVERYTHING.
WHAT'S SO GREAT ABOUT EYE OF NEWT?
EYE OF NEWT
THESE AREN'T FROM JUST ANY OLD NEWT, WRINKLES.
THESE ARE THE EYES OF NOTOPHTHALMUS VIRIDESCENS!
WHOA.
that's supposed to mean something to me, isn't it?

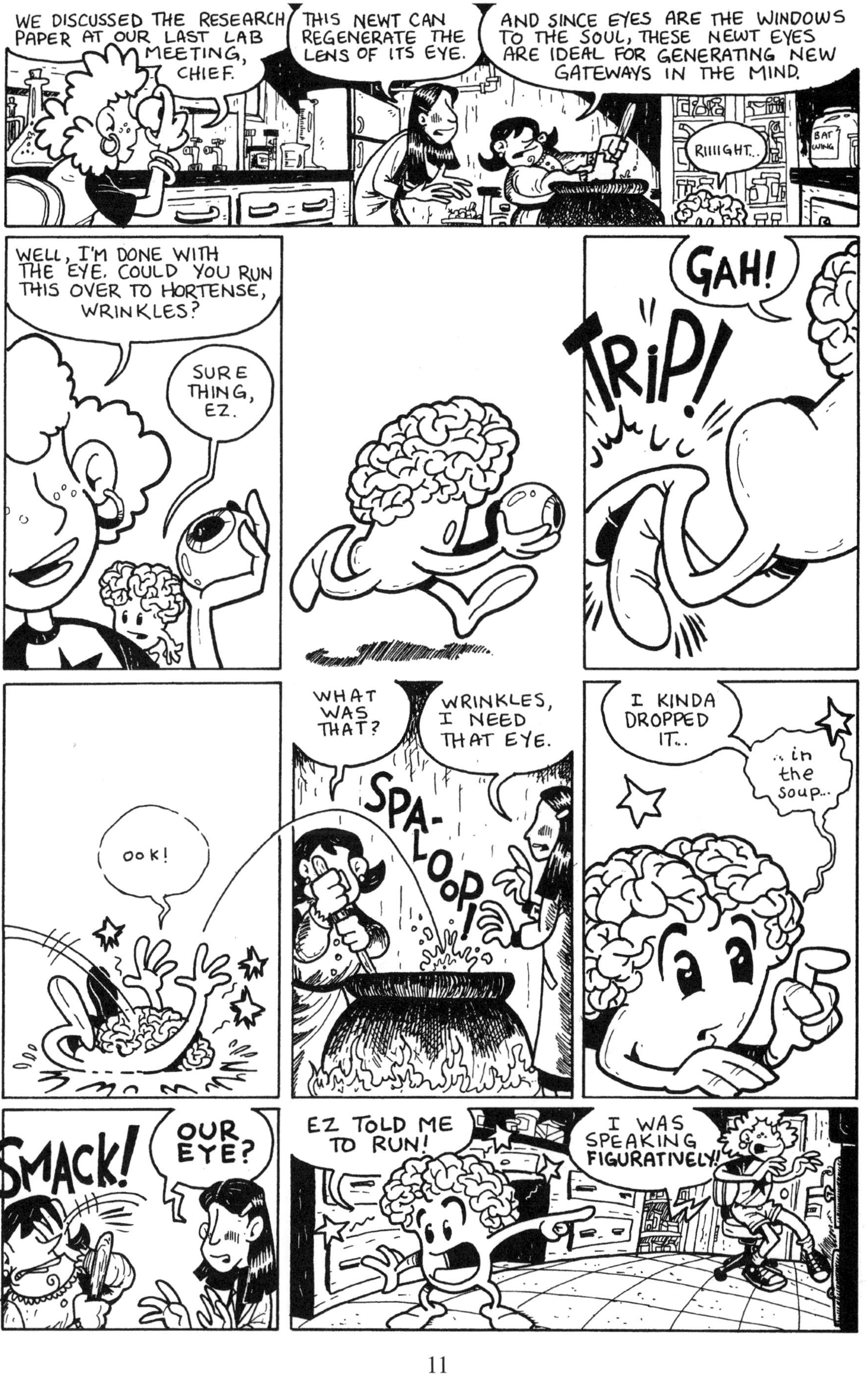
WE DISCUSSED THE RESEARCH PAPER AT OUR LAST LAB MEETING, CHIEF.
THIS NEWT CAN REGENERATE THE LENS OF ITS EYE.
AND SINCE EYES ARE THE WINDOWS TO THE SOUL, THESE NEWT EYES ARE IDEAL FOR GENERATING NEW GATEWAYS IN THE MIND.
RIIIIGHT...
BAT WING
WELL, I'M DONE WITH THE EYE. COULD YOU RUN THIS OVER TO HORTENSE, WRINKLES?
SURE THING, EZ.
GAH!
TRIP!
OOK!
WHAT WAS THAT?
WRINKLES, I NEED THAT EYE.
SPA-LOOP!
I KINDA DROPPED IT...
...in the soup...
SMACK!
OUR EYE?
EZ TOLD ME TO RUN!
I WAS SPEAKING **FIGURATIVELY**!

WHAT'S THE BIG DEAL? JUST REACH IN AND SCOOP IT OUT!
WE CAN'T. THIS IS DISTILLED IMAGINATION!
THE INTERIOR OF THIS POT IS AS EXPANSIVE AS ALL OF HUMAN THOUGHT!
THAT EYE COULD BE ANYWHERE IN SPACE AND TIME....
CAN'T YOU JUST GET THE SPARE?
SPARE? THERE'S NO SPARE!
YOU CAN DISTILL IMAGINATION BUT YOU CAN'T MAKE AN EXTRA MAGIC EYE?
YOU'LL HAVE TO GO IN AND GET IT, SPORT.
ME? I'M JUST THE LAB ASSISTANT!
WELL, WE CERTAINLY CAN'T GO LOOKING FOR OUR EYE WITHOUT OUR EYE, CAN WE?
i guess not...
TAKE THESE NEWT EYES. YOU CAN USE THEM TO OPEN GATEWAYS IN TIME, SPACE AND THOUGHT AS YOU SEARCH.
EYE -o- NEWT
a little lower.
HOW DO THEY WORK?
JUST THINK OF WHERE YOU WANT TO GO AND THEN EAT ONE.
bleagh...
EYE -o- NEWT
AND TAKE THIS, TOO. IT'S MY LATEST INVENTION. I CALL IT THE IMPROBA-BUBBLE.

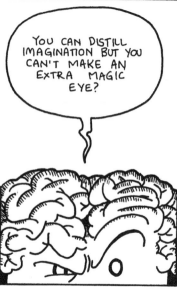

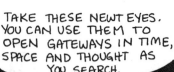

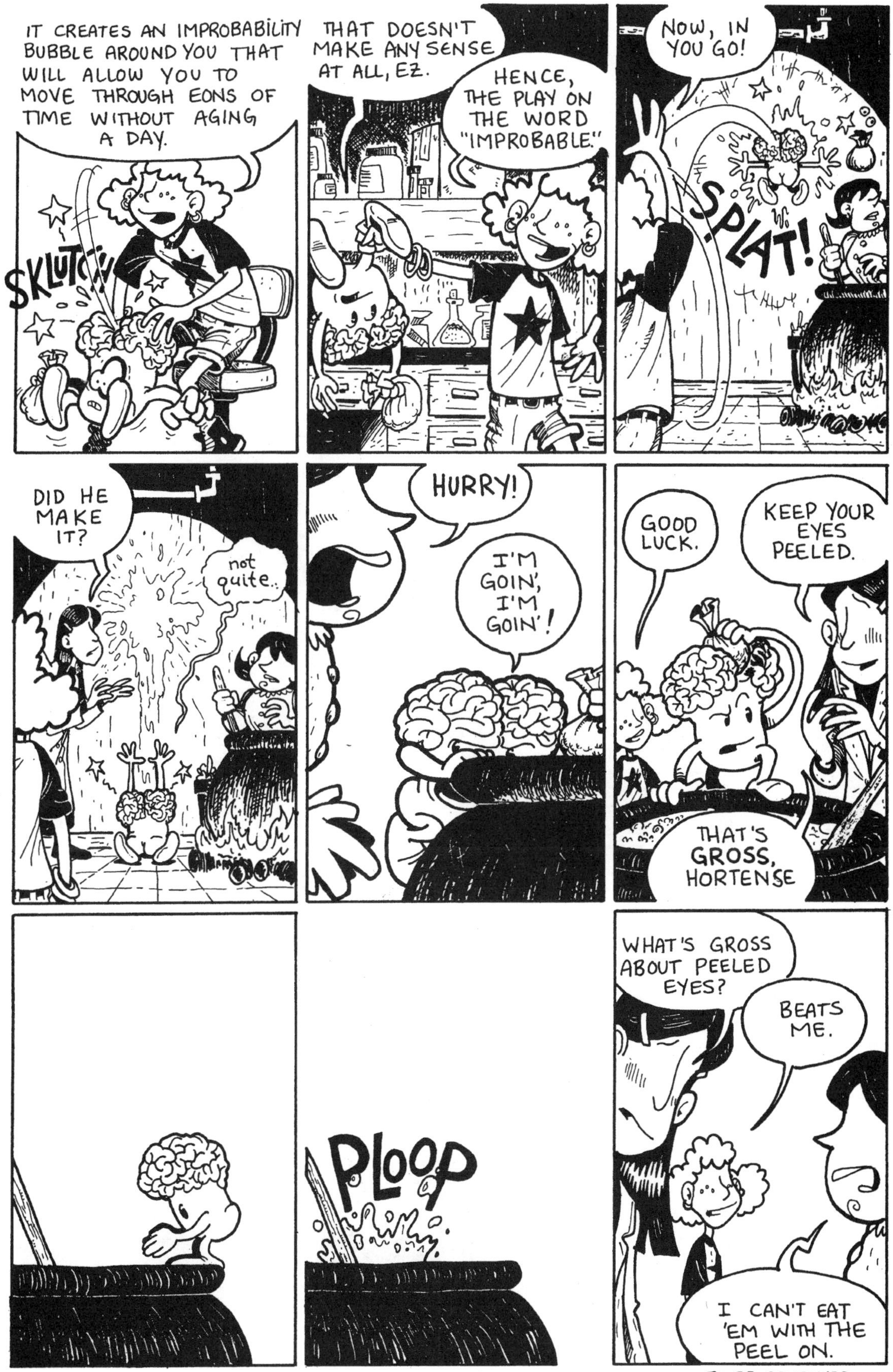
IT CREATES AN IMPROBABILITY BUBBLE AROUND YOU THAT WILL ALLOW YOU TO MOVE THROUGH EONS OF TIME WITHOUT AGING A DAY.
SKLUTCH
THAT DOESN'T MAKE ANY SENSE AT ALL, EZ.
HENCE, THE PLAY ON THE WORD "IMPROBABLE."
NOW, IN YOU GO!
SPLAT!
DID HE MAKE IT?
not quite..
HURRY!
I'M GOIN', I'M GOIN'!
GOOD LUCK.
KEEP YOUR EYES PEELED.
THAT'S GROSS, HORTENSE
PLOOP
WHAT'S GROSS ABOUT PEELED EYES?
BEATS ME.
I CAN'T EAT 'EM WITH THE PEEL ON.

TO BE CONTINUED...

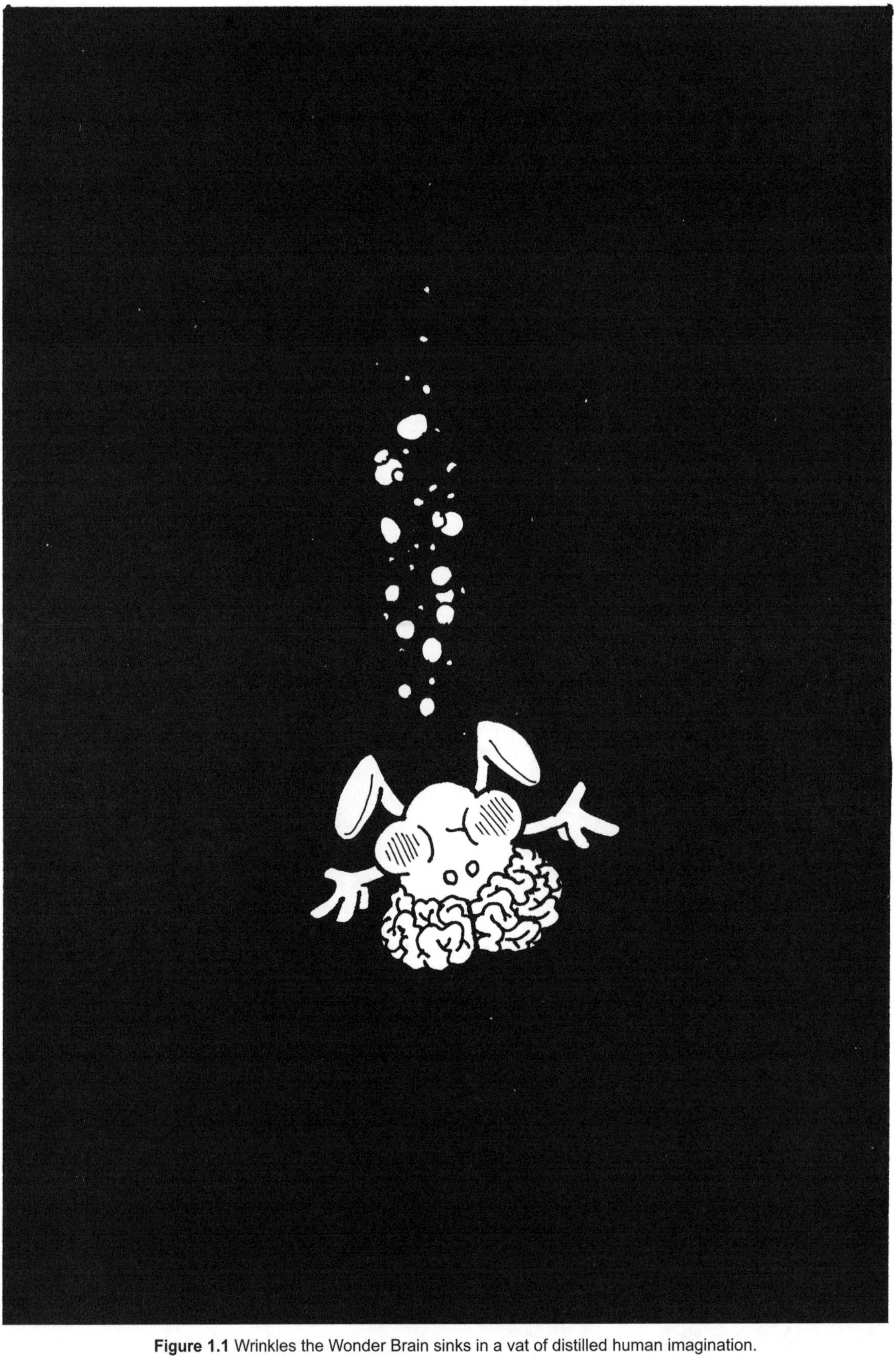

Figure 1.1 Wrinkles the Wonder Brain sinks in a vat of distilled human imagination.

Chapter Two: An Appetite for Evolution

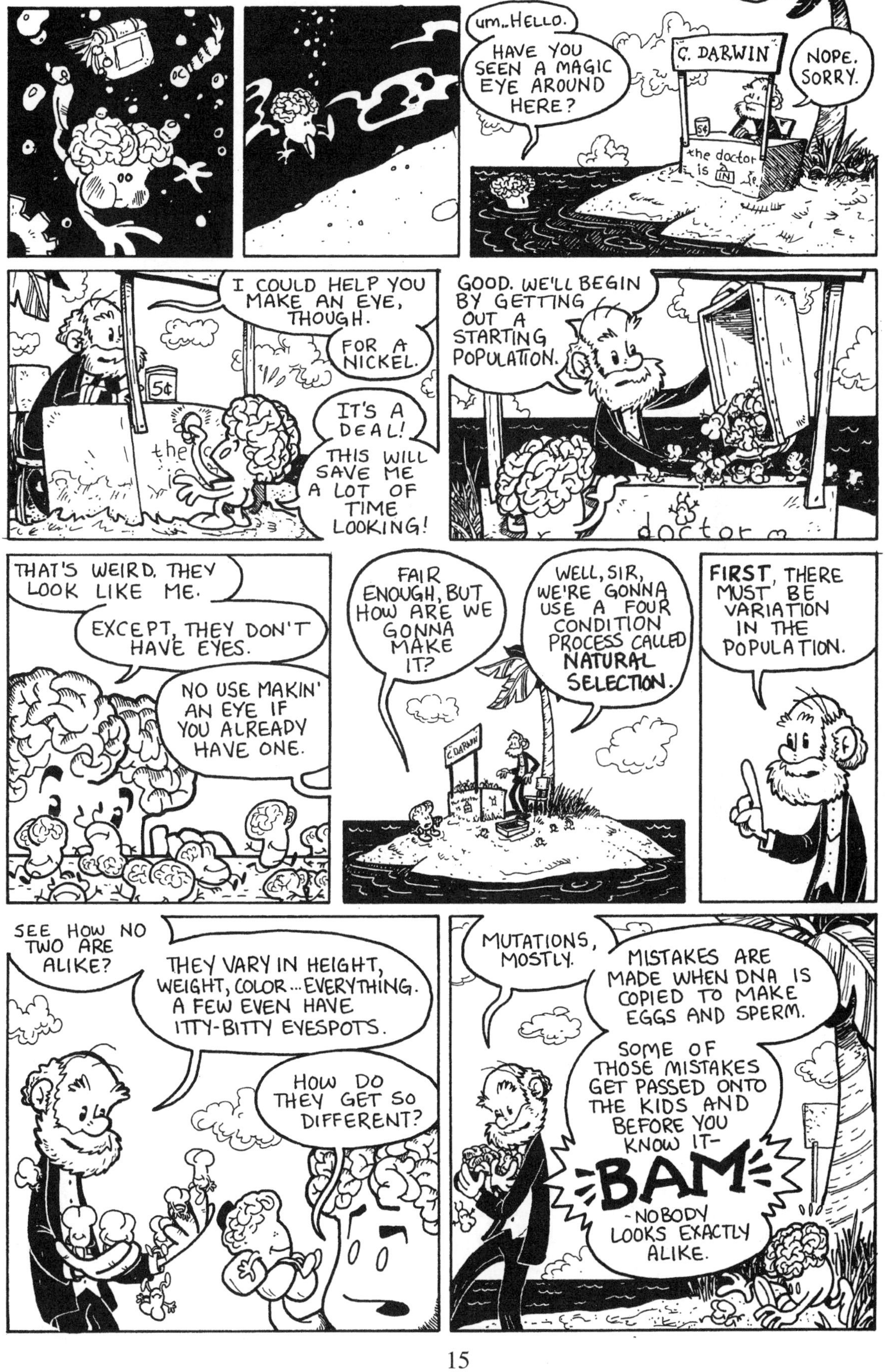
um..HELLO.
HAVE YOU SEEN A MAGIC EYE AROUND HERE?
C. DARWIN
5¢
the doctor is IN
NOPE. SORRY.
I COULD HELP YOU MAKE AN EYE, THOUGH.
FOR A NICKEL.
IT'S A DEAL!
THIS WILL SAVE ME A LOT OF TIME LOOKING!
GOOD. WE'LL BEGIN BY GETTING OUT A STARTING POPULATION.
THAT'S WEIRD. THEY LOOK LIKE ME.
EXCEPT, THEY DON'T HAVE EYES.
NO USE MAKIN' AN EYE IF YOU ALREADY HAVE ONE.
FAIR ENOUGH, BUT HOW ARE WE GONNA MAKE IT?
WELL, SIR, WE'RE GONNA USE A FOUR CONDITION PROCESS CALLED NATURAL SELECTION.
FIRST, THERE MUST BE VARIATION IN THE POPULATION.
SEE HOW NO TWO ARE ALIKE?
THEY VARY IN HEIGHT, WEIGHT, COLOR... EVERYTHING. A FEW EVEN HAVE ITTY-BITTY EYESPOTS.
HOW DO THEY GET SO DIFFERENT?
MUTATIONS, MOSTLY.
MISTAKES ARE MADE WHEN DNA IS COPIED TO MAKE EGGS AND SPERM.
SOME OF THOSE MISTAKES GET PASSED ONTO THE KIDS AND BEFORE YOU KNOW IT-
BAM
-NOBODY LOOKS EXACTLY ALIKE.

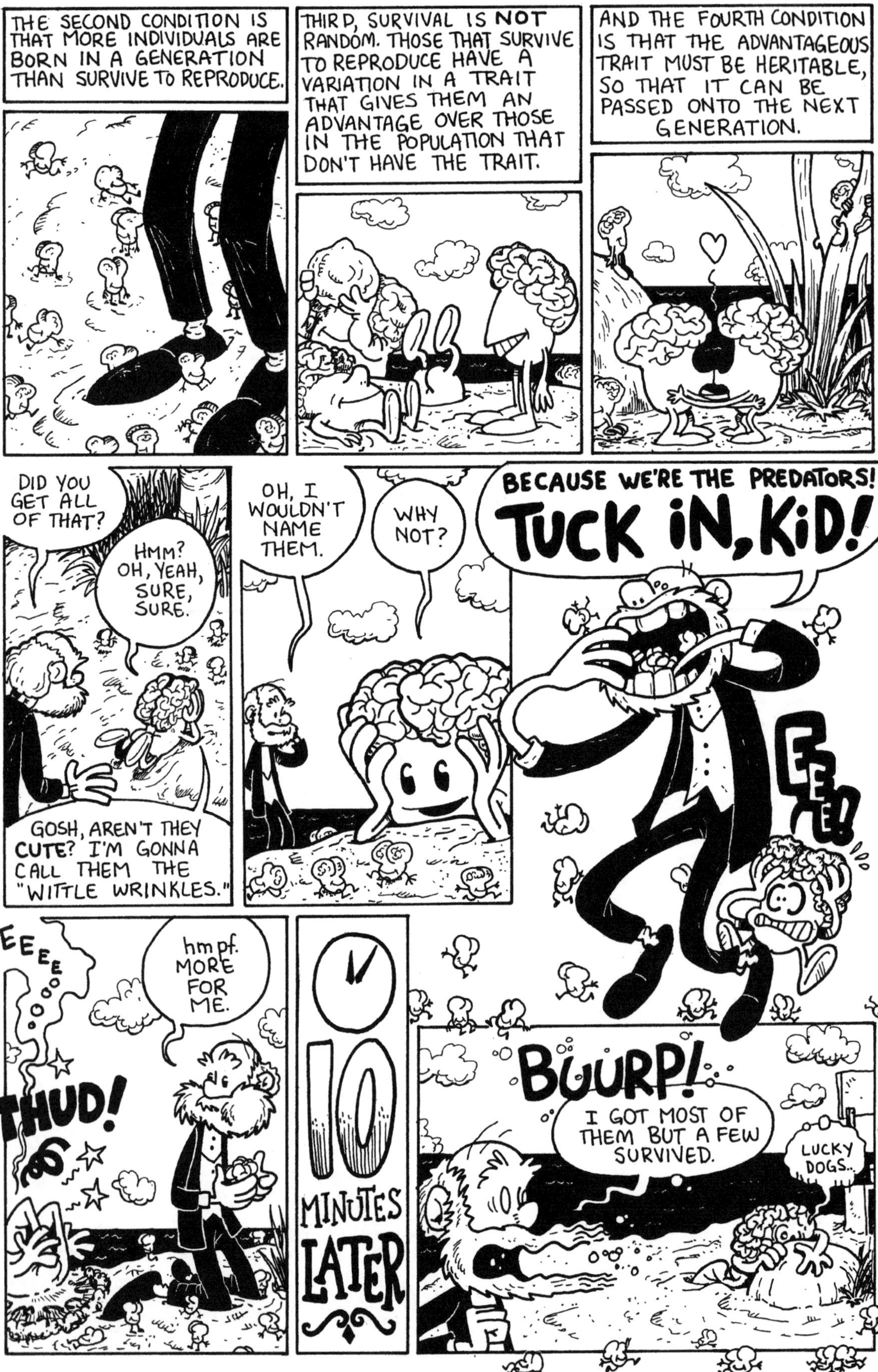
THE SECOND CONDITION IS THAT MORE INDIVIDUALS ARE BORN IN A GENERATION THAN SURVIVE TO REPRODUCE.
THIRD, SURVIVAL IS **NOT** RANDOM. THOSE THAT SURVIVE TO REPRODUCE HAVE A VARIATION IN A TRAIT THAT GIVES THEM AN ADVANTAGE OVER THOSE IN THE POPULATION THAT DON'T HAVE THE TRAIT.
AND THE FOURTH CONDITION IS THAT THE ADVANTAGEOUS TRAIT MUST BE HERITABLE, SO THAT IT CAN BE PASSED ONTO THE NEXT GENERATION.
DID YOU GET ALL OF THAT?
HMM? OH, YEAH, SURE, SURE.
GOSH, AREN'T THEY **CUTE**? I'M GONNA CALL THEM THE "WITTLE WRINKLES."
OH, I WOULDN'T NAME THEM.
WHY NOT?
BECAUSE WE'RE THE PREDATORS! TUCK IN, KID!
EEE!
EEEE
THUD!
hmpf. MORE FOR ME.
10 MINUTES LATER
BUURP!
I GOT MOST OF THEM BUT A FEW SURVIVED.
LUCKY DOGS..

IT MAY HAVE BEEN **LUCK**. OR, THE SURVIVORS MAY HAVE SOMETHING THE OTHERS DIDN'T.

LIKE **WHAT**?

WELL, MOST OF THE SURVIVORS HAVE THOSE EYESPOTS. MAYBE THEY HELPED IN THEIR STRUGGLE TO SURVIVE.

CAN AN EYESPOT FORM AN IMAGE LIKE OUR EYES?

DEAR ME, NO. IT CAN ONLY TELL THEM IF THE LIGHTS ARE ON OR OFF.

PFFT. THEN WHAT **GOOD** IS IT?

WELL, WHEN YOU'RE FIGHTING FOR SURVIVAL, **ANY** VISION IS BETTER THAN **NO** VISION AND ANY IMPROVEMENT, HOWEVER SLIGHT, IS AN ADVANTAGE.

NOW, WE'LL PUT THE SURVIVORS IN A BOX, PLAY A LITTLE SOFT MUSIC AND LET NATURE TAKE ITS COURSE. **RRROWW RROWW!**

YER GIVIN' ME THE WILLIES, SIR.

5¢

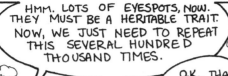

1 YEAR LATER

DID THAT SAY "ONE YEAR LATER?!?"

YEP.

I LIKE THE BEARD.

ACK!

HMM. LOTS OF EYESPOTS, NOW. THEY MUST BE A HERITABLE TRAIT. NOW, WE JUST NEED TO REPEAT THIS SEVERAL HUNDRED THOUSAND TIMES.

O.K., THAT SOUNDS G—.

how many times..?

Dig in!

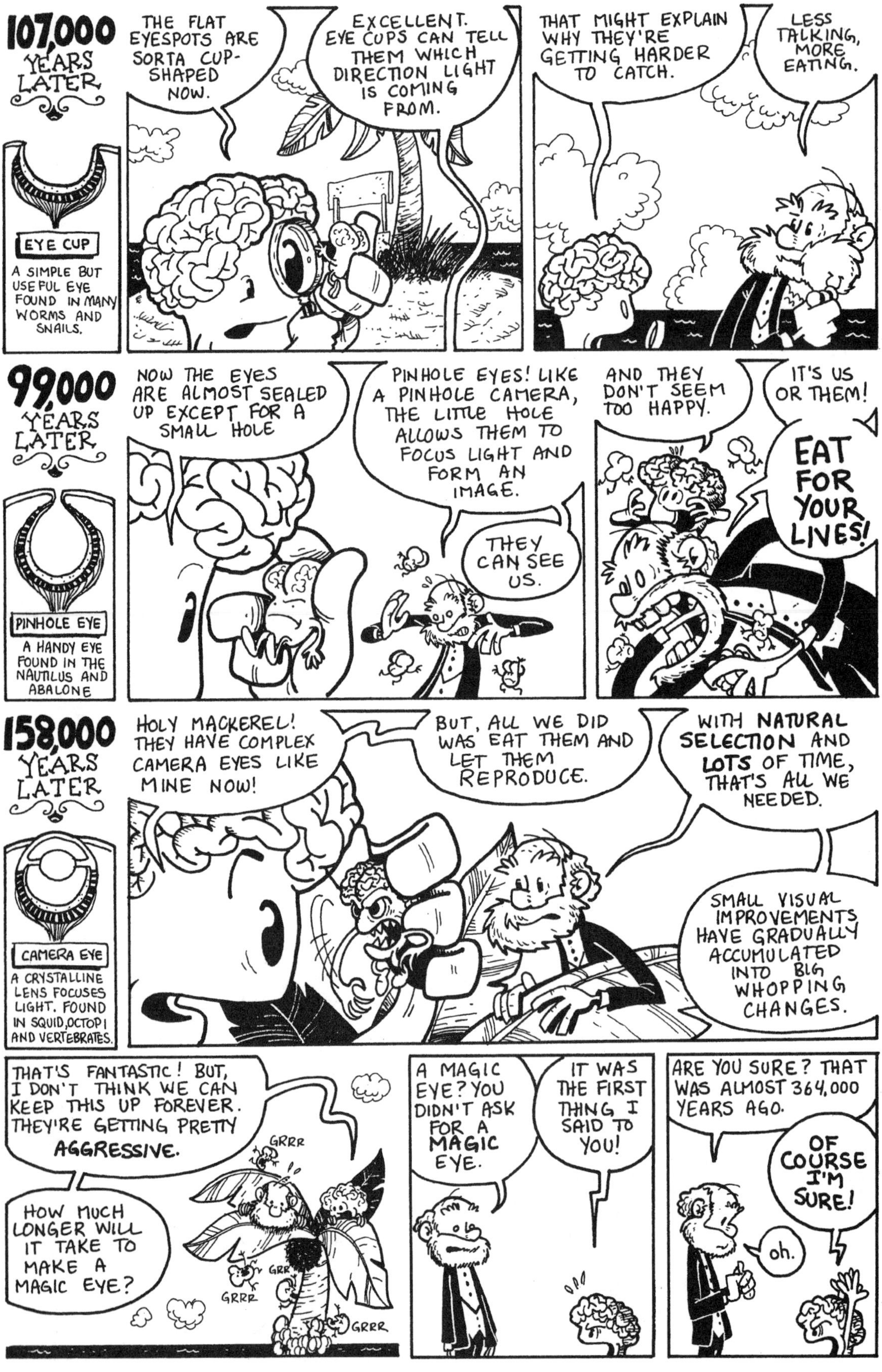
107,000 YEARS LATER
EYE CUP
A SIMPLE BUT USEFUL EYE FOUND IN MANY WORMS AND SNAILS.
THE FLAT EYESPOTS ARE SORTA CUP-SHAPED NOW.
EXCELLENT. EYE CUPS CAN TELL THEM WHICH DIRECTION LIGHT IS COMING FROM.
THAT MIGHT EXPLAIN WHY THEY'RE GETTING HARDER TO CATCH.
LESS TALKING, MORE EATING.
99,000 YEARS LATER
PINHOLE EYE
A HANDY EYE FOUND IN THE NAUTILUS AND ABALONE
NOW THE EYES ARE ALMOST SEALED UP EXCEPT FOR A SMALL HOLE
PINHOLE EYES! LIKE A PINHOLE CAMERA, THE LITTLE HOLE ALLOWS THEM TO FOCUS LIGHT AND FORM AN IMAGE.
THEY CAN SEE US.
AND THEY DON'T SEEM TOO HAPPY.
IT'S US OR THEM!
EAT FOR YOUR LIVES!
158,000 YEARS LATER
CAMERA EYE
A CRYSTALLINE LENS FOCUSES LIGHT. FOUND IN SQUID, OCTOPI AND VERTEBRATES.
HOLY MACKEREL! THEY HAVE COMPLEX CAMERA EYES LIKE MINE NOW!
BUT, ALL WE DID WAS EAT THEM AND LET THEM REPRODUCE.
WITH NATURAL SELECTION AND LOTS OF TIME, THAT'S ALL WE NEEDED.
SMALL VISUAL IMPROVEMENTS HAVE GRADUALLY ACCUMULATED INTO BIG WHOPPING CHANGES.
THAT'S FANTASTIC! BUT, I DON'T THINK WE CAN KEEP THIS UP FOREVER. THEY'RE GETTING PRETTY AGGRESSIVE.
GRRR
HOW MUCH LONGER WILL IT TAKE TO MAKE A MAGIC EYE?
GRR
GRRR
GRRR
A MAGIC EYE? YOU DIDN'T ASK FOR A MAGIC EYE.
IT WAS THE FIRST THING I SAID TO YOU!
ARE YOU SURE? THAT WAS ALMOST 364,000 YEARS AGO.
OF COURSE I'M SURE!
oh.

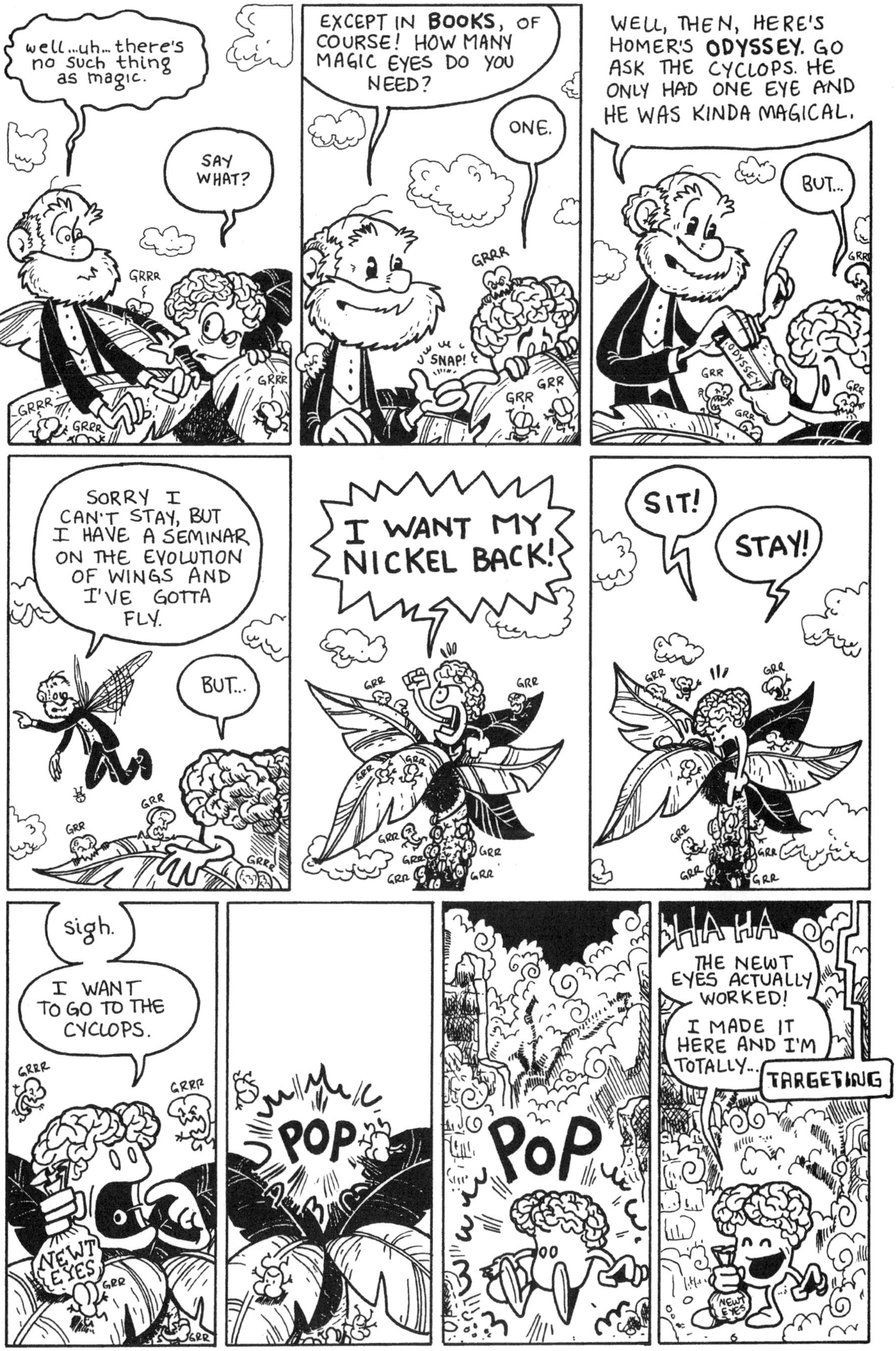
well...uh...there's no such thing as magic.
SAY WHAT?
GRRR
GRRR
GRRR
GRRR
EXCEPT IN BOOKS, OF COURSE! HOW MANY MAGIC EYES DO YOU NEED?
ONE.
SNAP!
GRRR
GRR
GRR
WELL, THEN, HERE'S HOMER'S ODYSSEY. GO ASK THE CYCLOPS. HE ONLY HAD ONE EYE AND HE WAS KINDA MAGICAL.
BUT...
ODYSSEY
GRR
GRR
SORRY I CAN'T STAY, BUT I HAVE A SEMINAR ON THE EVOLUTION OF WINGS AND I'VE GOTTA FLY.
BUT...
GRR
GRR
I WANT MY NICKEL BACK!
GRR
GRR
SIT!
STAY!
GRR
GRR
sigh.
I WANT TO GO TO THE CYCLOPS.
GRRR
GRRR
NEWT EYES
GRR
POP
POP
HA HA
THE NEWT EYES ACTUALLY WORKED!
I MADE IT HERE AND I'M TOTALLY...
TARGETING
NEWT EYES

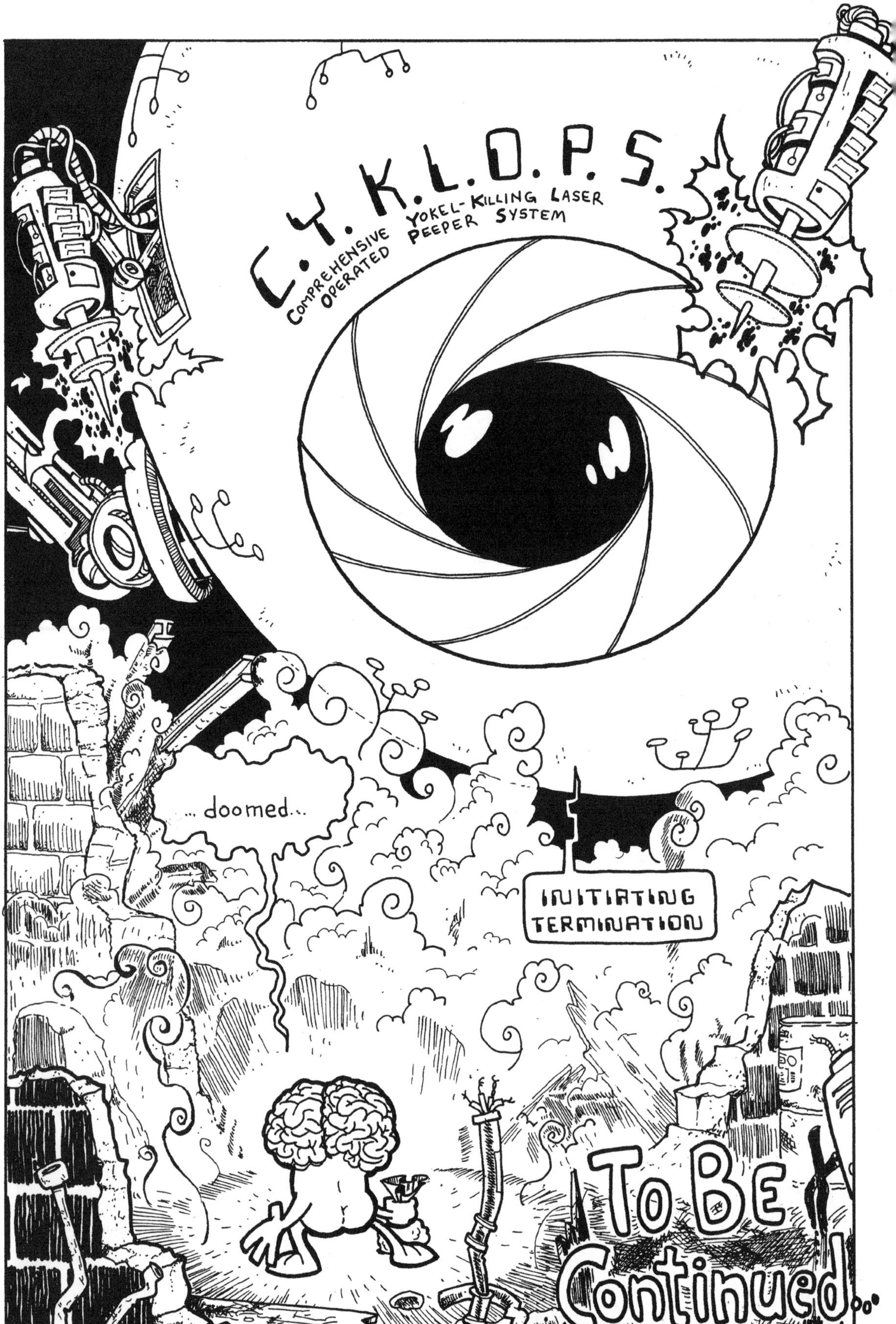
C.Y.K.L.O.P.S.
COMPREHENSIVE YOKEL-KILLING LASER OPERATED PEEPER SYSTEM
... doomed...
INITIATING TERMINATION
To Be Continued...

Evolving Eyes

"I have called this principle, by which each slight variation, if useful, is preserved, by the term Natural Selection"

-Charles Darwin, from *On the Origin of Species*

"How extremely stupid for me not to have thought of that!"

-T. H. Huxley on reading *On the Origin of Species*

Testing Ideas

The ancient Egyptians believed that a dung beetle rolled the sun across the sky everyday. Having **observed** the daily movements of the sun and the activities of a beetle rolling a dung ball, they formulated the **hypothesis** that a giant beetle pushed the sun in a similar fashion. Since they stopped short of systematically testing this idea, it became their belief, not a scientific explanation.

Science requires a few more steps beyond hypothesis formation. The first is performing **experiments** to test the idea. Experiments produce results called **data** that may support or refute a hypothesis. Using a sophisticated telescope and detailed satellite images of the sun would be one way to test whether a giant beetle (presumably wearing oven mitts) is responsible for old Sol's daily migration. To date, astronomers haven't spotted any, and they are now fairly confident that beetles have little to nothing to do with the movement of celestial bodies. Thus, the data collected refute the giant scarab hypothesis.

Systematically testing hypotheses is one of the primary ways in which scientists attempt to describe the natural world. That process assumes that there are natural explanations for the phenomena that we experience. We now explain the movement of stars and planets in terms of gravity, inertia, acceleration, rotation and revolution.

Just as scientists have looked for ways to explain the changes in the heavens, they have also looked for ways to explain changes in life on earth. A number of naturalists before Charles Darwin (including his poet grandfather) had suggested that living things evolved over time. But it was not until Darwin proposed a testable mechanism for evolution that the way we view life on earth was changed forever.

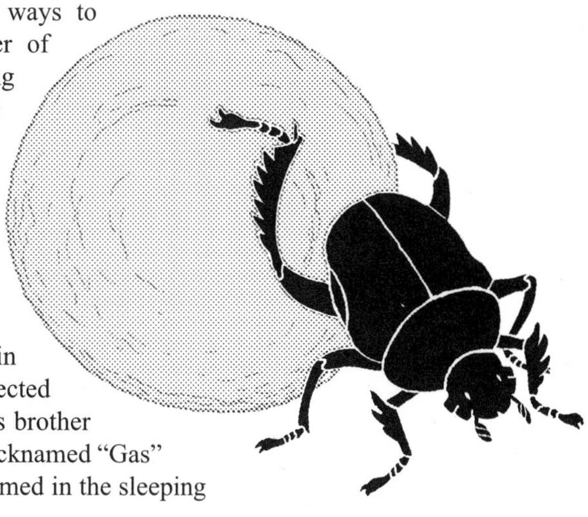

Evolution and Natural Selection

From a very early age, Charles Darwin was a naturalist and experimentalist. He collected bird eggs and beetles. He set up a lab with his brother Erasmus in a shed in their backyard and was nicknamed "Gas" for the stinky chemistry experiments he performed in the sleeping dorm of his boarding school. He noticed things, wrote them down and sought connections and explanations. These skills combined with his robust curiosity and patience would help him revolutionize how scientists viewed life on earth.

Darwin spent five years travelling the world on *HMS Beagle* as the ship's naturalist. In that time he had a chance to see a variety of animals living in a wide variety of different climates and ecosystems. This experience gave him a perspective on plant and animal species that few naturalist before him had. After his voyage, he wrote volumes about the specimens he collected and his observations on natural history. From those observations, he formulated a testable hypothesis for how evolution occurs. He called his mechanism **Natural Selection**, and we can break it into four primary postulates. Darwin felt that evolution can occur if the following conditions exist:

Charles Darwin
1809-1882

1. There is variation in the population
2. More individuals are born into a generation than survive to reproduce.
3. Those that survive to reproduce tend to have some advantage over those that do not.
4. Some of those advantages must be heritable.

The power of Darwin's theory is its simplicity. The basic idea is that those with advantages tend to have a better chance of surviving to reproduce and pass their advantageous traits onto the next generation.

When he proposed natural selection in his book *On the Origin of Species* in 1859, Darwin's hypothesis faced a critical scientific community ready to challenge the data. Yet, in the 148 years since then, natural selection has survived intense scientific scrutiny and has been experimentally supported innumerable times. When a hypothesis is supported by a substantial amount of accurate data, it is referred to as a **theory**. Though considered highly reliable, a theory is not set in stone and the possibility always exists that new data might be found that contradicts it. When that happens, the theory in question may need to be revised or completely abandoned.

Although researchers continue to add nuances to evolutionary theory, there has been no compelling evidence to contradict it. Biologists are quite confident that the Theory of Natural Selection explains a fundamental way in which life evolves.

Adaptations

Advantages that increase the long-term probability that an organism will survive to reproduce are referred to as **adaptations**. Adaptations can be **anatomical** features like an eye, **physiological** processes such as the ability of nerves to conduct electrical signals, and **behavioral** traits like reflexively turning toward a loud sound.

Those organisms with the best adaptations tend to do better in the long-term - the key word here being *tend*. An advantage is no guarantee of success. Having slightly better eyes than everyone else doesn't do you much good if you get blind-sided by a bus. Advantage or no, there is a small element of luck (good or bad) tied up in everyone's survival. But, taking that as a given, having slightly better eyes, a bigger brain or some other advantage can come in handy when you are competing with others for resources such as food and mates.

Mutations

So where do adaptations come from? How do some organisms get these "slight advantages" we keep mentioning? They start as goof-ups in the DNA called **mutations**. When animals make their sperm and eggs and plants make their pollen and ova, they have to copy their DNA. In the process, sometimes things are copied incorrectly.

Imagine having to transcribe the contents of your local library. Omissions and misspellings would be inevitable. When these mistakes happen copying DNA, there are three possible outcomes: First, the mistake may be **lethal**, in which case the embryo will not be viable. Second, the copying error might be **neutral**. In other words, the change has no effect on the organism. Third, there is the possibility that the mutation will be **beneficial**.

To consider how a small change in the DNA sequence can alter a gene, it is important to think of genes as bits of information, like sentences. Imagine our gene is the following sentence:

let's make an eye.

Now, we copy it several times and stick it into our sperm and eggs. What happens if we copy one of the letters incorrectly? We might get something that makes no sense, or changes the meaning completely, such as

*let's **b**ake an eye.*

Or we might get something that is a slight improvement, like

Let's make an eye.

Unfortunately, an organism cannot plan improvements in its genes. Mutations occur randomly. We cannot predict where or when they will pop up. So, how could a random process like this lead to the evolution of an elaborate adaptation like your camera eye? It couldn't.

If evolution were an exclusively random process, the evolution of sophisticated organisms like beetles and oak trees would be extremely unlikely. But mutation isn't working alone. Natural selection is its partner. Mutation is a *random* process that generates the raw material on which natural selection acts in a *highly directed* fashion.

Consider Darwin's quote about natural selection: "…Each slight variation, if useful, is preserved…" The flip side of that is that slight variations that are harmful are not preserved. Natural selection is, by definition, selective. The process weeds out what doesn't work and preserves what does. Sophisticated adaptations like the eye are the product of small incremental improvements in vision that have accumulated over vast amounts of time.

Selective Pressures

So, how does natural selection pick who stays and who goes? The process relies upon **selective agents** that apply **selective pressures** to a population of organisms. Predation in the preceding Wrinkles story was the selective agent. The miniature versions of Wrinkles with better eyes escaped the predators and those with weaker vision did not. Selective pressures can be **biotic** (living) or **abiotic** (non-living). Predation is a biotic selective pressure, because predators are living organisms. Climate is an example of an abiotic selective pressure.

Selective pressures sort organisms based on the organisms' **phenotypes**. A phenotype is the outward, physical expression of one's genes. In other words, the phenotype is the body and behavior that an organism's genes build. Thus, the group of miniature Wrinkles that survived Darwin's predatory onslaught had slightly different eye phenotypes than those that were eaten. Different phenotypes occur because all organisms have different sets of genes. An organism's unique set of genes is called its **genotype**. All genotypes are unique, but closely related organisms (like two humans) have fewer differences between their genotypes than more distantly related organisms (like a human and an earthworm).

Gene Pools and Populations

Although natural selection exerts pressure on individuals, evolution occurs at the population level. A **population** is an interbreeding community of organisms. The total genetic information in a population is called a **gene pool**. When organisms breed, the genes in the gene pool get mixed up and passed onto the next generation. If everybody in the population has the same chance to survive and nobody with new genes migrates in, then the gene pool won't change much.

In the preceding story, Charles Darwin and Wrinkles the Wonder Brain gobbled up phenotypes with less well-developed eyes in a population, thus removing the genotypes that built those phenotypes. Thus, the genes that code for the less sophisticated eyes will be removed from the population and change the make-up of the gene pool. When the gene pool changes, the types of phenotypes you see in the succeeding generations will change as well.

A change in the genetic make-up of a population from generation to generation is the modern definition of **evolution**. Consequently, we say that populations evolve. Individuals do not evolve. A drowning person cannot grow gills any more than a gazelle fleeing a cheetah can sprout wings and fly away. Thus, evolution is typically a relatively slow process (although populations of organisms like bacteria can evolve quite quickly). If only slight variations are being preserved from generation to generation in a population, then it will take a long time for a population to evolve a sophisticated adaptation like a camera eye. Fortunately, time is on our side.

Deep Time

If we want small variations to accumulate into big adaptive changes, we are going to need a lot of time. In fact, for evolution by natural selection to occur, we often need millions or billions of years.

Early in Darwin's career, most Western scientists believed that the earth was a little over 6000 years old. That changed when advances in the field of geology in the late 1700s and early 1800s yielded data indicating that the earth was quite a bit older. In the late 18th century, James Hutton advanced a theory called **uniformitarianism** (which was later expanded upon by Charles Lyell in the book *Principles of Geology*). Hutton and Lyell proposed that the small geological changes that we witness occurring now (such as the slow deposition or erosion of soil) have been happening for eons and are responsible for the landforms we see. The research of both men indicated that rocks form very slowly and that big geological features like mountains resulted from small incremental changes as geological forces slowly pushed up the earth's crust. Modern measurements confirm that the plates making up the earth's crust move 1-17 cm per year. According to data collected by the U.S. Geological Survey, the Himalayan Mountains rise by about 1 cm every year (a pace of about 10km per million years).

Current estimates place the earth's age at approximately 4.5 billion years. This figure has been corroborated by numerous different experiments from geology, chemistry and physics. Such an expansive sweep of time would be more than sufficient to move mountains and allow the critters scurrying on their landscape to evolve gradually.

Can't We Go Any Faster?

Not all creatures need loads of time to go through substantial evolutionary changes. Most animals like penguins and tulip trees have generation times that are measured in years. Thus, small changes in a population require considerable time to accumulate. Not so for the most successful living things on earth.

Bacteria, which can be found in virtually every conceivable habitat on the planet, deep inside the earth and high in the atmosphere, reproduce by splitting in two and can have very short generation times. The fastest reproducing bacteria can double their numbers in 15 minutes, although most have generation times measured in hours or a day. Thus, small changes in each generation can accumulate quite rapidly.

One example of this is seen in the evolution of antibiotic

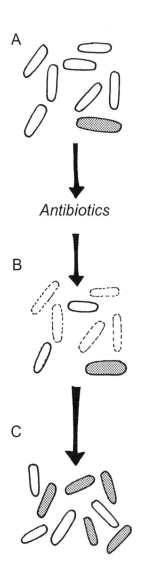

Figure 2.1 Small change, big problem. A) A small mutation makes a few bacteria in a population antibiotic resistant (gray bacteria). B) When antibiotics are applied, most of the non-resistant bacteria (white) are killed and those that are antibiotic resistant are not. C) As a result of the treatment, the genetic make-up of the next generation has changed and more resistant bacteria are present. The evolution of antibiotic resistant bacteria is a major concern for health care providers.

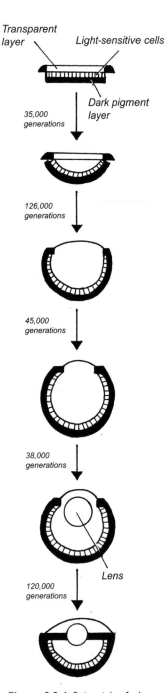

Transparent layer

Light-sensitive cells

Dark pigment layer

35,000 generations

126,000 generations

45,000 generations

38,000 generations

Lens

120,000 generations

Figure 2.2 A flat patch of photosensitive tissue becomes a camera eye very rapidly when there is a constant selective pressure for improved ability to form an image. Modified form Nilsson and Pelger (1994)

resistance, a growing problem for health care providers (Fig. 2.1). Antibiotics are designed to kill bacteria in a sick person. But if a few of those bacteria have a mutation that protects them from the antibiotic, they might survive and reproduce. Thus, the antibiotic is a selective agent selectively killing some and leaving those with resistance alive. If one continues to expose the bacteria to the antibiotic, one can cause a shift in the genetic make-up of the population, so that most of the bacteria are resistant and the antibiotic is rendered ineffective.

Automatic Camera Eye

So, how long would it take to evolve a camera eye? Not that long, actually. The years needed to evolve an eye as cited in the preceding story are taken from a study done by Dan-Erik Nilsson and Susanne Pelger in 1994.

Nilsson and Pelger ran a computer simulation of eye evolution. In their simulation, they wanted to see how long it took an elaborate camera eye to evolve from a small patch of photosensitive cells. These patches can be found in some flatworms and are considered to be characteristic of an ancient, ancestral visual apparatus.

In their experiment, they started with a flat patch of photosensitive cells that sat atop a dark pigment layer and were protected by a transparent layer above. Increased spatial resolution was an advantage (thus selected for) in the model, but they only allowed a 0.005% change in the shape of the eye from one generation to the next. This is a very small change (they referred to it as a pessimistic number, meaning that in nature changes would probably be larger from one generation to next) and would have led to very slow evolution.

Under these conservative conditions, the computer model evolved a camera eye from a small patch of photoreceptive cells in fewer than 400,000 generations (Fig. 2.2). If we assume one year per generation, then a camera eye could evolve remarkably quickly - so quickly, in fact, that they would seem to appear instantaneously in the fossil record. As we noted above, it takes a long time for rock to form. Layers of rock in the earth's crust aren't like the growth rings of a tree. You don't see a layer of rock for each of earth's 4.5 billion years. Instead, you see layers that were made over several thousands of years. These leaps in the geological record are on the order of about 500,000 years. Thus, a sophisticated eye that took fewer than 400,000 years to evolve might seem to appear out of nowhere in the fossil record. In fact, such a sudden appearance occurs between the rocks of the Precambrian Period and the Cambrian in an event called the Cambrian Explosion.

For Your Consideration

1. Imagine your flashlight won't work. Propose several hypotheses to account for the failure. What experiments would you conduct to test your hypotheses? What kind of data would you collect?

2. It is the nature of scientific study that any given hypothesis can be absolutely refuted but cannot be absolutely proven. Discuss this concept using the hypothesis: *The sun rises every morning.*

3. What distinguished Darwin's contribution to evolutionary theory from that of his scientific predecessors? How did this contribution help establish evolution as a scientific theory as opposed to a personal belief system?

4. If a mutation occurs in a bacterium's DNA that confers antibiotic resistance and there are no antibiotics around, is it an adaptation? Why or why not? Discuss the concepts of phenotype, genotype, selective pressure, gene pool, population and evolution in terms of antibiotic resistant bacteria.

5. The geological record is composed of several layers of rock that generally contain fossil animals and plants that are radically different from those in adjacent layers. At one time, the prevailing explanation for this was that the world had been periodically destroyed and recreated. How might the work of Nilsson and Pelger offer a scientific explanation for the radical changes in flora and fauna seen among different layers of rock?

Chapter Three: If Looks Could Kill

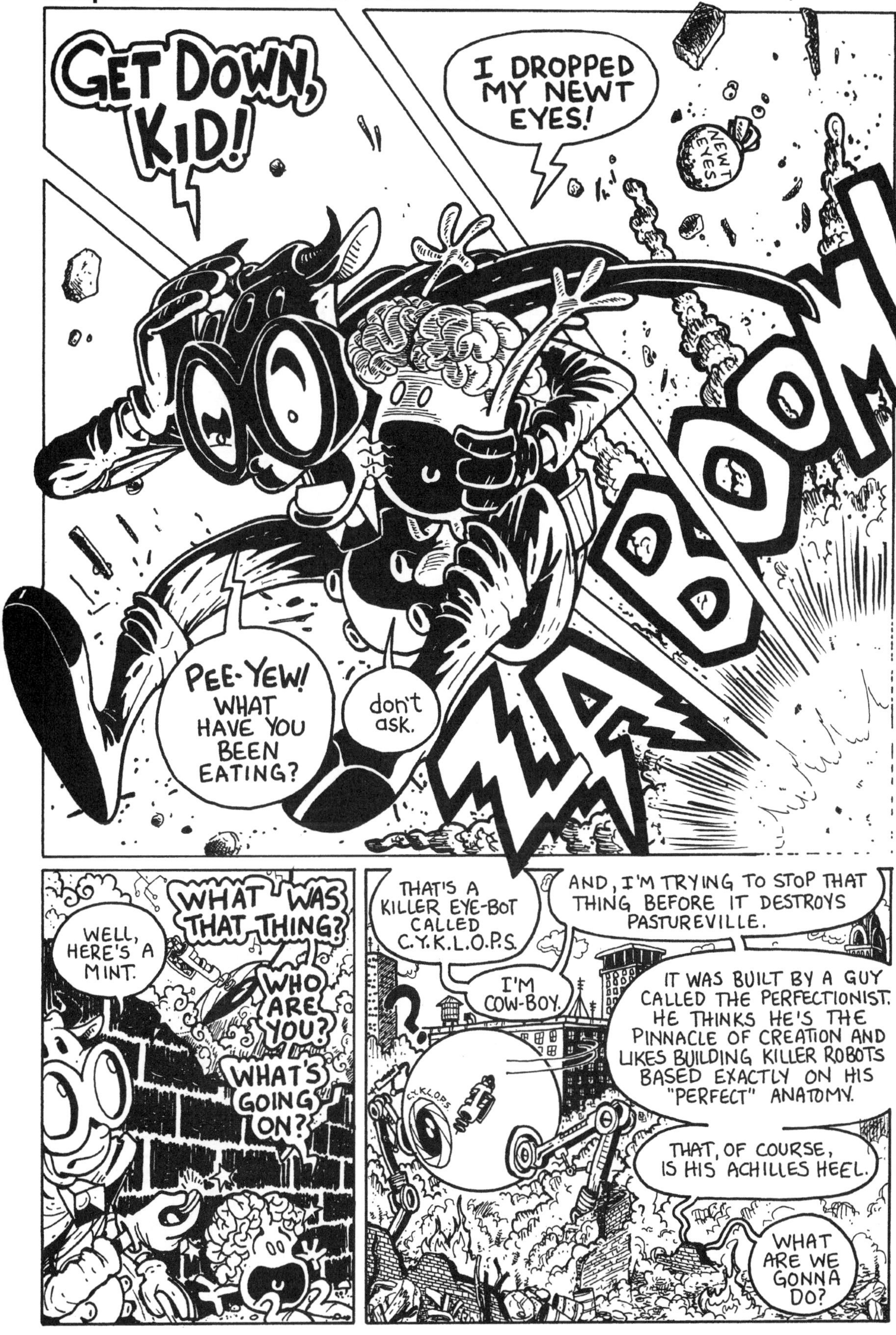
GET DOWN, KID!
I DROPPED MY NEWT EYES!
NEWT EYES
BOOM!
ZAP
PEE-YEW! WHAT HAVE YOU BEEN EATING?
don't ask.
WHAT WAS THAT THING?
WELL, HERE'S A MINT.
WHO ARE YOU?
WHAT'S GOING ON?
THAT'S A KILLER EYE-BOT CALLED C.Y.K.L.O.P.S.
AND, I'M TRYING TO STOP THAT THING BEFORE IT DESTROYS PASTUREVILLE.
I'M COW-BOY.
IT WAS BUILT BY A GUY CALLED THE PERFECTIONIST. HE THINKS HE'S THE PINNACLE OF CREATION AND LIKES BUILDING KILLER ROBOTS BASED EXACTLY ON HIS "PERFECT" ANATOMY.
C.Y.K.L.O.P.S.
THAT, OF COURSE, IS HIS ACHILLES HEEL.
WHAT ARE WE GONNA DO?

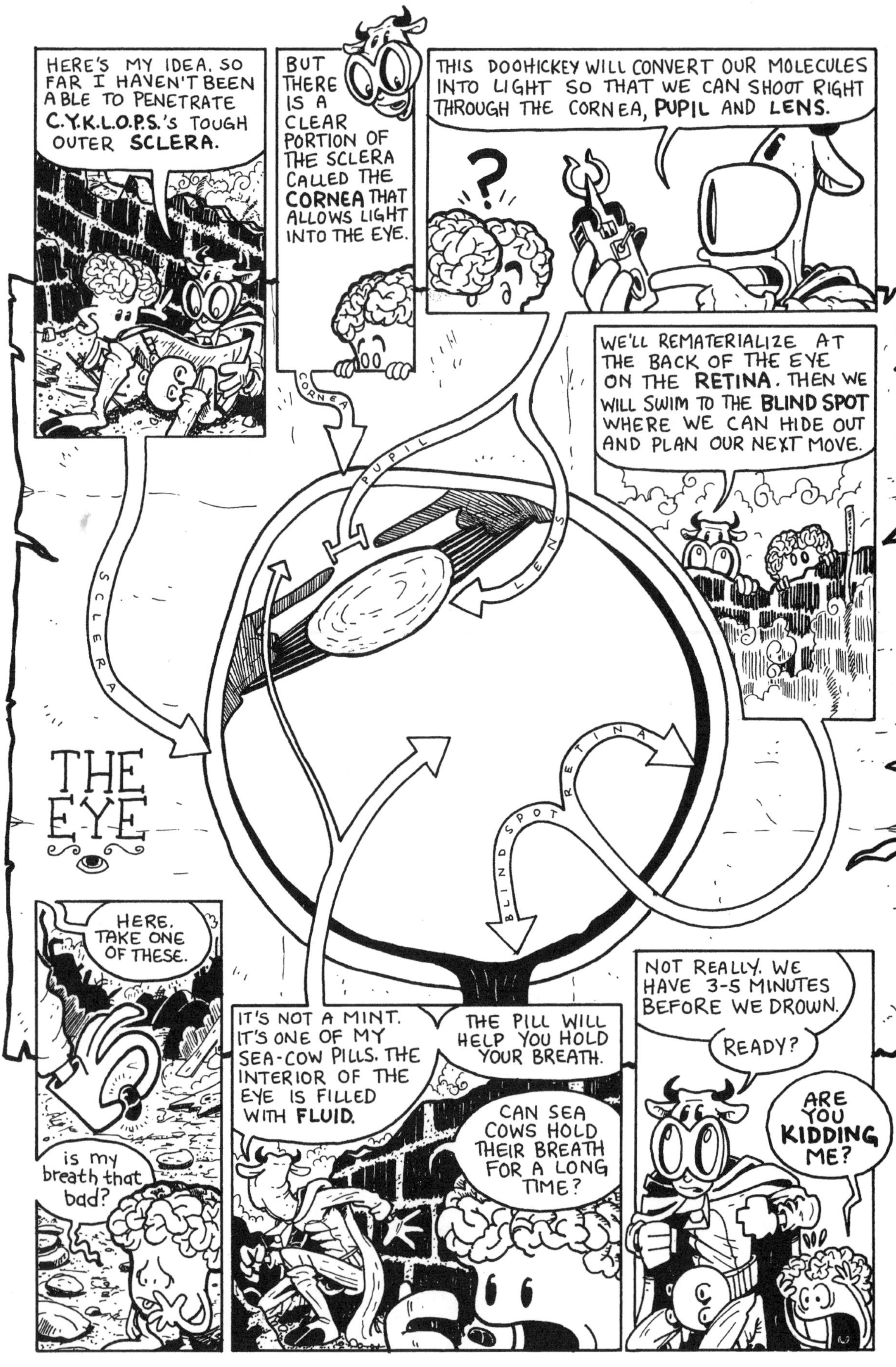
HERE'S MY IDEA. SO FAR I HAVEN'T BEEN ABLE TO PENETRATE C.Y.K.L.O.P.S.'s TOUGH OUTER SCLERA.
BUT THERE IS A CLEAR PORTION OF THE SCLERA CALLED THE CORNEA THAT ALLOWS LIGHT INTO THE EYE.
THIS DOOHICKEY WILL CONVERT OUR MOLECULES INTO LIGHT SO THAT WE CAN SHOOT RIGHT THROUGH THE CORNEA, PUPIL AND LENS.
?
WE'LL REMATERIALIZE AT THE BACK OF THE EYE ON THE RETINA. THEN WE WILL SWIM TO THE BLIND SPOT WHERE WE CAN HIDE OUT AND PLAN OUR NEXT MOVE.
CORNEA
PUPIL
LENS
SCLERA
RETINA
BLIND SPOT
THE EYE
HERE. TAKE ONE OF THESE.
is my breath that bad?
IT'S NOT A MINT. IT'S ONE OF MY SEA-COW PILLS. THE INTERIOR OF THE EYE IS FILLED WITH FLUID.
THE PILL WILL HELP YOU HOLD YOUR BREATH.
CAN SEA COWS HOLD THEIR BREATH FOR A LONG TIME?
NOT REALLY. WE HAVE 3-5 MINUTES BEFORE WE DROWN.
READY?
ARE YOU KIDDING ME?

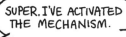

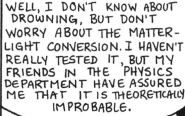
SUPER. I'VE ACTIVATED THE MECHANISM.

ALL WE HAVE TO DO IS STAND HERE UNTIL THE EYE-BOT TARGETS US.

IF WE TIME OUR LIGHT CONVERSION JUST AS THE EYE-BOT FIRES, THE PERFECTIONIST WILL THINK WE'RE DEAD AND WE'LL HAVE TIME TO DESTROY THE EYE-BOT FROM THE INSIDE.

THIS IS CRAZY. IF YOUR TIMING IS OFF, WE'LL BE FRIED.

AND IF THIS DOES WORK, WE'LL PROBABLY DROWN IN THAT THING.

WELL, I DON'T KNOW ABOUT DROWNING, BUT DON'T WORRY ABOUT THE MATTER-LIGHT CONVERSION. I HAVEN'T REALLY TESTED IT, BUT MY FRIENDS IN THE PHYSICS DEPARTMENT HAVE ASSURED ME THAT IT IS THEORETICALLY IMPROBABLE.

IMPROBABLE? IMPROBABLE IS BAD!

ARE YOU SURE?

TARGETING.

ZZA-BOOM

ugh. I feel kinda light-headed...

QUIT JOKING AROUND. WE'RE PASSING THROUGH THE CORNEA AND LENS AND WE NEED TO FOCUS!

DING

POP!

POP!

SHEESH. IT'S LIKE SWIMMING THROUGH JELLO.

THIS WAY.

BLIND SPOT

FOVEA

NICE OF HIM TO LABEL THINGS.

THIS IS THE RETINA. IT'S A NETWORK OF CELLS THAT COVERS THE ENTIRE INSIDE OF THE EYE.

THIS IS WHERE LIGHT IS CONVERTED INTO AN ELECTRICAL SIGNAL THE BRAIN CAN UNDERSTAND.

EXCEPT HERE AT THE BLIND SPOT, OF COURSE.

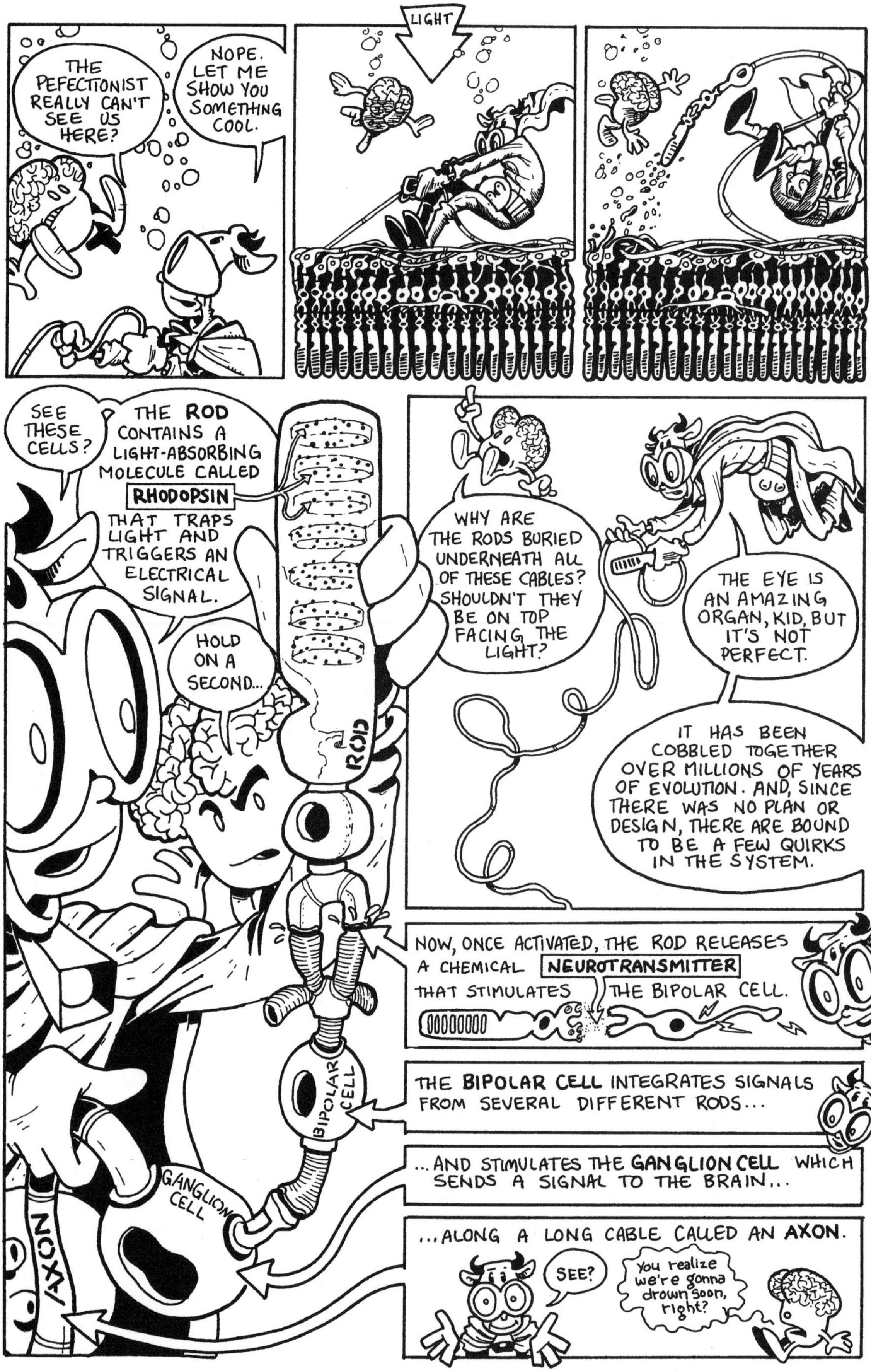
THE PEFECTIONIST REALLY CAN'T SEE US HERE?
NOPE. LET ME SHOW YOU SOMETHING COOL.
LIGHT
SEE THESE CELLS?
THE ROD CONTAINS A LIGHT-ABSORBING MOLECULE CALLED RHODOPSIN THAT TRAPS LIGHT AND TRIGGERS AN ELECTRICAL SIGNAL.
HOLD ON A SECOND...
ROD
WHY ARE THE RODS BURIED UNDERNEATH ALL OF THESE CABLES? SHOULDN'T THEY BE ON TOP FACING THE LIGHT?
THE EYE IS AN AMAZING ORGAN, KID, BUT IT'S NOT PERFECT.
IT HAS BEEN COBBLED TOGETHER OVER MILLIONS OF YEARS OF EVOLUTION. AND, SINCE THERE WAS NO PLAN OR DESIGN, THERE ARE BOUND TO BE A FEW QUIRKS IN THE SYSTEM.
NOW, ONCE ACTIVATED, THE ROD RELEASES A CHEMICAL NEUROTRANSMITTER THAT STIMULATES THE BIPOLAR CELL.
BIPOLAR CELL
THE BIPOLAR CELL INTEGRATES SIGNALS FROM SEVERAL DIFFERENT RODS...
...AND STIMULATES THE GANGLION CELL WHICH SENDS A SIGNAL TO THE BRAIN...
GANGLION CELL
AXON
...ALONG A LONG CABLE CALLED AN AXON.
SEE?
You realize we're gonna drown soon, right?

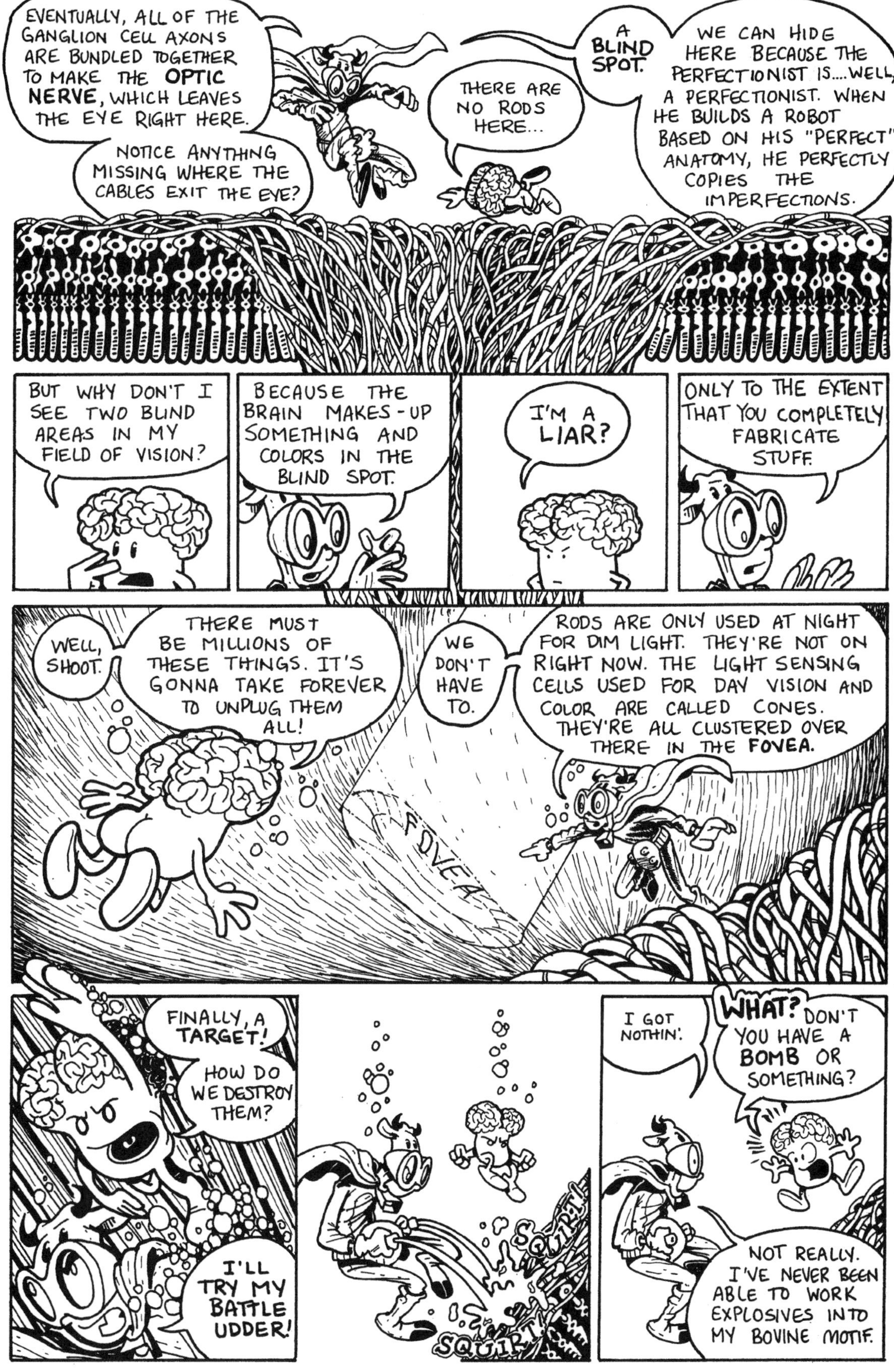
EVENTUALLY, ALL OF THE GANGLION CELL AXONS ARE BUNDLED TOGETHER TO MAKE THE OPTIC NERVE, WHICH LEAVES THE EYE RIGHT HERE.
NOTICE ANYTHING MISSING WHERE THE CABLES EXIT THE EYE?
THERE ARE NO RODS HERE...
A BLIND SPOT.
WE CAN HIDE HERE BECAUSE THE PERFECTIONIST IS....WELL, A PERFECTIONIST. WHEN HE BUILDS A ROBOT BASED ON HIS "PERFECT" ANATOMY, HE PERFECTLY COPIES THE IMPERFECTIONS.
BUT WHY DON'T I SEE TWO BLIND AREAS IN MY FIELD OF VISION?
BECAUSE THE BRAIN MAKES-UP SOMETHING AND COLORS IN THE BLIND SPOT.
I'M A LIAR?
ONLY TO THE EXTENT THAT YOU COMPLETELY FABRICATE STUFF.
WELL, SHOOT.
THERE MUST BE MILLIONS OF THESE THINGS. IT'S GONNA TAKE FOREVER TO UNPLUG THEM ALL!
WE DON'T HAVE TO.
RODS ARE ONLY USED AT NIGHT FOR DIM LIGHT. THEY'RE NOT ON RIGHT NOW. THE LIGHT SENSING CELLS USED FOR DAY VISION AND COLOR ARE CALLED CONES. THEY'RE ALL CLUSTERED OVER THERE IN THE FOVEA.
FOVEA
FINALLY, A TARGET!
HOW DO WE DESTROY THEM?
I'LL TRY MY BATTLE UDDER!
SQUIRT!
SQUIRT!
I GOT NOTHIN'.
WHAT? DON'T YOU HAVE A BOMB OR SOMETHING?
NOT REALLY. I'VE NEVER BEEN ABLE TO WORK EXPLOSIVES INTO MY BOVINE MOTIF.

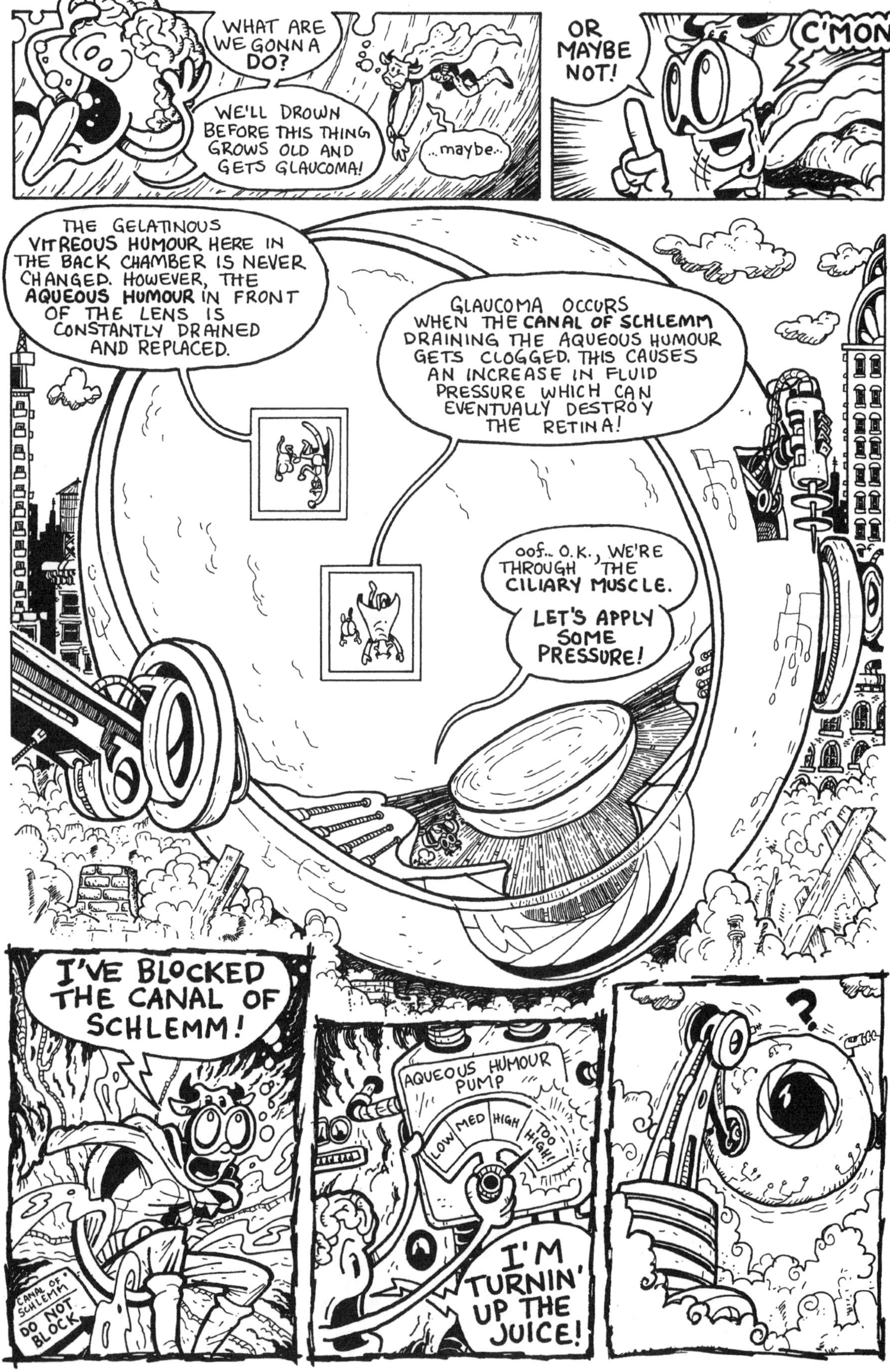
WHAT ARE WE GONNA DO?
WE'LL DROWN BEFORE THIS THING GROWS OLD AND GETS GLAUCOMA!
...maybe...
OR MAYBE NOT!
C'MON!
THE GELATINOUS VITREOUS HUMOUR HERE IN THE BACK CHAMBER IS NEVER CHANGED. HOWEVER, THE AQUEOUS HUMOUR IN FRONT OF THE LENS IS CONSTANTLY DRAINED AND REPLACED.
GLAUCOMA OCCURS WHEN THE CANAL OF SCHLEMM DRAINING THE AQUEOUS HUMOUR GETS CLOGGED. THIS CAUSES AN INCREASE IN FLUID PRESSURE WHICH CAN EVENTUALLY DESTROY THE RETINA!
oof.. O.K., WE'RE THROUGH THE CILIARY MUSCLE.
LET'S APPLY SOME PRESSURE!
I'VE BLOCKED THE CANAL OF SCHLEMM!
CANAL OF SCHLEMM
DO NOT BLOCK
AQUEOUS HUMOUR PUMP
LOW
MED
HIGH
TOO HIGH!
I'M TURNIN' UP THE JUICE!
?

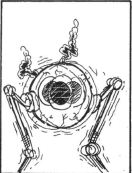

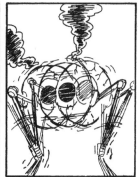

I CAN'T BELIEVE THAT WORKED.

YEAH, BUT AT WHAT PRICE? LOOK AT THESE DEVASTATED BUILDINGS!

DON'T WORRY ABOUT IT.

THIS IS THE ABANDONED WAREHOUSE DISTRICT. THE TOWN MAINTAINS IT FOR SITUATIONS JUST LIKE THIS.

NOW HELP ME LOOK FOR THE PERFECTIONIST.

AH-HA! THERE YOU ARE.

UNHAND ME!

WHAT THE--? THIS IS THE PINNACLE OF ALL CREATION?

I AM PERFECTION!

O.K, BILL, JUST SETTLE DOWN, WILLYA?

HEY! I FOUND MY MAGIC NEWT EYES!

NEW EYE

35

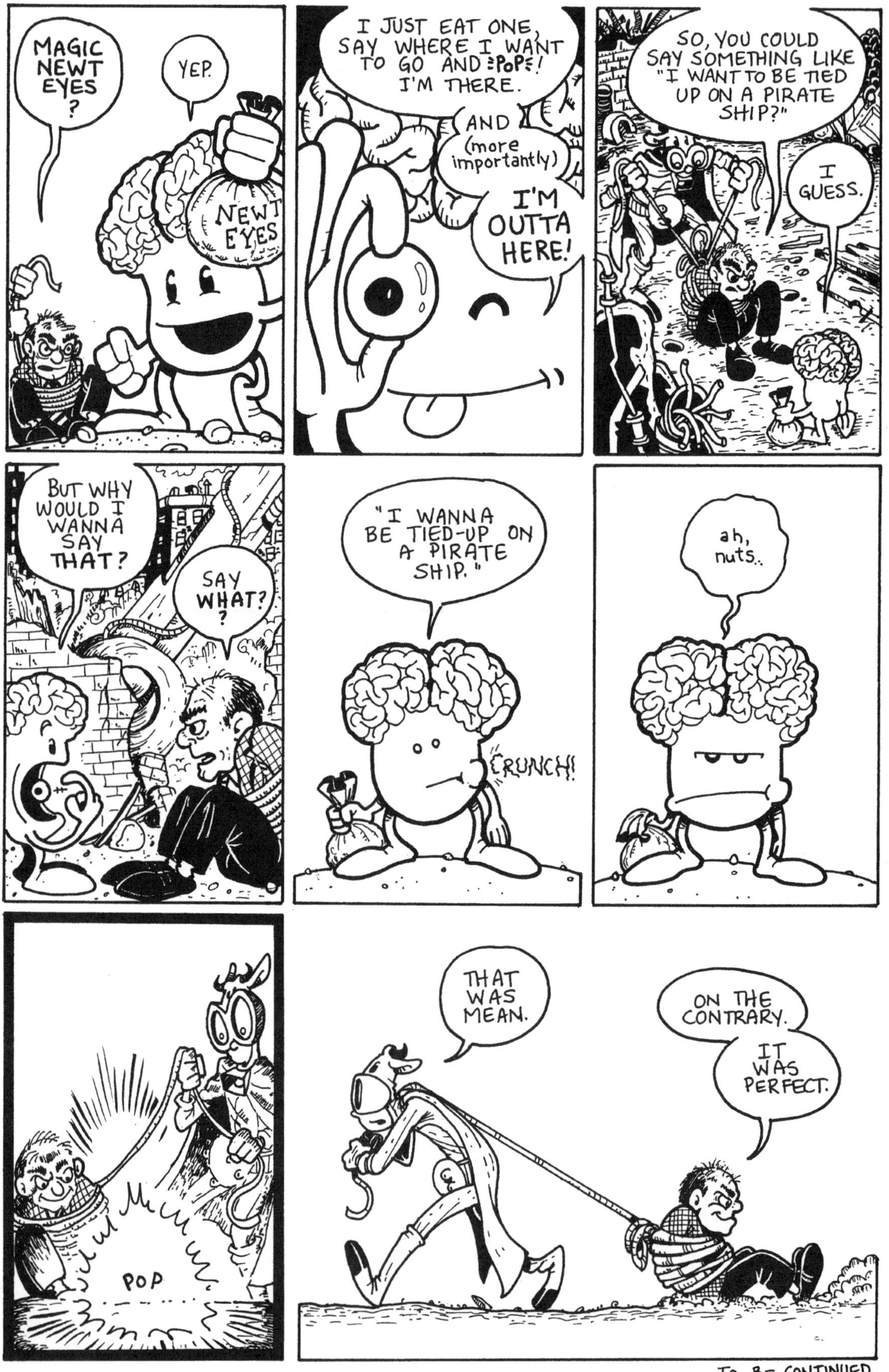
MAGIC NEWT EYES ?
YEP.
NEWT EYES
I JUST EAT ONE, SAY WHERE I WANT TO GO AND POP! I'M THERE.
AND (more importantly)
I'M OUTTA HERE!
SO, YOU COULD SAY SOMETHING LIKE "I WANT TO BE TIED UP ON A PIRATE SHIP?"
I GUESS.
BUT WHY WOULD I WANNA SAY THAT?
SAY WHAT? ?
"I WANNA BE TIED-UP ON A PIRATE SHIP."
CRUNCH!
ah, nuts..
POP
THAT WAS MEAN.
ON THE CONTRARY.
IT WAS PERFECT.
TO BE CONTINUED...

The Anatomy of Vision

The Birds and the Bees

Let me tell you about the birds and the bees - or their eyes, at least. Like many animals, birds and bees depend on vision to navigate, avoid being eaten, find food and choose mates, but, they accomplish these things with two very different types of eyes. You don't have to be a trained naturalist to differentiate between the **compound eye** of the common honey bee *Apis mellifera* and the massive yellow **camera eyes** of a bald eagle. Despite their differences, both eyes paint effective pictures of the world for their owners.

Eyes Run in Our Family

Biologists classify organisms based on how they look and their genetic similarities. Eagles are birds and birds belong to a group known as the vertebrates. **Vertebrates** have internal skeletons and a series of bones called vertebrae that run down their back and encase their spinal cord. You are a vertebrate. Assuming the vertebrate in question is not a blind cave fish or cave salamander, vertebrates have **camera eyes**, although the design of each varies based on the species' evolutionary history and ecological circumstances.

Honey bees are invertebrates. **Invertebrates** are multicellular animals without a backbone. This is a tremendously large group of animals that ranges from microscopic worms to the whale-sized giant squid! Insects belong to a sub-category of invertebrates known as the arthropods. The **arthropods** are classified as having external skeletons, jointed legs and no backbone. Arthropods have **compound eyes** which can vary in size, shape and complexity depending on the ecological circumstances and lifestyles of the arthropod in question.

When we consider the position of birds and bees on the family tree of life, we see that the branch that led to vertebrates split more than 500 million years ago from the branch that eventually led to arthropods. The common ancestor of these two lines probably did not have much in the way of visual apparatus. Thus, members of each line evolved their elaborate visual devices independently.

Compound eyes and camera eyes represent different solutions to the same ecological challenge: how to perceive light. Consequently, although they may not look very much alike, they share many of the same functional characteristics.

Let the Sunshine In

An eye's first job is to let the sunshine in. Most places on an animal's body are hard to see through, so for light to penetrate (and eventually be absorbed) there needs to be a transparent window someplace. In vertebrates, this region of the eye is called the **cornea** (Fig. 3.1A) and in insects it is called the **corneal lens** (Fig. 3.1C).

The "white of your eye" is a fibrous and relatively rigid structure called the **sclera** that gives the eye its shape. The cornea is a region of the sclera that has become transparent, in large part because it contains no blood vessels. Because of this, corneal transplants are the most successful type of transplant because the immune system has no way to reach the new cornea and reject it.

While the eye of an eagle is a single optical unit with only one cornea, the compound eye of a bee is composed of thousands of optical units called **ommatidia**, each with its own corneal lens (Fig. 3.1B-C). The corneal lens is a modified region of the bee's rigid exoskeleton that is devoid of most of its pigmentation.

Iris is a Very Good Pupil

In both birds and bees, once light has passed through the cornea or corneal lens, it must pass through another clear structure that acts, to a greater or lesser extent, to focus the light.

Light in the insect compound eye passes from the corneal lens immediately to the adjoining **crystalline cone** (Fig. 3.1C). In conjunction with the corneal lens, the crystalline cone bends incoming light and focuses it on the rhabdom at far end of the ommatidium.

The camera eye of a vertebrate also has a second focusing structure that works in conjunction with the cornea. However, they are not in direct physical contact. After light enters the eye through the cornea, it travels through the **aqueous humor** fluid of the front chamber of the eye and passes through the hole in the middle of the eye called the **pupil**. The pupil is formed by a circular muscle called the **iris** and can open and close to control the amount of light entering the eye.

In the dark, the pupil widens to allow as much light in as possible and in bright light it does the opposite. To see this happen, try the following experiment. Sit in the dark with a friend for a minute of two. Once your eyes have acclimated, shine a flashlight in your friend's eyes and watch his or her pupils contract. (You should probably warn your friend that you are going to do this or they might not be your friend for long.)

Once through the pupil, the light hits the oval-shaped **lens**. Traditionally we think of the lens as the structure that bends incoming light and focuses it on the retina at the back of the eye. However, the effectiveness of the lens in bending light depends on where you live.

I'm Having Trouble Focusing

In aquatic vertebrates like fishes, the lens is the primary means by which light is focused, but in terrestrial organisms like us, the cornea does most of the work. To understand why this is the case, it is important to bear in mind three important things: 1) the space between the cornea and lens is filled with a fluid (aqueous humor), 2) fluids are denser than air and 3) light travels faster through air than it does through water or a transparent solid like a lens.

When we see something, light has traveled through the air to

A
Pupil
Aqueous
Humor
Cornea
Iris
Lens
Sclera
Ciliary
Muscle
Vitreous
Humor
Optic
Disk
Pigmented
Layer
Fovea
Optic
Nerve
Retina
B

C
Corneal
Lens
Crystalline
Cone
Primary
Pigment
Cell
Secondary
Pigment
Cell
Retinula
Cell
Rhabdom

Figure 3.1 A) The human camera eye, B) a portion of the insect compound eye and C) a single ommatidium from the insect compound eye. (portions of this image after CSIRO 1970; Rossel 1989).

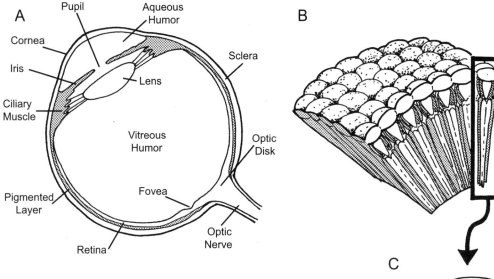

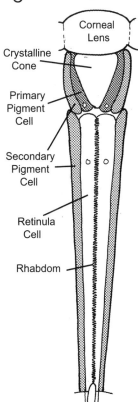

reach our eyes at a speed of 186,282.397 miles per second. When a wavefront of light passes through the curved surface of the cornea, two things happen. First, it slows down to 140,000 miles per second as it moves from the air into the much denser aqueous humor. Second, the light is bent and focused by the curved surface of the denser medium. This bending of light is called **refraction**.

Things are different for fishes. Light reaching their eyes passes from one fluid (the water) to another (the aqueous humour). This fluid-to-fluid transition doesn't slow the light and thus, doesn't bend or focus it much either. Consequently, fish rely upon the transition from the aqueous humour to the solid lens to slow the light and do most of the bending. Fish lenses slow light down to 124,000 miles per second. Because the lens is so thick, the light spends a relatively long time slogging through it and gets significantly refracted. By comparison, terrestrial vertebrates tend to have smaller, flatter lenses that are just responsible for fine-tuning focus.

You're Not Going Anywhere

Once the light is bent, it is focused on a structure where it can be absorbed and trigger a signal to be sent to the brain. In bees, the light in each ommatidium is focused on an area called the **rhabdom**, a place where the fingers of several neighboring **retinula cells** overlap (Fig. 3.1C). In an eagle, the light is focused on a layer of cells lining the back of the eye called the **retina** (Fig. 3.1A).

The cells of the rhabdom and retina both contain special molecules called **photopigments** that can absorb a photon of light. Once absorbed, the photon's energy causes the photopigment to change shape and activate a series of chemical reactions that will lead to an electrical change in the cell.

Of course, photons are quick little buggers and not every

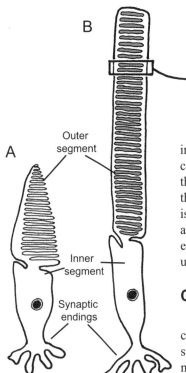

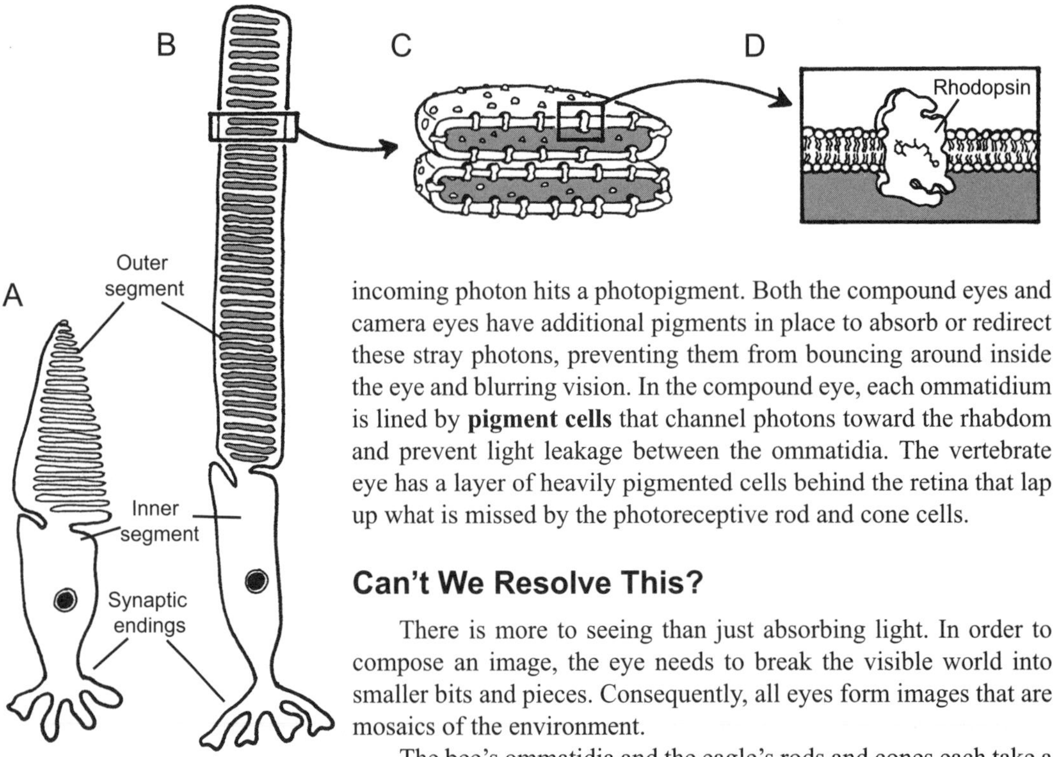

B

Outer segment

A

Inner segment

Synaptic endings

C

D

Rhodopsin

incoming photon hits a photopigment. Both the compound eyes and camera eyes have additional pigments in place to absorb or redirect these stray photons, preventing them from bouncing around inside the eye and blurring vision. In the compound eye, each ommatidium is lined by **pigment cells** that channel photons toward the rhabdom and prevent light leakage between the ommatidia. The vertebrate eye has a layer of heavily pigmented cells behind the retina that lap up what is missed by the photoreceptive rod and cone cells.

Can't We Resolve This?

There is more to seeing than just absorbing light. In order to compose an image, the eye needs to break the visible world into smaller bits and pieces. Consequently, all eyes form images that are mosaics of the environment.

The bee's ommatidia and the eagle's rods and cones each take a small piece of the big picture and the brain assembles them into an image. Just as the number of pixels in a computer monitor affects its resolution, the degree of detail of the image formed by the eye is determined by the size and number of ommatidia or cells. If there are only a few large pixels to compose the image, then each pixel will comprise a large piece of the picture and the image will lack detail and appear blocky. With higher numbers of smaller pixels, one can achieve greater detail. Eyes function on the same principle.

Rods, cones and ommatidia generate the pixels for a visual mosaic. In the human retina, there are about 100 million rods and cones but they are not distributed evenly (Fig. 3.3). While rods are found everywhere in the retina, they are absent from a small region in the center called the **fovea**. The fovea is densely packed with cones (which are only sparsely distributed throughout the rest of the retina) and this contributes to the formation of a high resolution image. Since rods are used primarily for night vision, we must focus mainly on the cones in the fovea to get a sense of visual acuity in the light.

The human fovea contains approximately 200,000 cones. Because of this high concentration, our fovea is the region of our keenest vision and color discrimination. But, as impressive as our vision is, an eagle's is even better. To be literally eagle-eyed means to have a fovea with approximately 1,000,000 cones. If you do the math, that makes their visual acuity five times greater than ours.

The resolution of compound eyes is usually much less than that of camera eyes. The compound eye of a honey bee only has

Figure 3.2 A) A cone cell from the vertebrate retina. Cones are used for day vision. In the human retina, there are three different types of cone cells, each responding preferentially to different wavelengths of light. Unlike the rod, the membranes of the cone's outer segment are continuous with the outer cell membrane and not self-contained, internal disks. B) Rod cell from a vertebrate retina. The rods and cones contain three segments. The outer segment of the rod contains stacks of membrane disks that are studded with photosensitive pigments. Rods are used for low-light vision. C) Two disks from a rod. D) The photosensitive pigment in the rod is called rhodopsin. It is a protein embedded in the disk membrane.

180,000
100,000
20,000
Number of rods or cones
Rods
Cones
80°
60°
40°
20°
0°
20°
40°
60°
80°
100°
180° of the curve of the retina

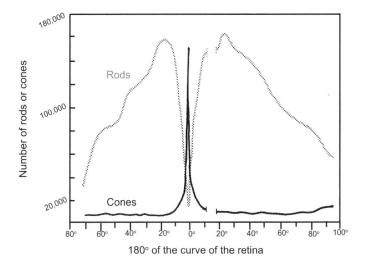

Figure 3.3. The distribution of rods and cones in the retina. In this diagram, the x-axis plots 180° of the curve of the retina. The fovea is plotted at 0°. Redrawn from Osterberg, 1935

about 4500 ommatidia with which to assemble a picture of the environment. Again, we see that this is a lot fewer than the eagle. But don't feel badly for the bee. Its eyes are much more effective at spotting fast-moving objects (like other bees).

As vertebrates that depend on vision so much, we have a tendency to think that bigger is better when it comes to eyes, and that has been true for the evolutionary survival of our species. But compound eyes of varying degrees of complexity are by far the most abundant type of eye in the animal kingdom. There are more species of beetles than species of birds and mammals combined, and every one of those beetles has a compound eye. So compound eyes may not paint the pretty picture our eyes do, but in evolutionary terms, their resolution has been more than sufficient for survival and great success.

Try To See It My Way

Camera and compound eyes aren't the only way to see the world, of course. Consider the figure of eye evolution from Nilsson and Pelger (Fig. 2.2). At one end of that continuum, we see the flat patch of photosensitive cells found in animals like flatworms, segmented worms and some crustaceans. At the other end of the spectrum, we have the camera eyes found in vertebrates, cephalopods (like squid and octopuses) and some jellyfish. And in between are a number of visual intermediates capable of forming images of varying complexity. These intermediate eyes are found throughout the animal kingdom and in a variety of ecological niches.

The functions of the visual intermediates vary. Flat and cupulate eyes can be found in worms, arthropods and vertebrates. They don't form images but they can be used by organisms to orient toward or away from light (a useful skill, if you are trying to avoid the bright open spaces filled with big, hungry predators). They may also be used to gauge day length, which can be useful in coordinating feeding and breeding behaviors.

Pinhole eyes are an elaboration of the cupulate eye. They contain a small aperture that can be used to focus light and work on the same principle as a pinhole camera. The small hole in the eye bends and focuses light to form an image on the photosensitive cells in the eye. The smaller the hole, the better the image resolution. But there is a trade-off to this approach: as the hole gets smaller, the image gets darker. Eventually, selection for additional increases in resolution (by making the hole smaller) is no longer favored because of lost image brightness. These eye can be found in ribbon worms, some arthropods and the ancient *Nautilus*.

There are several solutions to the ecological challenge of perceiving light. A survey of eyes in nature clearly demonstrates that it is incorrect to assume that the only eye worth having is an eye like ours. Natural selection does not work to make organisms more like us. It acts to preserve adaptations organisms need to survive in their environment. If a sedentary clam doesn't need an elaborate eye to sit and filter feed, then the economics of evolution will favor something simpler. Likewise, a predaceous squid will need far more sophisticated eyes to hunt at high speeds. And there are costs to having an eye. Eyes may not really be the gateway to the soul, but they can be a gateway for diseases. They are also vulnerable to predators. Under an organisms' unique environmental conditions, the costs of building an eye must be weighed against the needs of the animal.

For your consideration

1. Classify the following as either a vertebrate or invertebrate and explain your reasoning: tuna, earthworm, bear, crab, grasshopper, jellyfish, sponge, robin, octopus, tree frog, snake, shrimp, tapeworm, sea star and platypus.

2. Seals are aquatic mammals that evolved from land animals. Given that they spend much of their life living and hunting in the water, what differences would you hypothesize that you might see when comparing their eyes to those of a terrestrial relative? Why?

3. Imagine the early earth about four billion years ago when the most complex organisms were small, soft bodies critters with no eyes. Scientists like Dan-Erik Nilsson and Andrew Parker have suggested that the advent of an organism with a simple visual apparatus could have driven the evolution of eyes in other organisms, as well as of hard shells and body armor. Discuss how this might have happened, incorporating the concepts of adaptation and selective pressure into your answer.

4. Since the time of Darwin, a common refrain of opponents of the evolution of complex structures like the eye has been, "What good is half an eye?" What assumptions are the opponents making about what an eye is? Discuss why we might well answer that question, "Good enough, under the right conditions."

5. Consider Figure 3.3. Why is there a gap in both rod and cone curves between 15° and 20°?

Blind Spot Activity

Close your left eye and stare at Wrinkles with your right eye. Now move the page closer to your face keeping your right eye on Wrinkles the whole time. When the page is about a foot from your face, the magic eye should disappear. It will reappear if you continue moving the page closer to your face.

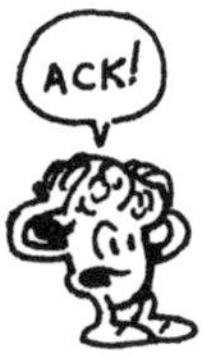
ACK!

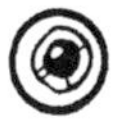

Wha' Happened?

As you move the page closer to your face, you eventually positioned the magic eye on the blind spot of your right eye. Since there are no rods and cones there, the image doesn't stimulate your retina. Your ever resourceful brain looks at the stimulation all around the blind spot and fills in the gap. Since the magic eye is surrounded by white, the brain colors in the area with white and the magic eye appears to disappear.

Chapter Four: See Quest

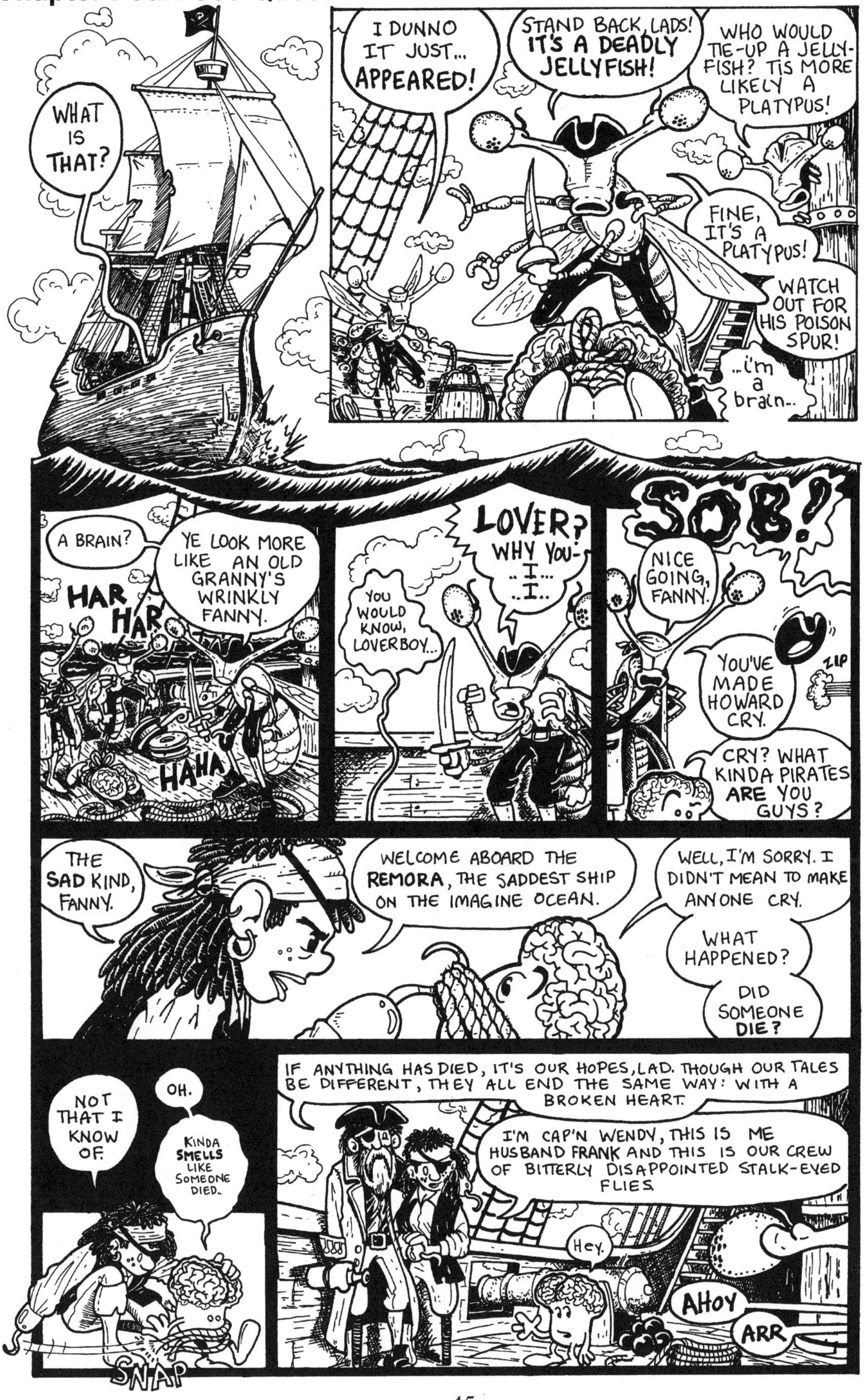
WHAT IS THAT?
I DUNNO IT JUST... APPEARED!
STAND BACK, LADS! IT'S A DEADLY JELLYFISH!
WHO WOULD TIE-UP A JELLY-FISH? TIS MORE LIKELY A PLATYPUS!
FINE, IT'S A PLATYPUS!
WATCH OUT FOR HIS POISON SPUR!
..i'm a brain..
A BRAIN?
YE LOOK MORE LIKE AN OLD GRANNY'S WRINKLY FANNY.
HAR HAR
HAHA
YOU WOULD KNOW, LOVERBOY...
LOVER? WHY YOU- ..I... ..I..
SOB!
NICE GOING, FANNY.
YOU'VE MADE HOWARD CRY.
ZIP
CRY? WHAT KINDA PIRATES ARE YOU GUYS?
THE SAD KIND, FANNY.
WELCOME ABOARD THE REMORA, THE SADDEST SHIP ON THE IMAGINE OCEAN.
WELL, I'M SORRY. I DIDN'T MEAN TO MAKE ANYONE CRY.
WHAT HAPPENED?
DID SOMEONE DIE?
NOT THAT I KNOW OF.
OH.
KINDA SMELLS LIKE SOMEONE DIED.
SNAP
IF ANYTHING HAS DIED, IT'S OUR HOPES, LAD. THOUGH OUR TALES BE DIFFERENT, THEY ALL END THE SAME WAY: WITH A BROKEN HEART.
I'M CAP'N WENDY, THIS IS ME HUSBAND FRANK AND THIS IS OUR CREW OF BITTERLY DISAPPOINTED STALK-EYED FLIES.
Hey.
AHOY
ARR

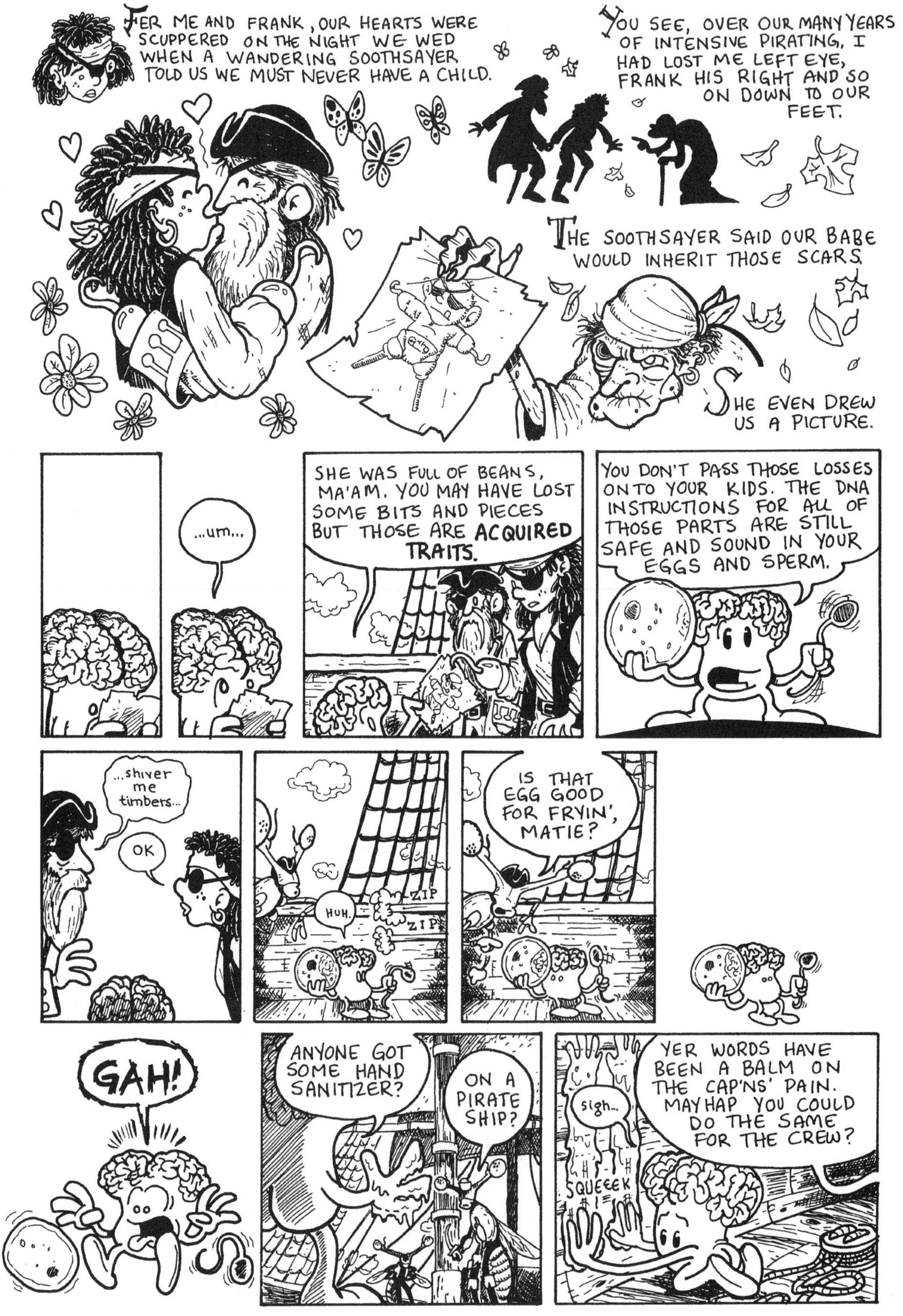
FER ME AND FRANK, OUR HEARTS WERE SCUPPERED ON THE NIGHT WE WED WHEN A WANDERING SOOTHSAYER TOLD US WE MUST NEVER HAVE A CHILD.
YOU SEE, OVER OUR MANY YEARS OF INTENSIVE PIRATING, I HAD LOST ME LEFT EYE, FRANK HIS RIGHT AND SO ON DOWN TO OUR FEET.
THE SOOTHSAYER SAID OUR BABE WOULD INHERIT THOSE SCARS.
SHE EVEN DREW US A PICTURE.
...um...
SHE WAS FULL OF BEANS, MA'AM. YOU MAY HAVE LOST SOME BITS AND PIECES BUT THOSE ARE **ACQUIRED TRAITS.**
YOU DON'T PASS THOSE LOSSES ONTO YOUR KIDS. THE DNA INSTRUCTIONS FOR ALL OF THOSE PARTS ARE STILL SAFE AND SOUND IN YOUR EGGS AND SPERM.
...shiver me timbers...
OK
HUH.
ZIP
ZIP
IS THAT EGG GOOD FOR FRYIN', MATIE?
GAH!
ANYONE GOT SOME HAND SANITIZER?
ON A PIRATE SHIP?
sigh...
SQUEEEK
YER WORDS HAVE BEEN A BALM ON THE CAP'NS' PAIN. MAYHAP YOU COULD DO THE SAME FOR THE CREW?

WELL, I GUESS THAT WOULD DEPEND ON WHAT THE PROBLEM IS.

AH, THEN IT'S A STORY YOU'LL BE WANTIN'!

WELL THEN, PREPARE YERSELF FOR THE TALE OF WOE AND **SEXUAL SELECTION** THAT BURDENS OUR SOULS.

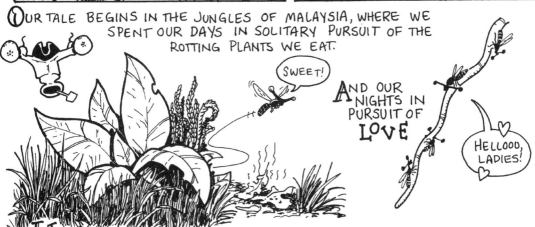

OUR TALE BEGINS IN THE JUNGLES OF MALAYSIA, WHERE WE SPENT OUR DAYS IN SOLITARY PURSUIT OF THE ROTTING PLANTS WE EAT.

SWEET!

AND OUR NIGHTS IN PURSUIT OF LOVE

HELLOOO, LADIES!

UNFORTUNATELY, LOVE DON'T COME EASY FOR STALK-EYED FLIES. NO, SIR, THERE'S FUSSIN', FIGHTIN', AND, ULTIMATELY FOR US, FAILURE.

Y'SEE, ME BOYO, LADS AND LASSIES ARE **DIFFERENT.**

NO FOOLIN'?

I'M NOT JUST TALKIN' ABOUT THEIR NAUGHTY BITS, **SMARTY.**

I'M TALKIN' ABOUT DIFFERENCES IN THE BITS THAT HAVE **NOTHIN'** TO DO WITH MAKIN' BABIES.

LIKE A MALE MOOSE'S ANTLERS

AYE, LAD, OR THESE ABSURD STALKS OUR EYES SIT ON.

WE CALL THESE DIFFERENCES **SEXUAL DIMORPHISMS**

THAT MEANS BOY FLIES HAVE MUCH BIGGER STALKS THAN GIRLIES.

BUT NOT ALL BOYS HAVE THE SAME SIZE EYE STALKS, IF YOU GET MY MEANING.

THERE'S VARIATION IN THE POPULATION

AYE, LAD! **VARIATION!**

AND **THAT** IS THE SOURCE OF OUR FLAGGIN' SPIRITS.

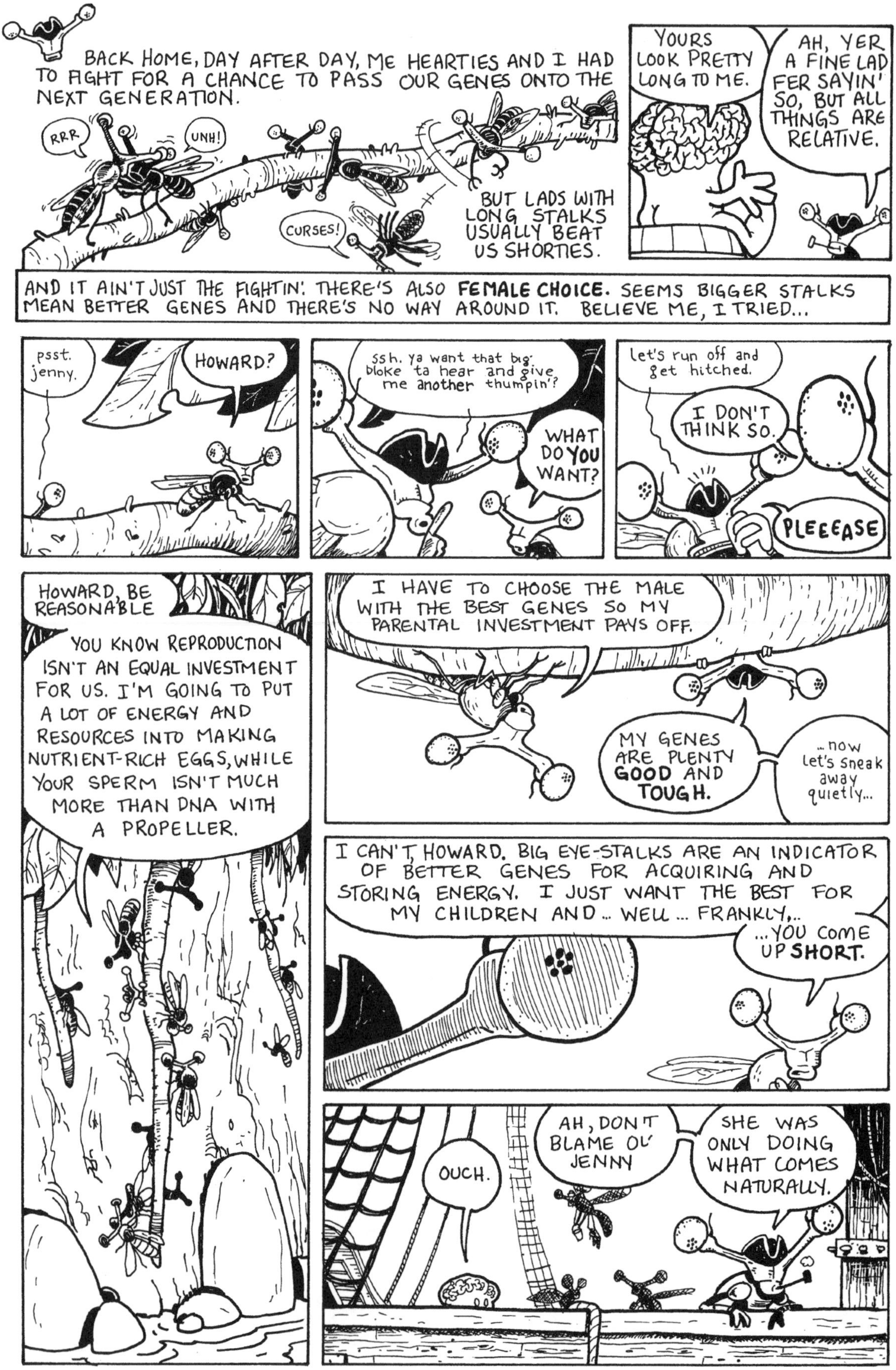
BACK HOME, DAY AFTER DAY, ME HEARTIES AND I HAD TO FIGHT FOR A CHANCE TO PASS OUR GENES ONTO THE NEXT GENERATION.
RRR
UNH!
CURSES!
BUT LADS WITH LONG STALKS USUALLY BEAT US SHORTIES.
YOURS LOOK PRETTY LONG TO ME.
AH, YER A FINE LAD FER SAYIN' SO, BUT ALL THINGS ARE RELATIVE.
AND IT AIN'T JUST THE FIGHTIN'. THERE'S ALSO FEMALE CHOICE. SEEMS BIGGER STALKS MEAN BETTER GENES AND THERE'S NO WAY AROUND IT. BELIEVE ME, I TRIED...
psst. jenny.
HOWARD?
ssh. ya want that big bloke ta hear and give me another thumpin'?
WHAT DO YOU WANT?
let's run off and get hitched.
I DON'T THINK SO.
PLEEEASE
HOWARD, BE REASONABLE
YOU KNOW REPRODUCTION ISN'T AN EQUAL INVESTMENT FOR US. I'M GOING TO PUT A LOT OF ENERGY AND RESOURCES INTO MAKING NUTRIENT-RICH EGGS, WHILE YOUR SPERM ISN'T MUCH MORE THAN DNA WITH A PROPELLER.
I HAVE TO CHOOSE THE MALE WITH THE BEST GENES SO MY PARENTAL INVESTMENT PAYS OFF.
MY GENES ARE PLENTY GOOD AND TOUGH.
...now let's sneak away quietly...
I CAN'T, HOWARD. BIG EYE-STALKS ARE AN INDICATOR OF BETTER GENES FOR ACQUIRING AND STORING ENERGY. I JUST WANT THE BEST FOR MY CHILDREN AND... WELL... FRANKLY,...
...YOU COME UP SHORT.
OUCH.
AH, DON'T BLAME OL' JENNY
SHE WAS ONLY DOING WHAT COMES NATURALLY.

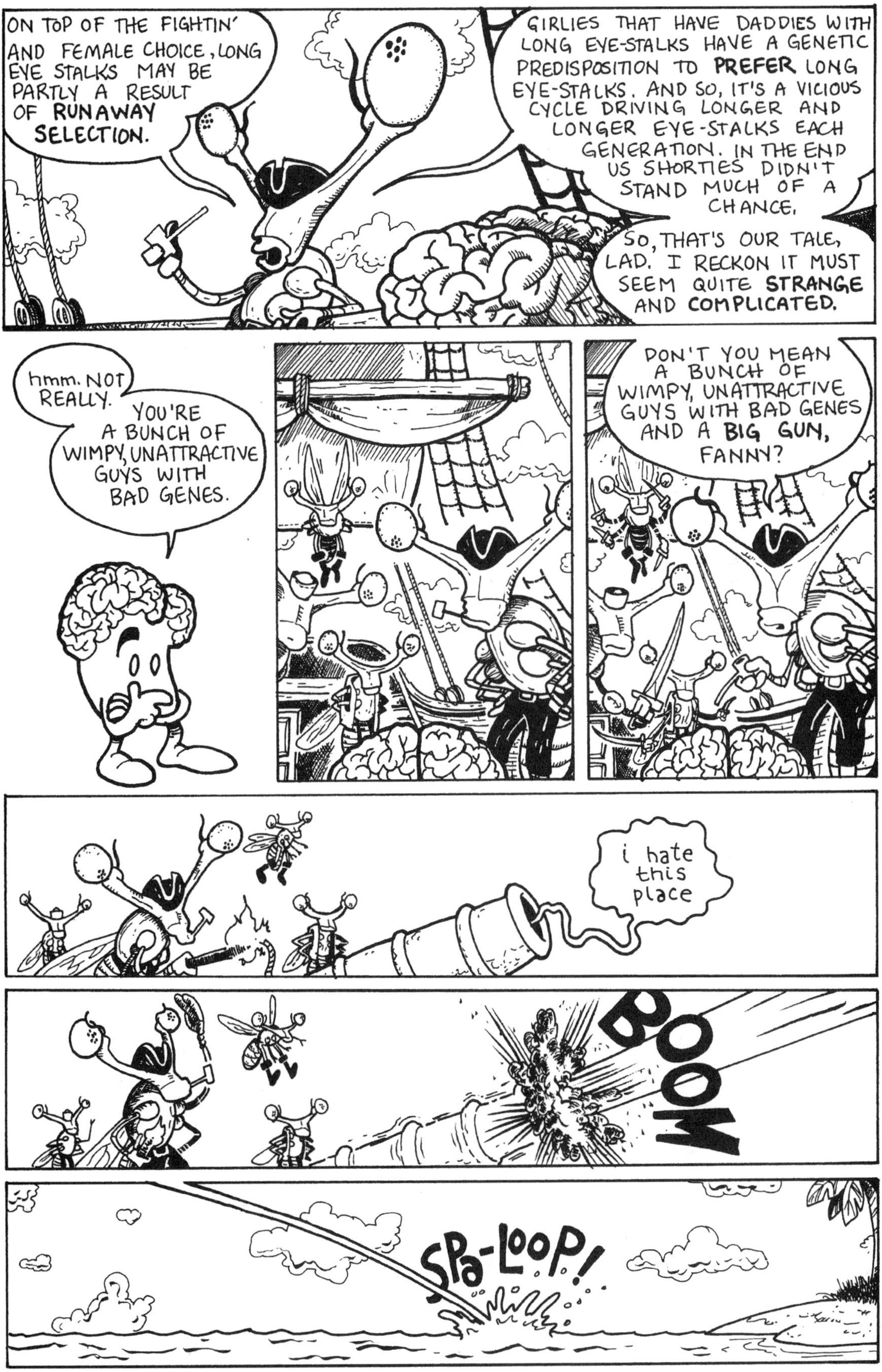
ON TOP OF THE FIGHTIN' AND FEMALE CHOICE, LONG EYE STALKS MAY BE PARTLY A RESULT OF **RUNAWAY SELECTION.**
GIRLIES THAT HAVE DADDIES WITH LONG EYE-STALKS HAVE A GENETIC PREDISPOSITION TO **PREFER** LONG EYE-STALKS. AND SO, IT'S A VICIOUS CYCLE DRIVING LONGER AND LONGER EYE-STALKS EACH GENERATION. IN THE END US SHORTIES DIDN'T STAND MUCH OF A CHANCE.
SO, THAT'S OUR TALE, LAD. I RECKON IT MUST SEEM QUITE **STRANGE** AND **COMPLICATED.**
hmm. NOT REALLY.
YOU'RE A BUNCH OF WIMPY, UNATTRACTIVE GUYS WITH BAD GENES.
DON'T YOU MEAN A BUNCH OF WIMPY, UNATTRACTIVE GUYS WITH BAD GENES AND A **BIG GUN,** FANNY?
i hate this place
BOOM
SPA-LOOP!

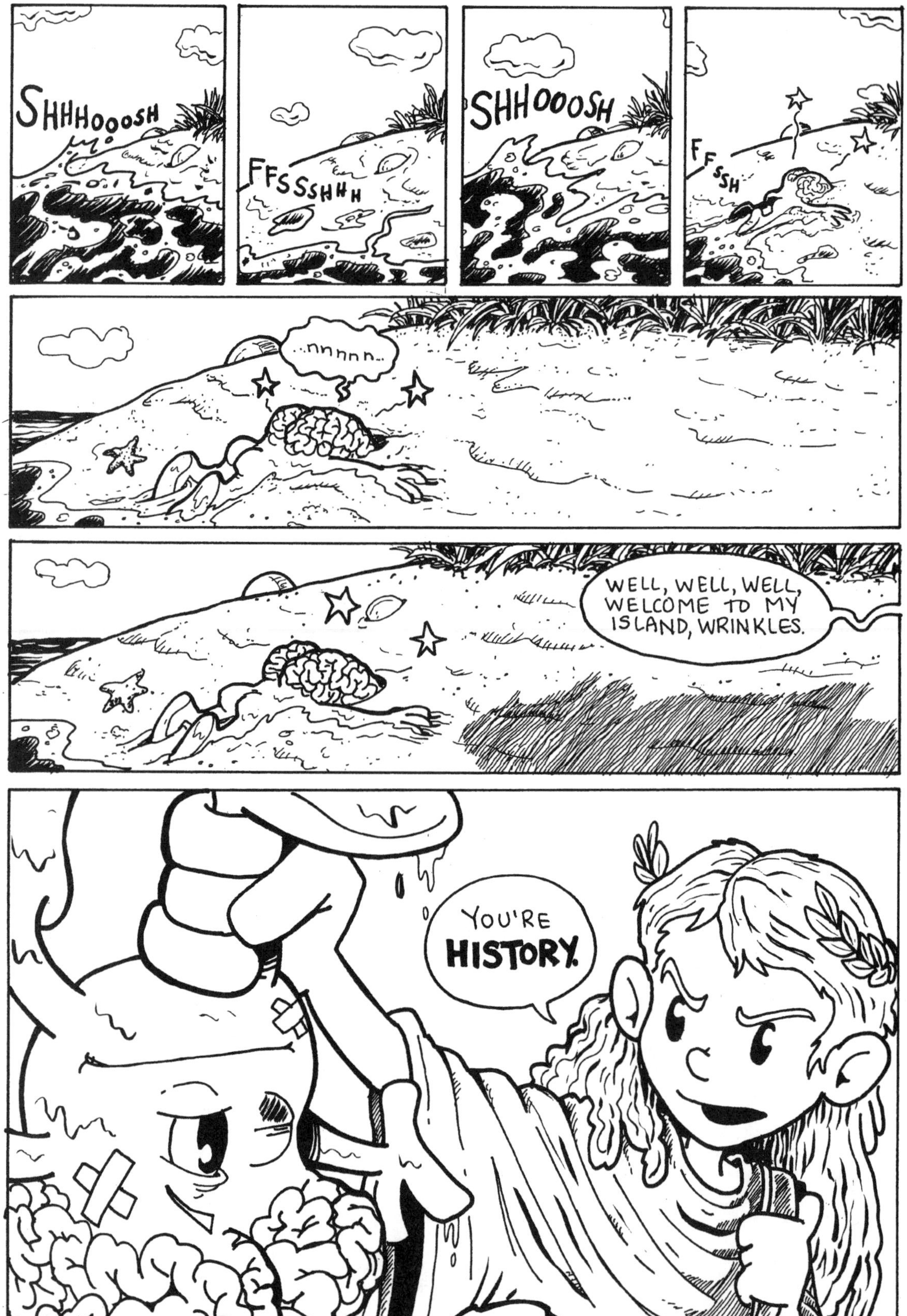
SHHHoooSH
FFSSSHHH
SHHOOOSH
FFSSH
...nnnnn...
WELL, WELL, WELL, WELCOME TO MY ISLAND, WRINKLES.
YOU'RE HISTORY.

TO BE CONTINUED...

Eye of the Beholder

News Flash: Males and Females are Different

Why do males and females of many species look so different? Obviously, members of each sex are issued different reproductive equipment to bring together eggs and sperm (collectively referred to as **gametes**). But what about differences that have nothing to do with an exchange of gametes? Why do male elephant seals have giant blubbery noses while female elephant seals do not? Why does a mallard have a conspicuous green noggin while the female coloration is much better camouflage? Why do males of a species of dung beetle from Ecuador have two horns while the females has none? These types of differences between the sexes are known as **sexual dimorphisms** (di = two, morph = shape) and Darwin proposed that they arise because of competition for mates.

Sexual Selection

Natural selection can be broken down into two types of selection. The first leads to differential abilities to survive and is known as **mortality selection**. The second leads to differential abilities to reproduce and is known as **sexual selection**. In the preceding chapters, we have talked about adaptations that help organisms survive long enough to reproduce. But surviving to reproductive age doesn't guarantee you will pass on your genes. Only ten percent of the male elephant seals on a beach will sire pups while the remaining 90% will fail to mate at all. In contrast, the majority of females reproduce. To understand why so many males fail, it is useful to think of mates as a resource. Organisms compete for food, water and space to survive. Why wouldn't they also complete for the mates required for reproduction? Sexual selection is the process by which variations in sexually dimorphic traits or behaviors give some individuals an advantage in obtaining mates.

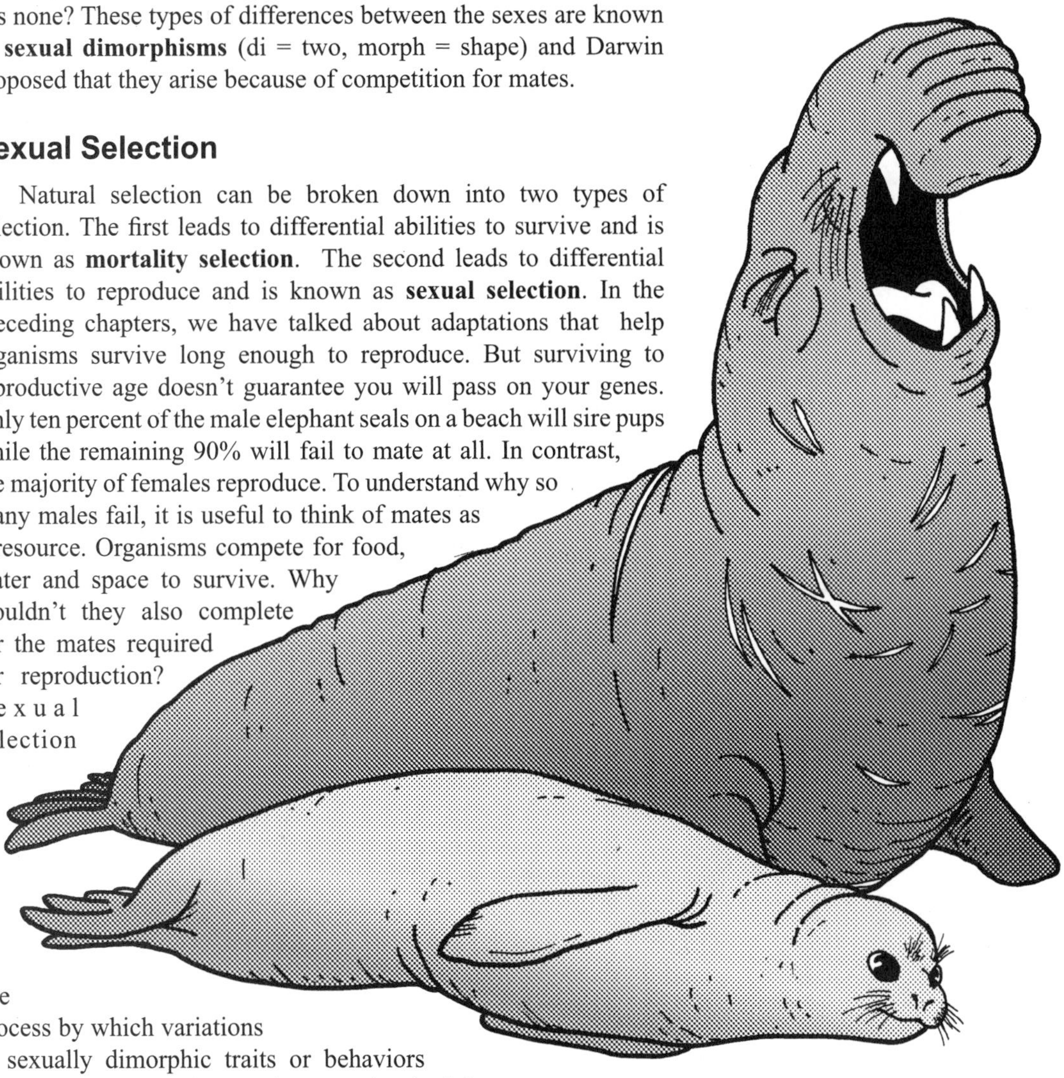

Figure 4.1 A male (big nose and big mouth) and female elephant seal.

In the case of the elephant seal, females prefer protected areas of beach to have their pups. Consequently, males capable of

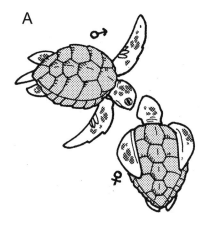

A

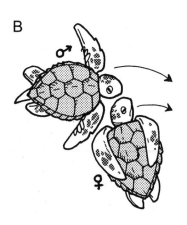

B

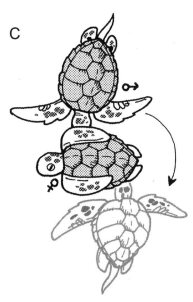

C

Figure 4.2 Courtship ritual of the loggerhead turtle. See text for description. Modified from Frick, et al (2000).

securing desirable beach front territories will have more luck with the ladies. Not surprisingly, the males that have the most success holding good territories are pretty big. They use their noses to trumpet warnings and threats to other males. This posturing can often dissuade smaller rivals. However, if another male thinks he stands a chance of driving the resident male from his property, the male elephant seals fight. This usually involves these massive animals rearing up and slamming their considerable bulk down upon their opponents while simultaneously driving their dagger-like teeth into their rival's neck. It can get bloody, but it's worth it. Successfully holding the territory means holding onto a harem of females with which to breed.

So why don't female elephant seals have big blubbery noses? Or, dagger-like teeth? The answer is, they don't need them. They aren't fighting for access to males, the males are fighting for access to the females. But, why fight in the first place?

How Much are You Willing to Invest?

Sexual selection can occur through a number of different mechanisms, but before we address them, we should stop to consider why it happens at all. What drives a system of differential reproductive success? The simple answer is investment. There is usually a disparity between what males and females invest in reproduction.

Neither male nor female loggerhead sea turtles provide any care for their young after the eggs are laid. After they exchange gametes, the male may go off to mate again. The female, however, must expend considerable metabolic energy to build a protective shell for each egg and provision them with the nutrient rich yolk. Then she drags herself out of the water, crawls up the beach, digs a big hole in the sand, lays her eggs (of which there may be hundreds) and covers them up. This is an exhausting process that exposes her to potential harm by terrestrial predators, including humans. Needless to say, if the female is going through all of that, she is going to be choosey about the father of her children!

To convince a female that his genes are worth the trouble, the smaller male loggerhead must perform a courtship behavior. He begins by circling the female as she floats facing him (Fig. 4.1A and B). After circling for awhile, he nuzzles her side (Fig. 4.1C) and bites her back flippers (Fig. 4.1D). He finishes by facing her and paddling his front flippers in a circular fashion (Fig. 4.1E). If she likes what she sees at this point, she might accept him (Fig. 4.1F). Or she might not, in which case the male might keep trying or eventually give up. This type of sexual selection, in which the female selects with whom she will or will not mate, is known as **female choice**.

What Does She See in That Guy?

What does a choosey female look for in a mate? Sometimes, she's looking for **direct benefits** such as she gets from a male with a good territory (as is the case with elephant seals) or a male that will stick around and help with the kids. Those are very tangible benefits. Sometimes, the benefits aren't as easy to spot. In some cases, females might be reading certain sexually dimorphic traits as indicators of **indirect benefits**, such as good genes. Female gray tree frogs prefer males that have longer calls. The males themselves don't offer the female anything directly (such as a good place to live or parental care). However, offspring of males with longer calls grow faster and are bigger when they go through metamorphosis than offspring of males with short calls. So, call length tells the female that the male has better genes for acquiring resources. By choosing males with longer calls, she is equipping her offspring with an adaptation that will give them a distinct advantage as they are competing for food.

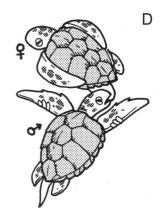

D

Of course, all of this choosing can get out of hand. **Runaway selection** describes a phenomenon in which female choice rapidly selects for more and more extravagant male features. Male stalk-eyed flies with longer eye-stalks tend to be better at acquiring resources. Thus the length of the eye stalk is an indication of good genes and as a result females show a preference for this trait. This preference appears to have a genetic basis and can be passed on to the female's offspring. Under these conditions, the females of the each generation will preferentially breed with the males with the longest eyestalks. It isn't hard to imagine how this selection will start to run away with itself and drive eyestalks of males in an population to elongate rapidly. As one might imagine, these flies expend more energy making and carrying around eye stalks and are easier targets for predators than flies without long eye stalks. However, the benefits of winning a mate and passing on one's genes more than compensate for the inconvenience and expenditure of energy.

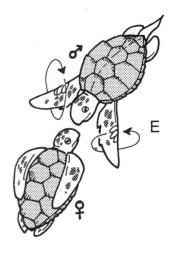

E

There are natural limits to runaway selection. If eye-stalks became so big that the male could not lift his head, that would severely curtail his ability to escape predators, find food and mate. The length of the eye-stalks are probably the result of a balancing act between sexual selection by females and mortality selection on males.

I'm a Fighter, Not a Lover!

Competition is another way to gain access to mates. This type of sexual selection can take on a number of different forms and can occur before, during or after the fertilization of the egg by the sperm. The most common form of competition is male **combat**, in which males fight to gain direct access to females or to defend a territory that females find attractive. To be winners, males must have sexually selected traits like bigger bodies or antlers to help them prevail against other males. In stalk-eyed flies, bigger eyestalks correlate with bigger overall size. So, it isn't surprising that when push literally comes to shove, bigger flies with bigger stalks prevail and get to reproduce.

F

But an exchange of gametes is still no guarantee that one's

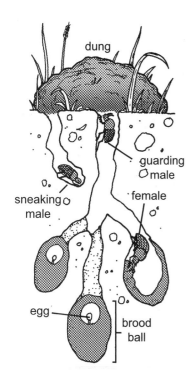

dung
guarding
male
sneaking
male
female
egg
brood
ball
Figure 4.3 Home sweet dung. A horned male dung beetle defends the entrance to his burrow as a female lays eggs in a brood ball made of dung. A tunneling hornless male is attempting to access the female by intercepting the burrow below the guarding male. Modified from Emlen (2000).

genes will get passed into the next generation. Females of many species can mate multiple times before their eggs are fertilized. **Sperm competition** is the phenomenon in which the sperm from multiple males scramble to get to an egg first. Males can respond to this competition in a number of ways. They can produce more sperm or sperm of varying sizes and shapes that are better adapted to compete in the female's reproductive tract.

Superior number or quality is not the only way sperm competition occurs. In some cases, mating order plays a role. In chimpanzees, the dominant male is often the last to mate with a female and his sperm is more likely to fertilize her eggs. Female insects can actually store a male's semen in a structure called the **spermatheca** for extended periods of time before she uses it to fertilize her eggs. In the event she encounters a male that she deems superior to her first mate, she can mate again. At that time, the first male's sperms can be displaced. Damselfly males have evolved a diverse array of appendages on their penises designed to scoop out a rival's sperm. To prevent this type of sperm displacement, several species of animals use a techniques called mate guarding. Male loggerhead turtles often stay connected to the female long after the exchange of gametes is complete to prevent another male access.

Infanticide is a competition strategy that is sometimes used after offspring have been born. Groups of langur monkeys consist of one male and his harem of females. Male langurs born into the harem must leave. To pass on their genes, these males must eventually depose an older male and take over his harem. When a langur has done this successfully, he will kill his rival's offspring so that all parental care and resources are invested exclusively in the offspring that he will soon sire.

Sensitive Guys

Our discussion, so far, has centered on female choice and male adaptations that develop via sexual selection. But it is best to consider sexual selection in more general terms. Specifically, sexual selection happens when the least-invested sex competes and the most-invested sex is choosey. When sexual selection occurs in nature, it is generally the females that are most invested (for many of the reasons outlined above), but there are occasions when this role is reversed.

Males of the firefly *Photinus* offer females a nuptial (or mating) gift called a **spermatophore**. The spermatophore is a gelatinous package composed of sperm and food for the developing eggs. During the breeding season, each *Photinus* firefly will mate several times. However, they do not eat during this time. So, each mating event diminishes their reserves and they aren't replenishing themselves with food. Consequently, over the course of the season, females become dependent upon the spermatophore's provisions for their developing eggs. At the same time, the male's spermatophores are becoming smaller and less abundant. Thus, at end of the season, female-female competition arises for spermatophores and males

A
B
C

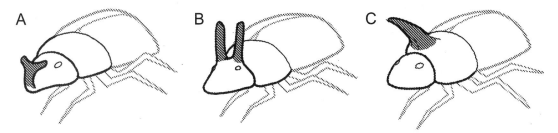

Figure 4.4 Numerous species of dung beetles have evolved horns. Depending on the species, those horns can develop on A) the front of the head, B) the back of the head or C) the thorax. However, when resources are allocated to building horns during development, fewer resources are available for neighboring organs such as eyes.

become selective in their choice of mates.

Tag-Team Selection

There comes a time in every young dung beetle's life to seek a mate. At this time, males and females head for the best pile of poop they can find. The female burrows under the dung and builds a network of chambers (Fig. 4.3). Each chamber will contain one egg and a provision of dung for the emerging beetle larva. While the female is working below, male dung beetles fight for an opportunity to mate with her. This is done by standing at the mouth of the burrow and defending it against other males. Males that successfully defend the burrow can periodically go down and mate with the female. As it would happen, males with bigger horns are better at securing a burrow than smaller males with small horns.

Dung beetles belong to the genus *Onthophagus,* in the scarab beetle family. This family contains in excess of 2000 species living in a variety of habitats across the globe. (Poop is everywhere, after all.) Most of the *Onthophagus* beetles have horns, but their location on the body varies from species to species. Members of some species have horns growing from the front of their head; others

Percent (%) of species with horns at each location
60
50
40
30
20
10
Diurnal
Nocturnal
Diurnal
Nocturnal
Diurnal
Nocturnal
Front of head
Back of head
Thorax
Horn location

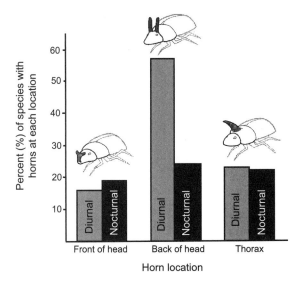

Figure 4.5 Association between horn size and ecology. When the location of the horn doesn't affect eye size (front of the head, thorax), there is no difference between the number of diurnal and nocturnal species with horns in that location. However, nocturnal beetles (who need to navigate in the dark) are significantly less likely to have horns on the back of their head. Modified form Emlen (2001).

have them growing from the back of their head; and still others have them growing out of their thorax (Fig. 4.4). These horns are sexually selected traits that are energetically costly to make and haul around. And, since they are part of the beetle's exoskeleton, they can't be shed at the end of the breeding season as deer shed their antlers. They also come with a developmental cost. Resources that are allocated to grow horns are not available for building other nearby structures. Thus, beetles with horns growing from the front of the head have smaller antennae than those without horns in the front. Those with horns at the back of the head have smaller eyes, and those with horns on the thorax have smaller wings.

This system is a fascinating example of the interplay between sexual selection and ecology. Horns are clearly something useful for combat and access to females, but they come at a cost. Consequently, mortality selection should select for the horn location that has the least impact on the species' ability to survive. This appears to be the case. Dung beetles active during the day have horns on the back of the head much more frequently than nocturnal species (Fig. 4.5). Bigger eyes are an advantage when trying to navigate the low-light conditions at night. Thus, though sexual selection may favor the evolution of horns in dung beetles, mortality selection would favor nocturnal beetles that grow them somewhere that doesn't make their eyes smaller.

All's Fair in Love and War
(or, Cheaters Never Prosper, Except When They Do)

Big horns are not the end of the story in dung beetle reproduction and sexual selection. Sometimes guile can more than compensate for a lack of horn size. A male dung beetle with small horns often digs his own tunnel under the dung in an attempt to intercept the network of tunnels the female has constructed (Fig. 4.3). If he can sneak in behind the horned male protecting the tunnels, he may successfully mate with the female below.

So, Why Aren't Acquired Traits Passed On?

In the preceding story, Wrinkles made Wendy and Frank very happy when he told them that their acquired traits wouldn't be passed onto their baby. But, why wouldn't they? The cells of your body can be divided into two broad categories: gametes and **somatic cells**. As we have established, gametes are sperm and egg cells. Somatic cells are all of the remaining cells in your body that aren't gemetes.

To understand why acquired traits aren't passed-on to offspring, let's imagine that you are reading a book about eyes. As you take in the information, you are subtly changing your brain. Specifically, you are altering the physical architecture and electrochemical activity of somatic cells in your brain called **neurons**. If you find the book thrilling, your brain may be forever changed and a lasting memory will be formed. You now know a great deal about eyes. Unfortunately, none of that will be passed onto your offspring because your studying has not altered the genetic material in your gametes. If you have kids, you will pass on the genes to build what will undoubtedly be a lovely brain, but you will not pass along any of the changes that you made in yours.

For Your Consideration

1. What other examples of sexual dimorphisms can you think of? How do you think each might affect its bearer's survival?

2. Rituals evolve among animals that engage in combat to gain access to mates and/or defend territories. What examples of behavioral rituals can you think of? Why do you suppose performing rituals prior to fighting might have some adaptive value?

3. Which aspects of human anatomy, physiology and behavior do you think may have been shaped by sexual selection? Explain.

4. In 1975, the biologist Amotz Zahavi hypothesized that evolution might lead to unusual examples of honest communication between animals. He called this hypothesis the Handicap Principle and it proposed that animals might evolve physical features that are burdensome or costly to honestly communicate their fitness to others. Discuss how this hypothesis might be used to explain various sexually dimorphic traits in nature.

Chapter Five: Clio's Island

I'M HISTORY?

YOU BETTER BELIEVE IT, BUSTER.

OF COURSE, AREN'T WE ALL?

WHU MP!!

HISTORY IN THE MAKING!

?

SORRY. I WAS JUST MESSIN' WITH YOU.

I DON'T GET MANY VISITORS, SO I GOTTA HAVE MY FUN.

...s'not funny to me..

YOU'RE RIGHT.

TRUCE?

I WON'T TEASE YOU IF YOU STOP ACTING HURT.

everybody knows brains don't have pain receptors, you big faker.

sigh.

o.k.

I'M CLIO, MUSE OF HISTORY.

WRINKLES.

I **KNOW.** I'VE HAD MY EYE ON YOU FOR AWHILE NOW.

YOU HAVE?

YEP. AND I'VE BEEN DYIN' TO ASK: WHY WRINKLES?

MY PARENTS LIKED DESCRIPTIVE NAMES.

THEY NAMED MY SISTER "JIGGLY PINKY POO."

NO, NO. WHY DO YOU **HAVE** WRINKLES?

OH, THAT.

HUUUUP

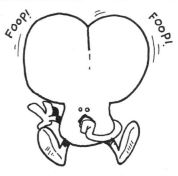

FOOP!

FOOP!

I GET IT, WRINKLES INCREASE YOUR SURFACE AREA.

LETS ME FOLD MORE BRAIN INTO A SMALL SKULL.

if I lived in a skull, that is..

SO, YOU COULD BE PRETTY SMART IF YOU WANTED?

WHAT DO YOU MEAN **COULD** BE?

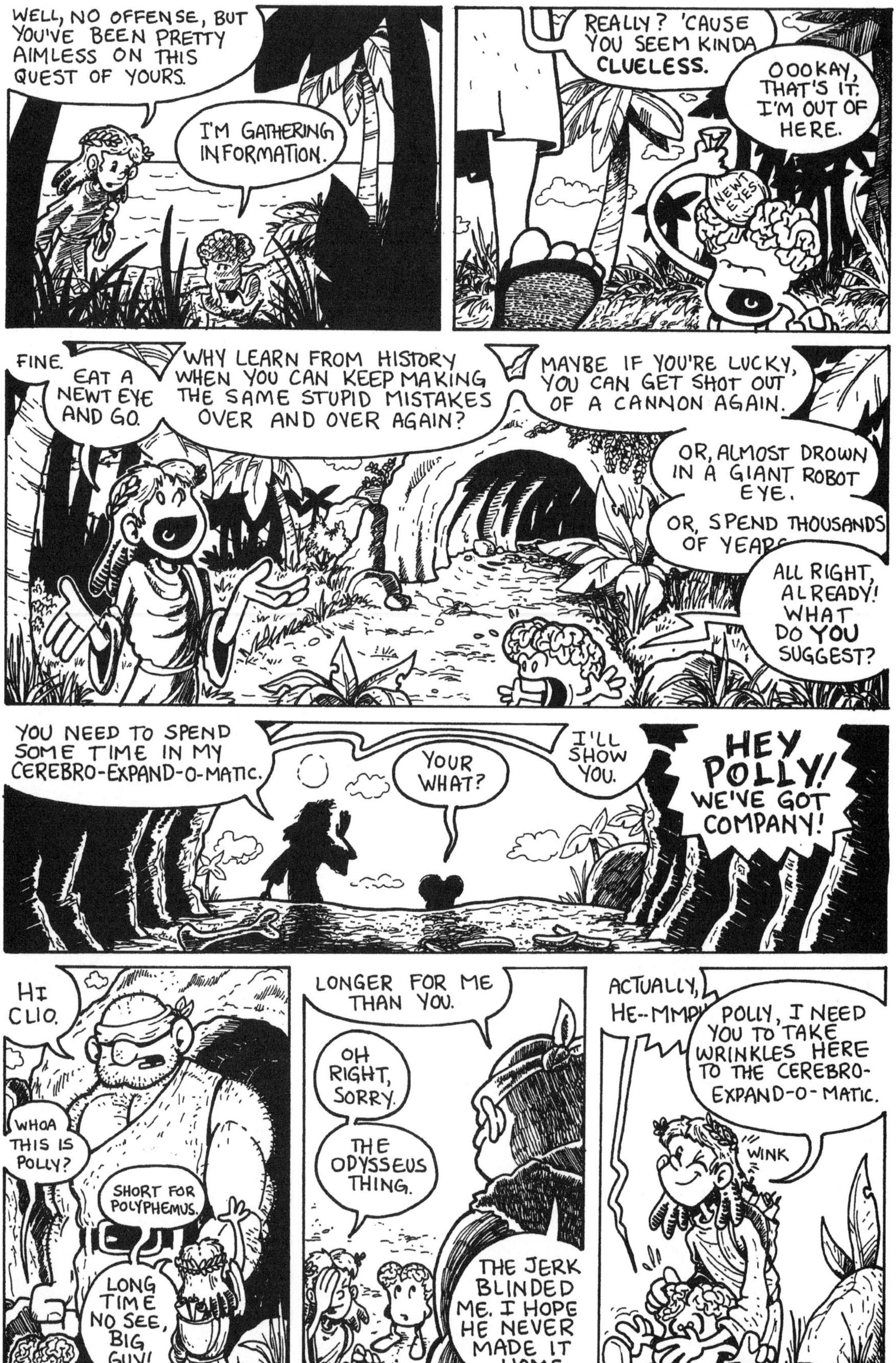
WELL, NO OFFENSE, BUT YOU'VE BEEN PRETTY AIMLESS ON THIS QUEST OF YOURS.
I'M GATHERING INFORMATION.
REALLY? 'CAUSE YOU SEEM KINDA CLUELESS.
OOOKAY, THAT'S IT. I'M OUT OF HERE.
NEWT EYES
FINE.
EAT A NEWT EYE AND GO.
WHY LEARN FROM HISTORY WHEN YOU CAN KEEP MAKING THE SAME STUPID MISTAKES OVER AND OVER AGAIN?
MAYBE IF YOU'RE LUCKY, YOU CAN GET SHOT OUT OF A CANNON AGAIN.
OR, ALMOST DROWN IN A GIANT ROBOT EYE.
OR, SPEND THOUSANDS OF YEARS
ALL RIGHT, ALREADY! WHAT DO YOU SUGGEST?
YOU NEED TO SPEND SOME TIME IN MY CEREBRO-EXPAND-O-MATIC.
YOUR WHAT?
I'LL SHOW YOU.
HEY POLLY! WE'VE GOT COMPANY!
HI CLIO.
WHOA THIS IS POLLY?
SHORT FOR POLYPHEMUS.
LONG TIME NO SEE, BIG GUY!
LONGER FOR ME THAN YOU.
OH RIGHT, SORRY.
THE ODYSSEUS THING.
THE JERK BLINDED ME. I HOPE HE NEVER MADE IT HOME.
ACTUALLY, HE--MMPH
POLLY, I NEED YOU TO TAKE WRINKLES HERE TO THE CEREBRO-EXPAND-O-MATIC.
WINK

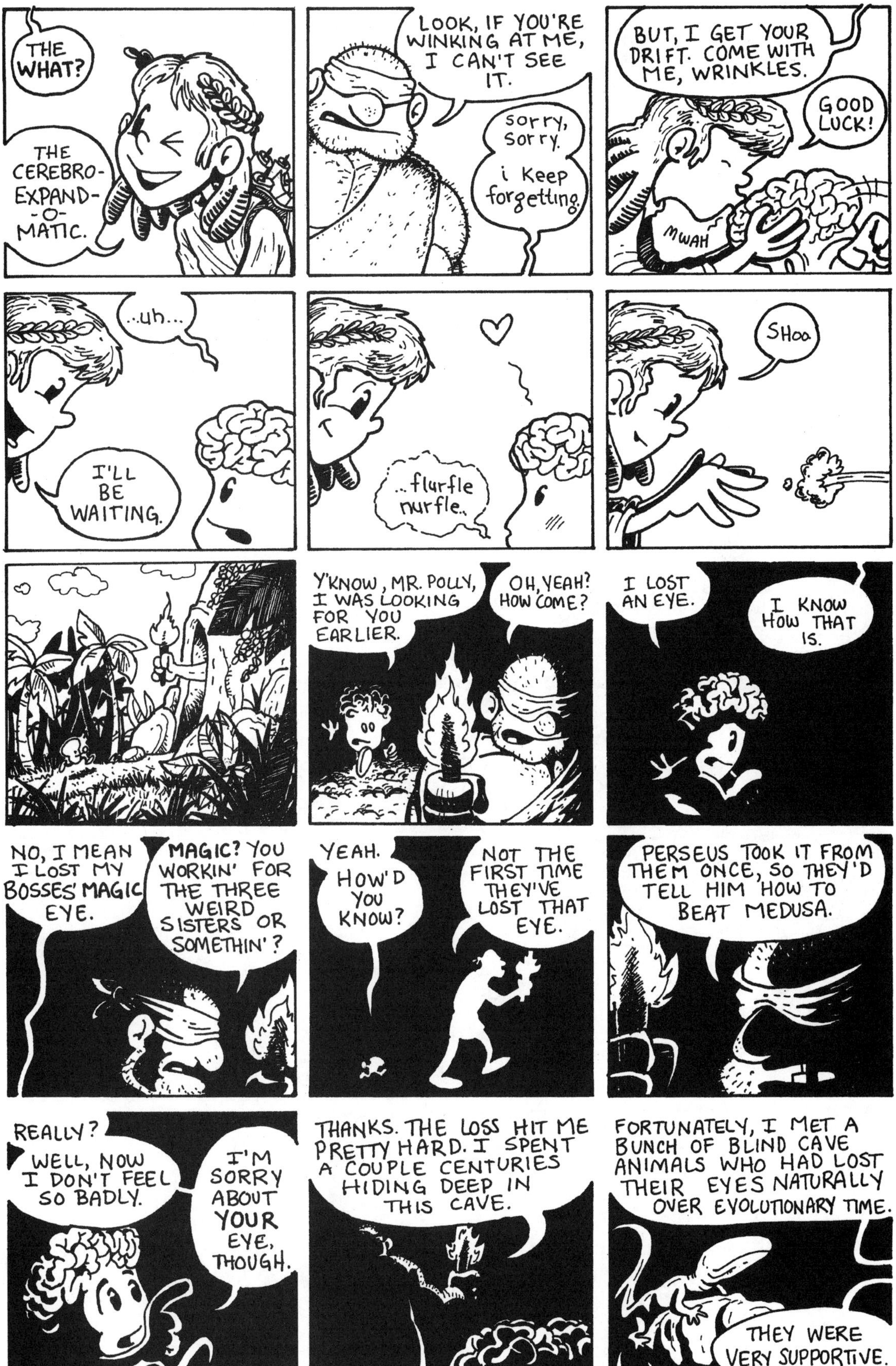
THE WHAT?
THE CEREBRO-EXPAND-O-MATIC.
LOOK, IF YOU'RE WINKING AT ME, I CAN'T SEE IT.
sorry, sorry.
i keep forgetting.
BUT, I GET YOUR DRIFT. COME WITH ME, WRINKLES.
GOOD LUCK!
MWAH
..uh...
I'LL BE WAITING.
...flurfle nurfle..
SHoo
Y'KNOW, MR. POLLY, I WAS LOOKING FOR YOU EARLIER.
OH, YEAH? HOW COME?
I LOST AN EYE.
I KNOW HOW THAT IS.
NO, I MEAN I LOST MY BOSSES' MAGIC EYE.
MAGIC? YOU WORKIN' FOR THE THREE WEIRD SISTERS OR SOMETHIN'?
YEAH.
HOW'D YOU KNOW?
NOT THE FIRST TIME THEY'VE LOST THAT EYE.
PERSEUS TOOK IT FROM THEM ONCE, SO THEY'D TELL HIM HOW TO BEAT MEDUSA.
REALLY?
WELL, NOW I DON'T FEEL SO BADLY.
I'M SORRY ABOUT YOUR EYE, THOUGH.
THANKS. THE LOSS HIT ME PRETTY HARD. I SPENT A COUPLE CENTURIES HIDING DEEP IN THIS CAVE.
FORTUNATELY, I MET A BUNCH OF BLIND CAVE ANIMALS WHO HAD LOST THEIR EYES NATURALLY OVER EVOLUTIONARY TIME.
THEY WERE VERY SUPPORTIVE.

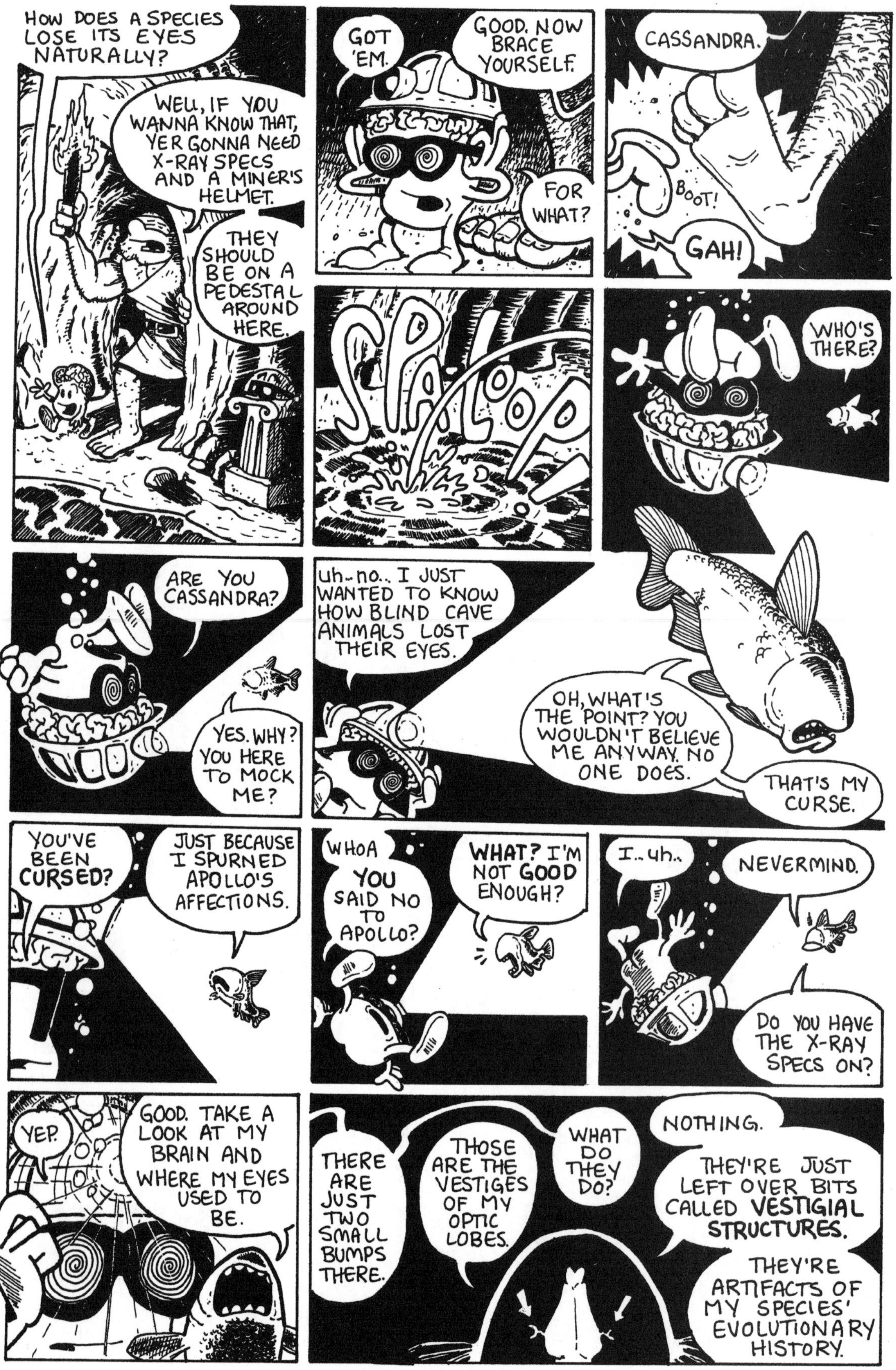
HOW DOES A SPECIES LOSE ITS EYES NATURALLY?
WELL, IF YOU WANNA KNOW THAT, YER GONNA NEED X-RAY SPECS AND A MINER'S HELMET.
THEY SHOULD BE ON A PEDESTAL AROUND HERE.
GOT 'EM.
GOOD. NOW BRACE YOURSELF.
FOR WHAT?
CASSANDRA.
BOOT!
GAH!
SPALOOP
WHO'S THERE?
ARE YOU CASSANDRA?
YES. WHY? YOU HERE TO MOCK ME?
uh.. no.. I JUST WANTED TO KNOW HOW BLIND CAVE ANIMALS LOST THEIR EYES.
OH, WHAT'S THE POINT? YOU WOULDN'T BELIEVE ME ANYWAY. NO ONE DOES.
THAT'S MY CURSE.
YOU'VE BEEN **CURSED**?
JUST BECAUSE I SPURNED APOLLO'S AFFECTIONS.
WHOA **YOU** SAID NO TO APOLLO?
WHAT? I'M NOT **GOOD** ENOUGH?
I.. uh..
NEVERMIND.
DO YOU HAVE THE X-RAY SPECS ON?
YEP.
GOOD. TAKE A LOOK AT MY BRAIN AND WHERE MY EYES USED TO BE.
THERE ARE JUST TWO SMALL BUMPS THERE.
THOSE ARE THE VESTIGES OF MY OPTIC LOBES.
WHAT DO THEY DO?
NOTHING.
THEY'RE JUST LEFT OVER BITS CALLED **VESTIGIAL STRUCTURES.**
THEY'RE ARTIFACTS OF MY SPECIES' EVOLUTIONARY HISTORY.

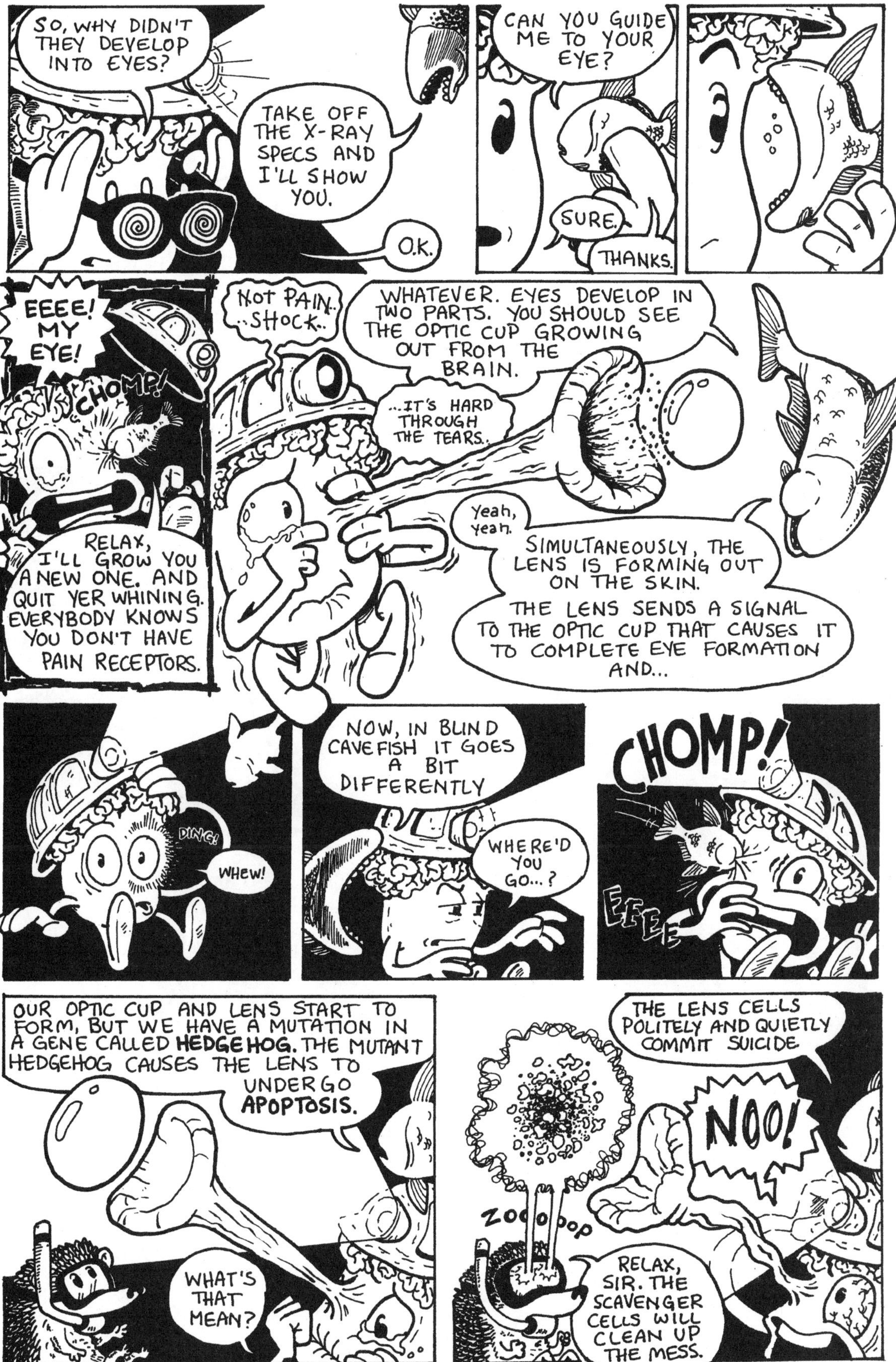

SO, WHY DIDN'T THEY DEVELOP INTO EYES?
TAKE OFF THE X-RAY SPECS AND I'LL SHOW YOU.
O.K.
CAN YOU GUIDE ME TO YOUR EYE?
SURE.
THANKS.
EEEE! MY EYE!
CHOMP!
RELAX, I'LL GROW YOU A NEW ONE. AND QUIT YER WHINING. EVERYBODY KNOWS YOU DON'T HAVE PAIN RECEPTORS.
NOT PAIN.. ..SHOCK..
WHATEVER. EYES DEVELOP IN TWO PARTS. YOU SHOULD SEE THE OPTIC CUP GROWING OUT FROM THE BRAIN.
...IT'S HARD THROUGH THE TEARS..
Yeah, yeah.
SIMULTANEOUSLY, THE LENS IS FORMING OUT ON THE SKIN.
THE LENS SENDS A SIGNAL TO THE OPTIC CUP THAT CAUSES IT TO COMPLETE EYE FORMATION AND...
DING!
WHEW!
NOW, IN BLIND CAVEFISH IT GOES A BIT DIFFERENTLY
WHERE'D YOU GO...?
CHOMP!
EEEE
OUR OPTIC CUP AND LENS START TO FORM, BUT WE HAVE A MUTATION IN A GENE CALLED HEDGEHOG. THE MUTANT HEDGEHOG CAUSES THE LENS TO UNDERGO APOPTOSIS.
WHAT'S THAT MEAN?
THE LENS CELLS POLITELY AND QUIETLY COMMIT SUICIDE.
NOO!
ZOOOOOP
RELAX, SIR. THE SCAVENGER CELLS WILL CLEAN UP THE MESS.

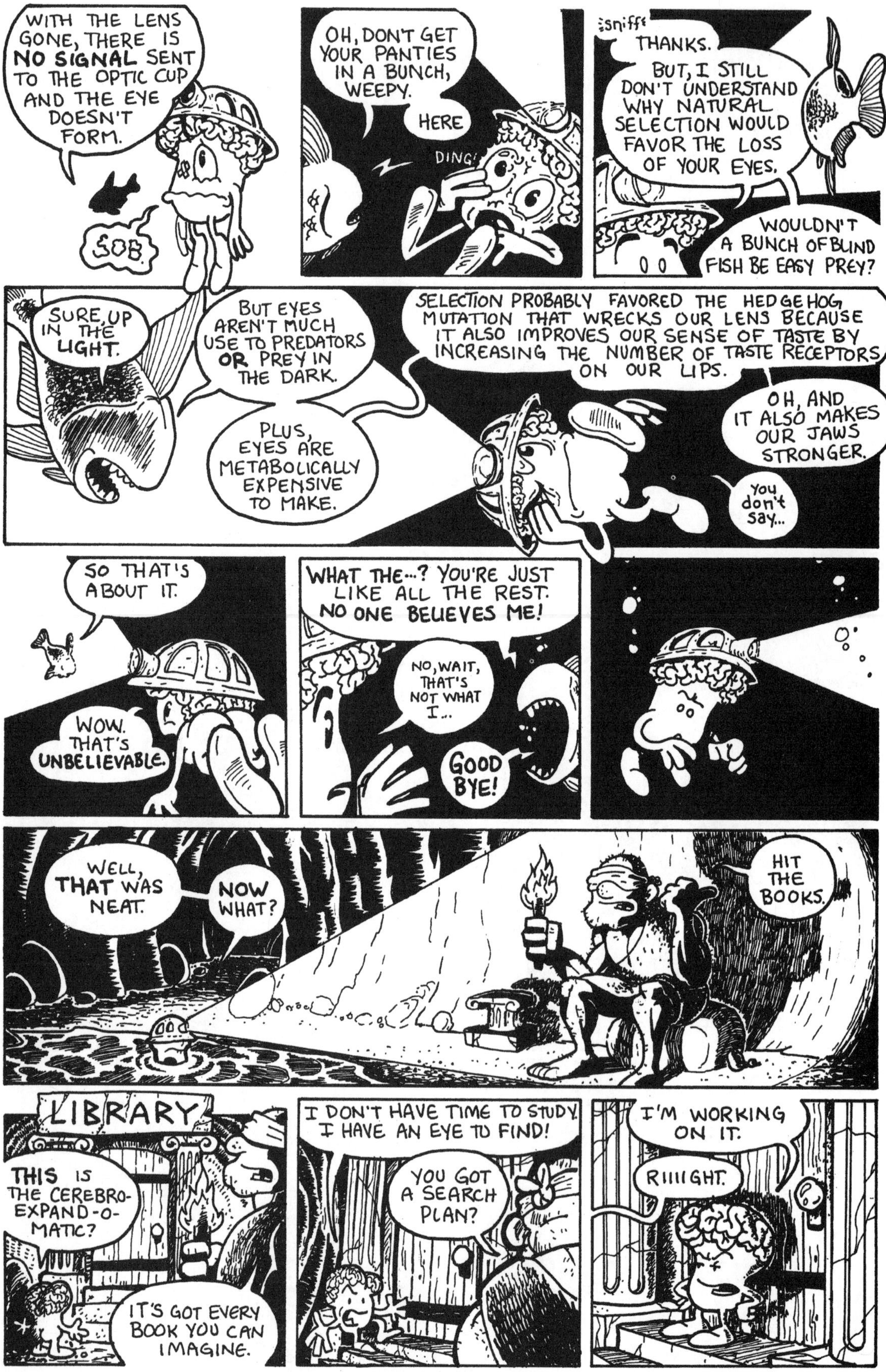
WITH THE LENS GONE, THERE IS NO SIGNAL SENT TO THE OPTIC CUP AND THE EYE DOESN'T FORM.
SOB.
OH, DON'T GET YOUR PANTIES IN A BUNCH, WEEPY.
HERE
DING!
sniff
THANKS.
BUT, I STILL DON'T UNDERSTAND WHY NATURAL SELECTION WOULD FAVOR THE LOSS OF YOUR EYES.
WOULDN'T A BUNCH OF BLIND FISH BE EASY PREY?
SURE, UP IN THE LIGHT.
BUT EYES AREN'T MUCH USE TO PREDATORS OR PREY IN THE DARK.
PLUS, EYES ARE METABOLICALLY EXPENSIVE TO MAKE.
SELECTION PROBABLY FAVORED THE HEDGEHOG MUTATION THAT WRECKS OUR LENS BECAUSE IT ALSO IMPROVES OUR SENSE OF TASTE BY INCREASING THE NUMBER OF TASTE RECEPTORS ON OUR LIPS.
OH, AND IT ALSO MAKES OUR JAWS STRONGER.
You don't say...
SO THAT'S ABOUT IT.
WOW. THAT'S UNBELIEVABLE.
WHAT THE...? YOU'RE JUST LIKE ALL THE REST. NO ONE BELIEVES ME!
NO, WAIT, THAT'S NOT WHAT I...
GOOD BYE!
WELL, THAT WAS NEAT.
NOW WHAT?
HIT THE BOOKS.
LIBRARY
THIS IS THE CEREBRO-EXPAND-O-MATIC?
IT'S GOT EVERY BOOK YOU CAN IMAGINE.
I DON'T HAVE TIME TO STUDY. I HAVE AN EYE TO FIND!
YOU GOT A SEARCH PLAN?
I'M WORKING ON IT.
RIIIIGHT.

THAT'S WHY CLIO SENT YOU HERE, KID.

YOU CAN SEE, BUT YOU GOT NO VISION.

huh.

THAT IS SO TRUE

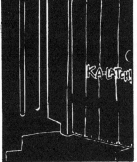

CREEEAK

KA-LTCH!

FIVE YEARS LATER

CREEEAK

CLANG!

DO YOU HEAR THAT?

IT'S COMIN' FROM THE CAVE.

CLANG! CLANG! CLANG! CLANG!

holy macaroni

YOU LIKE MY ROBO-BOD? NOW I CAN LOOK YOU IN THE EYE.

IS THIS ALL YOU WORKED ON?

HECK, NO. I READ EVERY BOOK IN THERE.

LEARN ANYTHING TO HELP YOU ON YOUR SEARCH?

NOT DIRECTLY, BUT I'M SMARTER AND STRONGER NOW, SO NO ONE'S GONNA MESS WITH ME ANYMORE.

FEEL.

IMPRESSIVE.

WHAT'S THE FATAL FLAW?

WHAT DO YOU MEAN?

WHAT'S THIS THING'S WEAKNESS?

THE STUPID DESIGN FLAW THAT TURNS IT INTO A WORTHLESS HUNK OF JUNK.

THERE ISN'T ANY.

TAP TAP

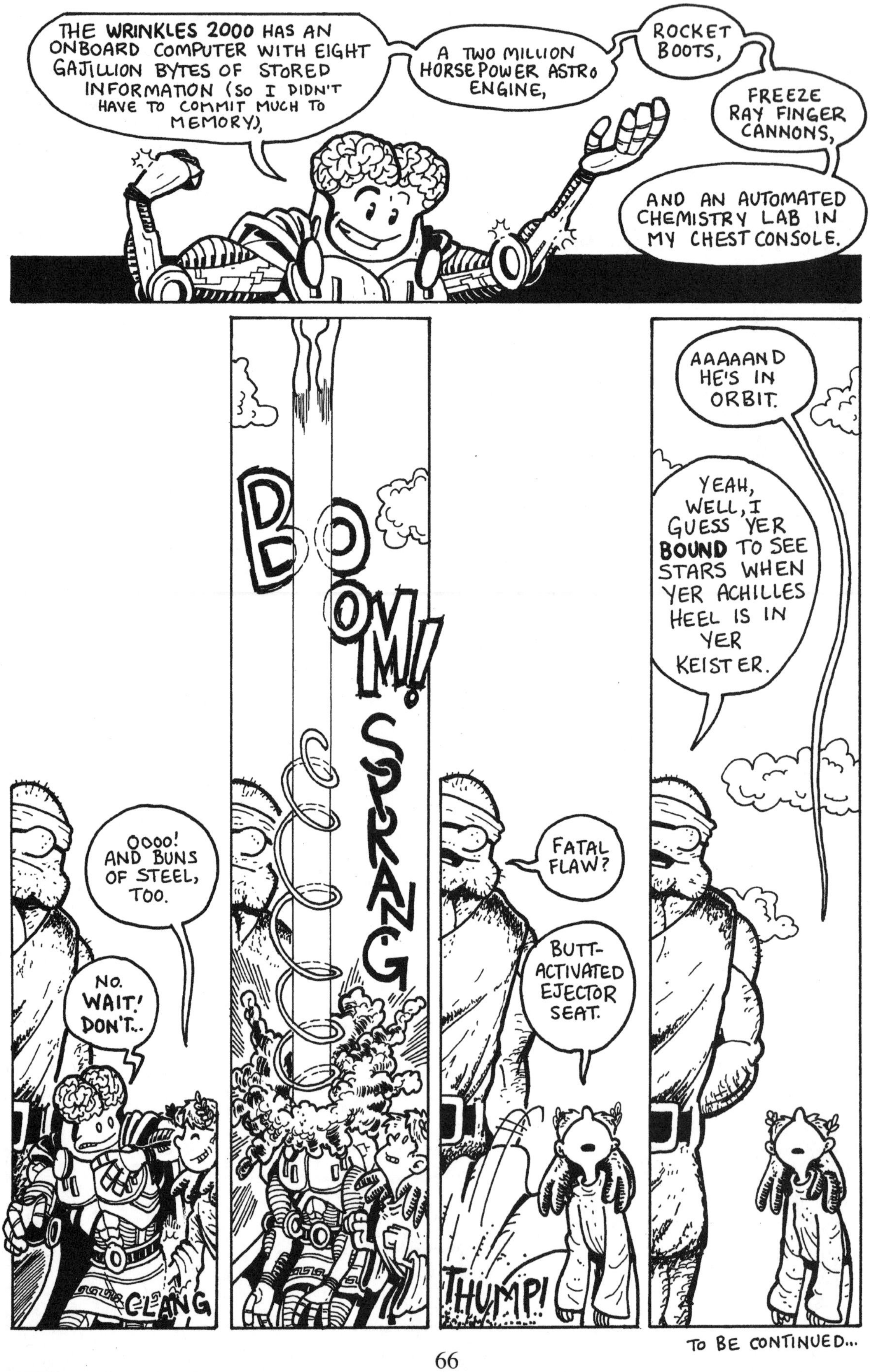
THE WRINKLES 2000 HAS AN ONBOARD COMPUTER WITH EIGHT GAJILLION BYTES OF STORED INFORMATION (SO I DIDN'T HAVE TO COMMIT MUCH TO MEMORY),
A TWO MILLION HORSEPOWER ASTRO ENGINE,
ROCKET BOOTS,
FREEZE RAY FINGER CANNONS,
AND AN AUTOMATED CHEMISTRY LAB IN MY CHEST CONSOLE.
OOOO! AND BUNS OF STEEL, TOO.
NO. WAIT! DON'T..
CLANG
BOOM!
SPRANG
FATAL FLAW?
BUTT-ACTIVATED EJECTOR SEAT.
THUMP!
AAAAAND HE'S IN ORBIT.
YEAH, WELL, I GUESS YER BOUND TO SEE STARS WHEN YER ACHILLES HEEL IS IN YER KEISTER.

TO BE CONTINUED...

An Eye on Development

The Central Dogma

An organism's DNA contains all of the information required to build its anatomical features and run its physiological processes. But how is that information accessed and used? How does a molecule of DNA exert its influence on the body? At a very basic level, DNA contains the recipes to make proteins. The process of making these proteins follows a very specific set of steps.

DNA (short for **deoxyribonucleic acid**) is a double-stranded molecule made of **nucleic acids** that is found in a small chamber inside an organism's cells called the **nucleus** (Fig. 5.1). Each DNA strand contains many regions known as **genes**. These genes are the recipes used to make specific proteins. The kitchen where these proteins are made is outside the nucleus in the cell's internal fluid (called the **cytoplasm)** and the cooks are small, protein building organelles called **ribosomes**. Now, when you or I use a recipe, we take it into the kitchen where we'll do the cooking. In the cell, however, we are not allowed to take the DNA recipes out of the nucleus and into the cytoplasmic kitchen. To get the recipes to where we make the proteins, the recipes must be copied and transported out of the nucleus.

Making a protein starts when the double-stranded DNA recipe is used as a template to make a single-stranded molecule of **RNA** (ribonucleic acid). This RNA is our copy of the DNA recipe for a protein and can leave the nucleus. Since the information in DNA and RNA is written in the same nucleic acid language, the process of making RNA from DNA is know as **transcription** (Fig. 5.2).

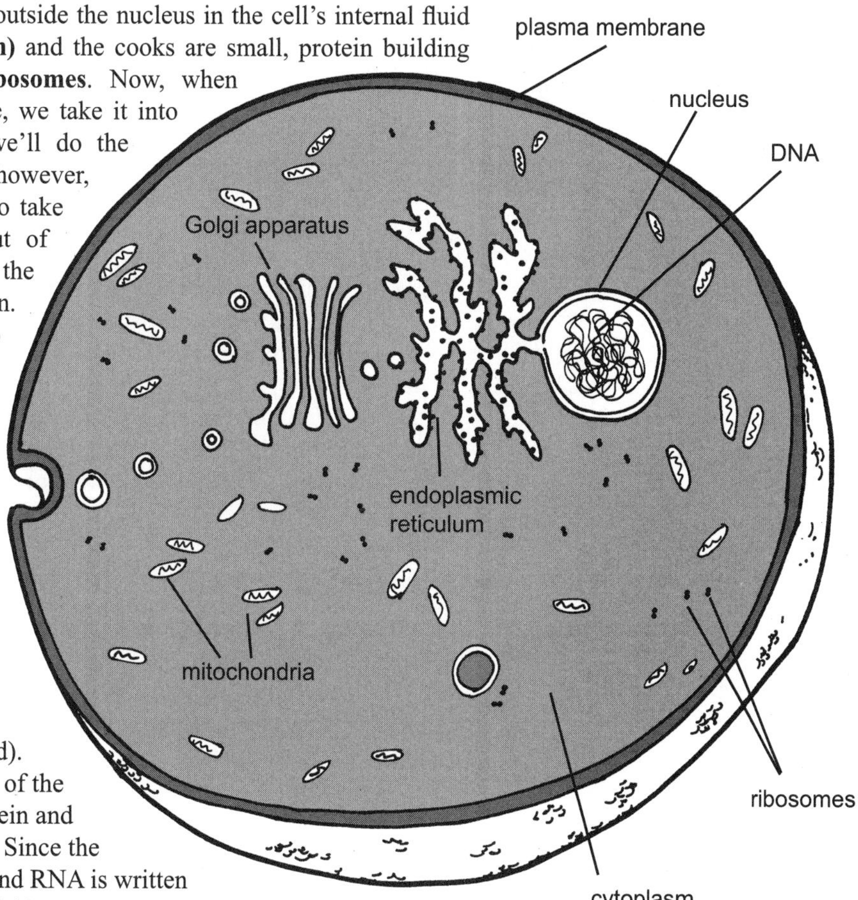
plasma membrane
nucleus
DNA
Golgi apparatus
endoplasmic
reticulum
mitochondria
ribosomes
cytoplasm

Figure 5.1 The animal cell is composed primarily of watery cytoplasm contained in a lipid plasma membrane. The genetic material (DNA) is contained in the membrane-bound nucleus.

Once transcribed, the RNA can move from the nucleus to the cytoplasm (the kitchen), where it is received by the ribosomes (the cooks). The ribosomes must now take the RNA recipe and build a protein molecule. However, proteins are not built of nucleic acids. They are composed of units known as **amino acids**. Thus, the

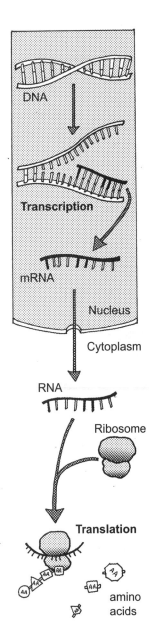

DNA

Transcription

mRNA

Nucleus

Cytoplasm

RNA

Ribosome

Translation

amino
acids

Figure 5.2 The Central Dogma of Biology. Information on a DNA molecule is transcribed into a molecule of RNA. The RNA then leaves the nucleus and enters the cytoplasm. In the cytoplasm, the information in the RNA molecule is translated into a protein by an organelle called a ribosome.

ribosomes must read the nucleic acid recipe and translate it into amino acid ingredients. This process of making proteins using RNA recipes is called **translation** (Fig 5.2).

This entire operation, which can be summarized as *DNA to RNA to protein*, is known as the **Central Dogma** of biology (Fig. 5.2). Of course, the process is a touch more complicated. Sometimes the protein needs to be tweaked before and after the translation process. These alterations, known as **pre-and post-translational modifications**, can include adding molecules to the protein that further refine the specificity of its function.

Development and Evolution

Organisms are constructed and run by the proteins encoded by their DNA. But is the Central Dogma all we need to understand about how a complex plant or animal is built? Not really. In between the DNA code for an animal and the animal itself is a long, complicated process known as **development**. During development, a single fertilized egg gives rise to billions of well-organized, specialized cells found in tissues (like muscles and bones), as well as to larger anatomical features such as eyes and appendages.

Just as building a house often requires several construction workers, it takes a multitude of genes to build an organism (25,000 for human, 13,700 for a fruit fly) and the activity of those genes, like the activity of construction workers, must be coordinated. If you tried to run the electricity for a house before the foundation was laid, the end result probably wouldn't be livable. Likewise, building an organism requires more than just pumping out a bunch of proteins. The production of these proteins must be coordinated so that they are only produced at the appropriate time and place. This coordination is carried out in the cell by regulatory genes. One interesting class of regulatory genes are the homeobox genes (or *hox* genes, for short).

Hox Genes

Hox genes are sometimes referred to as "master" genes and several have been identified in the animal kingdom. Perhaps the most fascinating thing about *hox* genes is that they are nearly the same in most critters. Despite significant differences in how eagles and bees look, the same *hox* genes seem to play the same general roles in directing the construction of specific structures (Fig. 5.3). A relevant example is the *pax*-6 gene. *Pax*-6 has been identified in nearly all animal species ranging from jellyfish to humans. In each case, it appears to play a role in directing the formation of the animal's eyes, whether it is the camera eyes of a jellyfish or the compound eyes of a dung beetle.

Of course, a lot can go wrong during the transition from a fertilized egg to a fully formed organism. This is why development is of so much interest to evolutionary biologists. It appears that most animals utilize the same basic tool kit of *hox* genes, but slight genotypic variations in how those *hox* genes function early

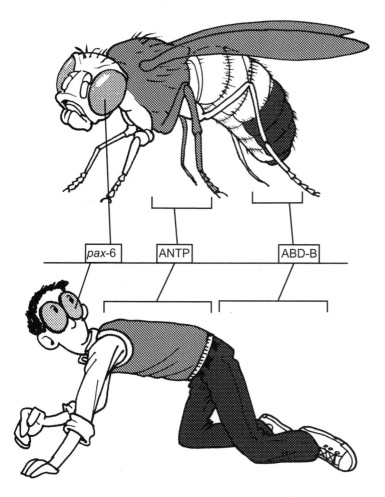

Figure 5.3 Hox genes in a fruit fly and a representative mammal. Hox genes control the development of an organism. Most multicellular animals share a very similar set of *hox* genes which perform similar functions in each animal. This illustration features three such developmental genes which guide the development of eyes (*pax*-6), the middle region of the organims (ANTP) and their anterior portions (ABD-B).

in development can have significant effects downstream on the phenotype. To visualize how this might happen, imagine you are an archer and you shoot an arrow 100 feet. If you shift your aim by just one inch, your next shot will land almost three feet away from the first one. A mutation in a *hox* gene (called a **homeotic mutation**) can result in regulatory changes that alter the fate of an entire structure. Mutations in the fruit fly *hox* gene *antennapedia*, for example, can cause legs to grow where antenna should be and vice versa.

Odysseus Gets Sheepish

Polyphemus was the Cyclops encountered by Odysseus in Homer's epic poem *The Odyssey*. In that tale, Polyphemus caught Odysseus and his crew trespassing in his cave, trapped the interlopers and ate six of them. To escape, Odysseus and his men stabbed Polyphemus' eye out with a big, pointy stick. With Polyphemus blinded, our heros slipped past him when he opened the cave to put his flock out to pasture. Though Polyphemus felt the back of each animal for riders, he missed Odysseus and his men, who had strapped themselves to the bellies of Polyphemus' sheep.

The connection between sheep and the Cyclops isn't just mythological. It's developmental. In 1968, researchers described a phenomenon in which baby sheep were stillborn with a single central eye. Clearly something had interfered with their development, but what was it? The culprit turned out to be a chemical found in the lily *Veratrum californicum* called cyclopomine. When a pregnant ewe grazed on this lily during a critical time in her offspring's development, the cyclopomine blocked the activity of a gene known as *Sonic hedgehog* (*Shh*). The protein product of *Shh* diffuses between neighboring cells and stimulates the organization of tissues of the head into neat left and right sides. When *Shh* activity is blocked during development, developing eyes fail to separate and cyclopic sheep are born.

No Chemicals Added

In blind cave fishes, eye development is inhibited and no eye forms. However, unlike the sheep described above, the alteration of eye development in blind cave fishes is not due to some outside chemical agent; instead, it appears to be the result of selection for a mutation of a gene called *hedgehog* (not to be mistaken for *Sonic hedgehog*). The mutant version of *hedgehog* in these fishes interferes with *pax-6*, the *hox* gene that directs eye development. This interference blocks the development of eyes and promotes stronger jaws and more taste receptors.

This mechanism for the loss of eyes in cave fishes is significant because it dispels the notion that eyes are lost because of disuse. Though often invoked, disuse was never a compelling explanation for the loss of eyes in cave animals because there is no gene for "disuse" that could be selected for in nature. By contrast, the *hedgehog* mutation in blind cave fishes could be selected for strongly.

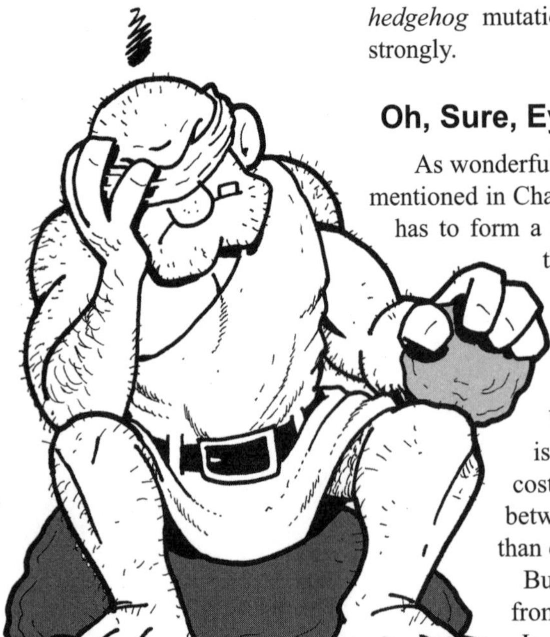

Oh, Sure, Eyes are Great, BUT...

As wonderful as eyes are, they do have their down side. As we mentioned in Chapter 3, in order to let light into the eye, the body has to form a thin spot in it's protective outer layer. As such, the eyes are a relative easy avenue into the body for bacteria, viruses and parasites. They are also weak spots that are often exploited by predators. On top of all of that, eyes are metabolically expensive to make and maintain. Sheesh. Why bother with them in the first place? The answer is that the benefits of vision usually outweigh the costs. In evolutionary terms, there is a **trade-off** between the adaptive value eyes provide and the less than desirable costs.

But blind cave fishes don't get any visual benefit from their eyes, so they are only left with the costs. In a case like this, the mutation in *hedgehog* that inhibits eye development would provide an obvious adaptive value for cave fishes that had it. And the case for selection is made even stronger when we consider that they exchange eyes for something that could come in quite handy in the dark (stronger jaws and more sensitive taste reception).

He Would Have Missed Anyway

After they escaped the cyclops' cave, Odysseus and his men hightailed it to their ship. But, once they were safely aboard and rowing away, Odysseus' cockiness got the better of his common sense and he decided to taunt Polyphemus. The enraged Polyphemus blindly charged toward the shore and started chucking boulders at Odysseus' ship. There were a few near misses, but in the end Odysseus and his crew managed to get away.

The fact that the blinded Polyphemus almost hit Odysseus' ship might make you think that he could have clobbered Odysseus and his men if only he'd had his eye. Maybe, but probably not. You need **depth perception** to hit a target at a distance and depth perception requires binocular vision. **Binocular vision** is the product of two closely-spaced eyes on the front of the face that provide slightly different pictures of the world. What your right eye sees is shifted a touch to the right relative to the picture seen by your left eye. Your brain uses these two different images to gauge how far away something is and uses that information to calculate how hard to throw something (a boulder, for example). So, Polyphemus probably wouldn't have been very good at hitting the mark even before he got a big pointy stick in his eye.

For Your Consideration

1. If the gene *pax-6* guides eye development in eagles and bees, then why do you supposed their eyes look so different?

2. The RNA that leaves the nucleus is called messenger RNA (mRNA for short). Why?

3. Explain the difference between transcription and translation.

4. Use a basketball to test the power of binocular vision. Shoot 20 free throws and record your misses and makes. Now, cover one eye with a pirate eye patch and shoot the same number. Compare your data with a friend. Are there any differences?

Chapter Six: Fun with Mr. Sun

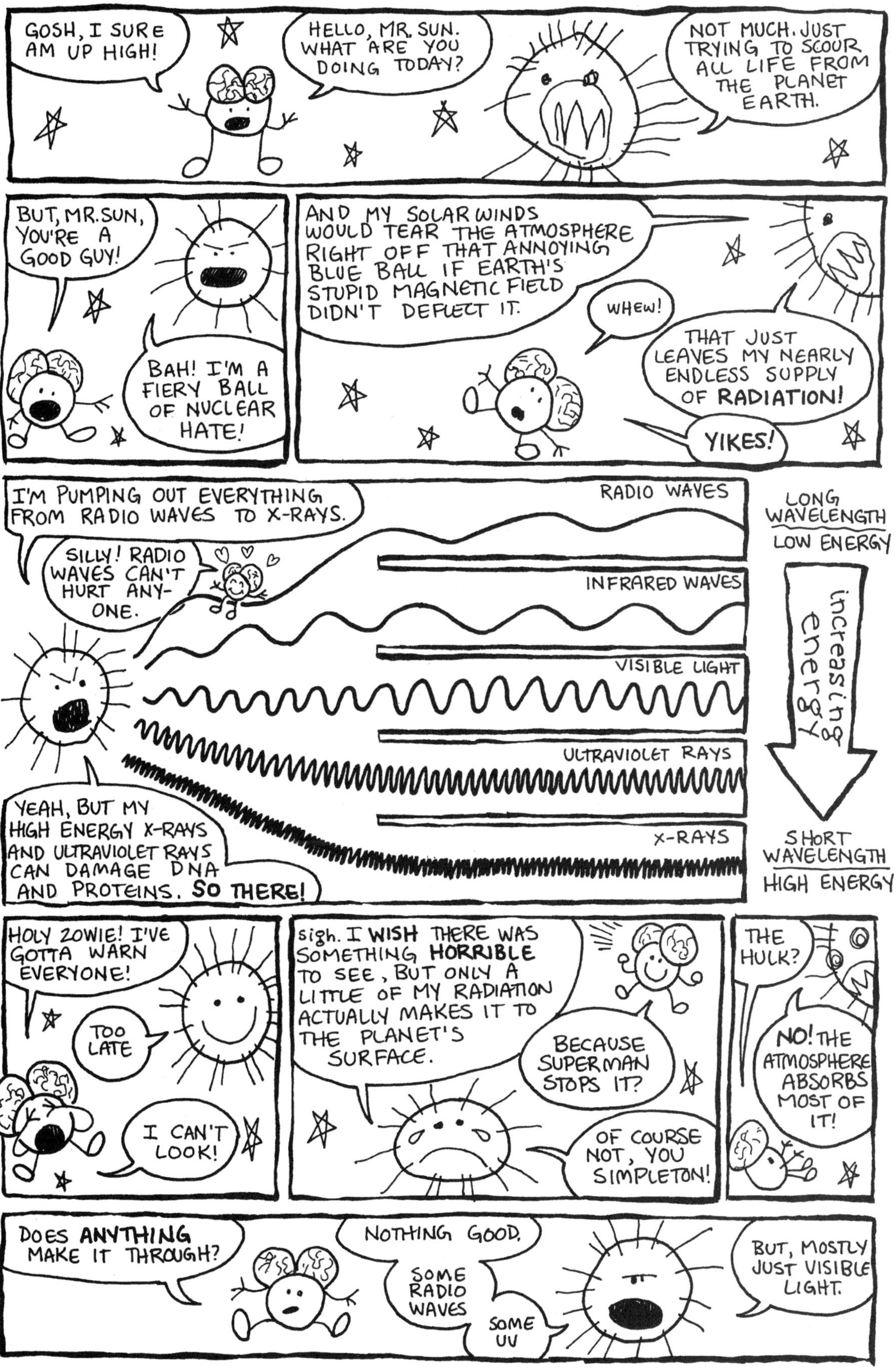

GOSH, I SURE AM UP HIGH!
HELLO, MR. SUN. WHAT ARE YOU DOING TODAY?
NOT MUCH. JUST TRYING TO SCOUR ALL LIFE FROM THE PLANET EARTH.
BUT, MR. SUN, YOU'RE A GOOD GUY!
BAH! I'M A FIERY BALL OF NUCLEAR HATE!
AND MY SOLAR WINDS WOULD TEAR THE ATMOSPHERE RIGHT OFF THAT ANNOYING BLUE BALL IF EARTH'S STUPID MAGNETIC FIELD DIDN'T DEFLECT IT.
WHEW!
THAT JUST LEAVES MY NEARLY ENDLESS SUPPLY OF **RADIATION!**
YIKES!
I'M PUMPING OUT EVERYTHING FROM RADIO WAVES TO X-RAYS.
SILLY! RADIO WAVES CAN'T HURT ANYONE.
RADIO WAVES
INFRARED WAVES
VISIBLE LIGHT
ULTRAVIOLET RAYS
X-RAYS
LONG WAVELENGTH
LOW ENERGY
increasing energy
SHORT WAVELENGTH
HIGH ENERGY
YEAH, BUT MY HIGH ENERGY X-RAYS AND ULTRAVIOLET RAYS CAN DAMAGE DNA AND PROTEINS. **SO THERE!**
HOLY ZOWIE! I'VE GOTTA WARN EVERYONE!
TOO LATE
I CAN'T LOOK!
sigh. I **WISH** THERE WAS SOMETHING **HORRIBLE** TO SEE, BUT ONLY A LITTLE OF MY RADIATION ACTUALLY MAKES IT TO THE PLANET'S SURFACE.
BECAUSE SUPERMAN STOPS IT?
OF COURSE NOT, YOU SIMPLETON!
THE HULK?
NO! THE ATMOSPHERE ABSORBS MOST OF IT!
DOES **ANYTHING** MAKE IT THROUGH?
NOTHING GOOD.
SOME RADIO WAVES
SOME UV
BUT, MOSTLY JUST VISIBLE LIGHT.

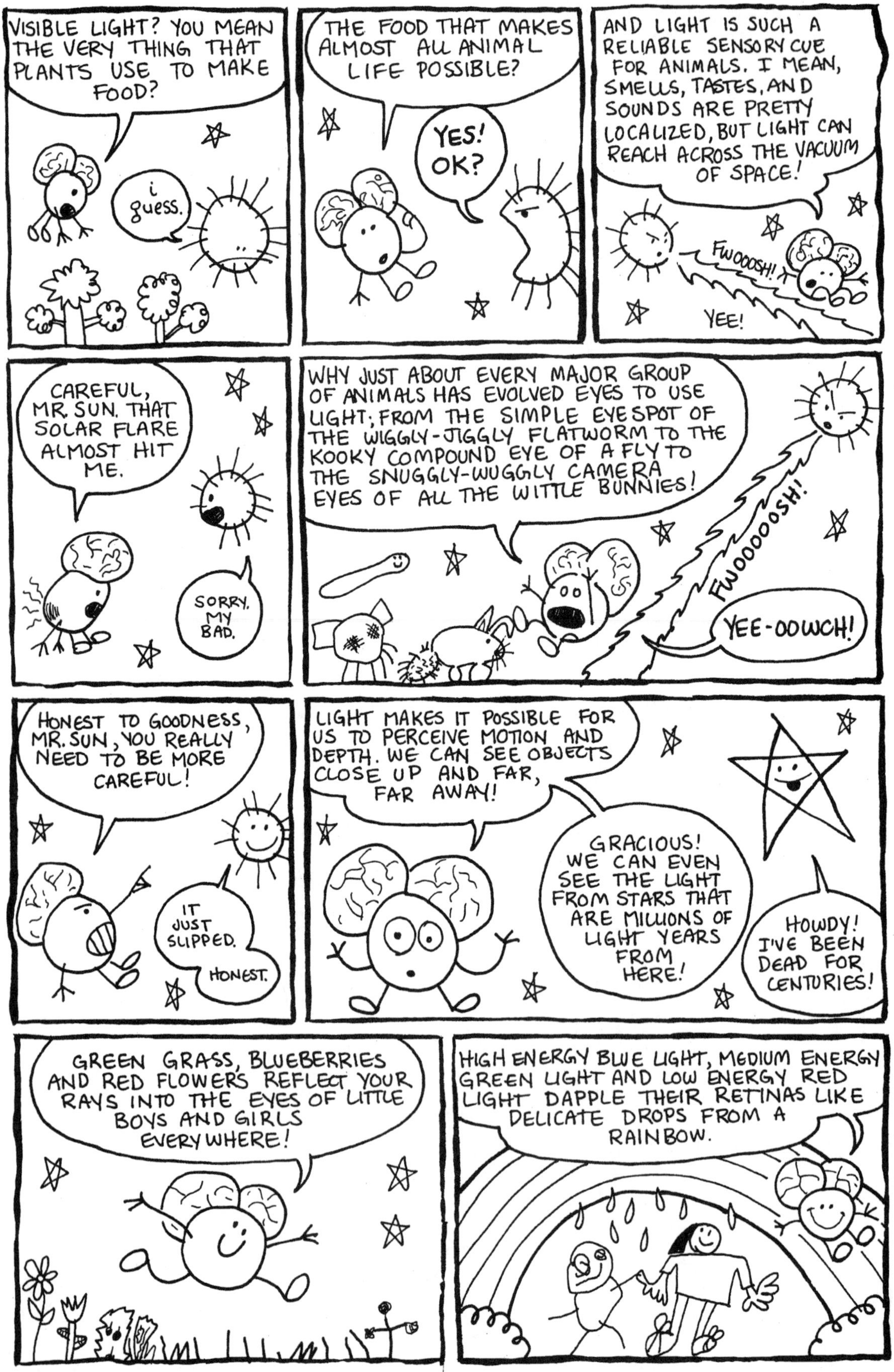
VISIBLE LIGHT? YOU MEAN THE VERY THING THAT PLANTS USE TO MAKE FOOD?
i guess.
THE FOOD THAT MAKES ALMOST ALL ANIMAL LIFE POSSIBLE?
YES! OK?
AND LIGHT IS SUCH A RELIABLE SENSORY CUE FOR ANIMALS. I MEAN, SMELLS, TASTES, AND SOUNDS ARE PRETTY LOCALIZED, BUT LIGHT CAN REACH ACROSS THE VACUUM OF SPACE!
FWOOOSH!
YEE!
CAREFUL, MR. SUN. THAT SOLAR FLARE ALMOST HIT ME.
SORRY. MY BAD.
WHY JUST ABOUT EVERY MAJOR GROUP OF ANIMALS HAS EVOLVED EYES TO USE LIGHT; FROM THE SIMPLE EYESPOT OF THE WIGGLY-JIGGLY FLATWORM TO THE KOOKY COMPOUND EYE OF A FLY TO THE SNUGGLY-WUGGLY CAMERA EYES OF ALL THE WITTLE BUNNIES!
FWOOOOOSH!
YEE-OOWCH!
HONEST TO GOODNESS, MR. SUN, YOU REALLY NEED TO BE MORE CAREFUL!
IT JUST SLIPPED.
HONEST.
LIGHT MAKES IT POSSIBLE FOR US TO PERCEIVE MOTION AND DEPTH. WE CAN SEE OBJECTS CLOSE UP AND FAR, FAR AWAY!
GRACIOUS! WE CAN EVEN SEE THE LIGHT FROM STARS THAT ARE MILLIONS OF LIGHT YEARS FROM HERE!
HOWDY! I'VE BEEN DEAD FOR CENTURIES!
GREEN GRASS, BLUEBERRIES AND RED FLOWERS REFLECT YOUR RAYS INTO THE EYES OF LITTLE BOYS AND GIRLS EVERYWHERE!
HIGH ENERGY BLUE LIGHT, MEDIUM ENERGY GREEN LIGHT AND LOW ENERGY RED LIGHT DAPPLE THEIR RETINAS LIKE DELICATE DROPS FROM A RAINBOW.

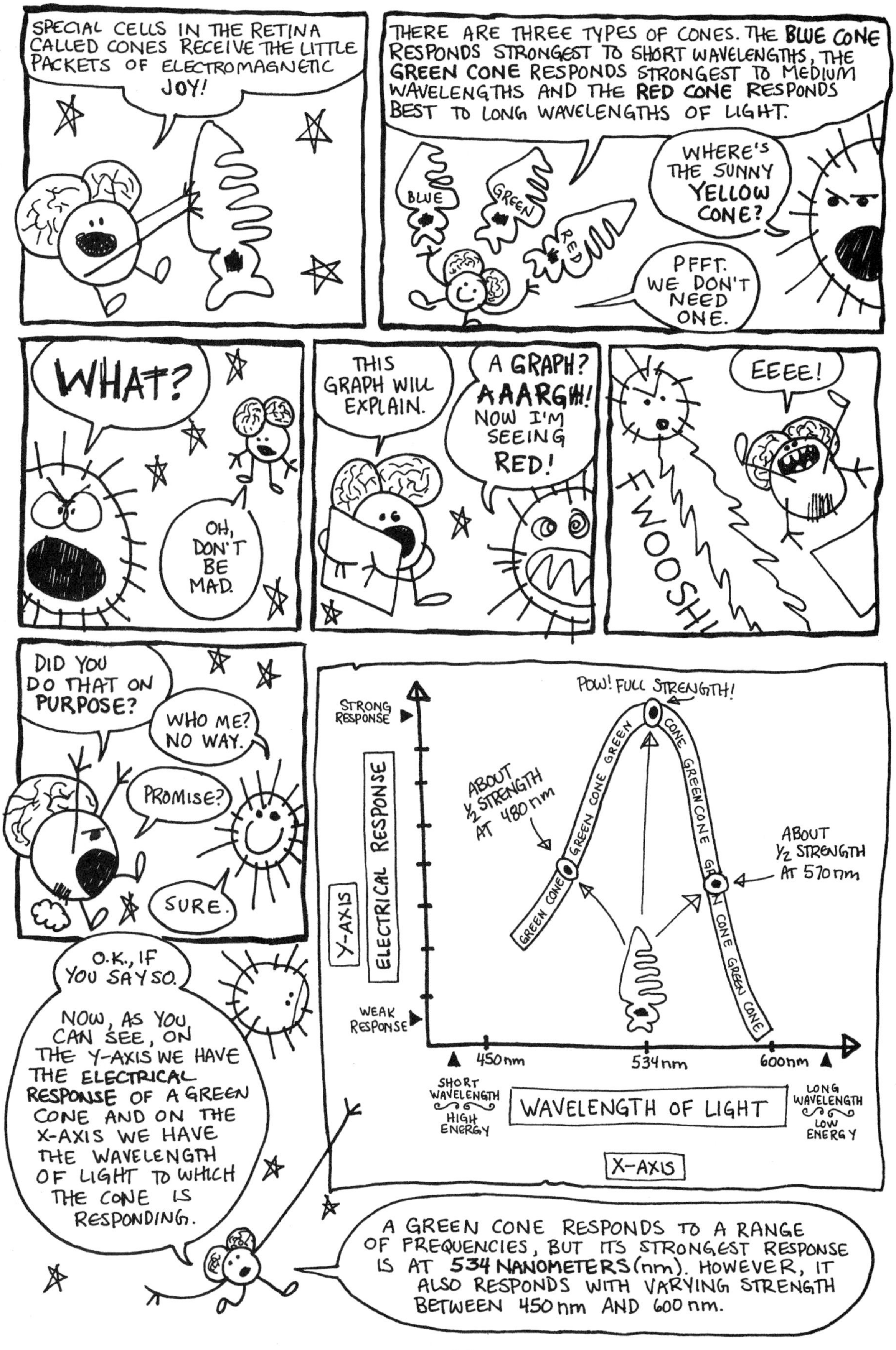
SPECIAL CELLS IN THE RETINA CALLED CONES RECEIVE THE LITTLE PACKETS OF ELECTROMAGNETIC JOY!
THERE ARE THREE TYPES OF CONES. THE BLUE CONE RESPONDS STRONGEST TO SHORT WAVELENGTHS, THE GREEN CONE RESPONDS STRONGEST TO MEDIUM WAVELENGTHS AND THE RED CONE RESPONDS BEST TO LONG WAVELENGTHS OF LIGHT.
BLUE
GREEN
RED
WHERE'S THE SUNNY YELLOW CONE?
PFFT. WE DON'T NEED ONE.
WHAT?
OH, DON'T BE MAD.
THIS GRAPH WILL EXPLAIN.
A GRAPH? AAARGH! NOW I'M SEEING RED!
EEEE!
FWOOSH!
DID YOU DO THAT ON PURPOSE?
WHO ME? NO WAY.
PROMISE?
SURE.
POW! FULL STRENGTH!
STRONG RESPONSE
WEAK RESPONSE
Y-AXIS
ELECTRICAL RESPONSE
ABOUT ½ STRENGTH AT 480 nm
ABOUT ½ STRENGTH AT 570 nm
GREEN CONE GREEN CONE GREEN CONE GREEN CONE GREEN CONE GREEN CONE GREEN CONE
450 nm
534 nm
600 nm
SHORT WAVELENGTH HIGH ENERGY
WAVELENGTH OF LIGHT
LONG WAVELENGTH LOW ENERGY
X-AXIS
O.K., IF YOU SAY SO.
NOW, AS YOU CAN SEE, ON THE Y-AXIS WE HAVE THE ELECTRICAL RESPONSE OF A GREEN CONE AND ON THE X-AXIS WE HAVE THE WAVELENGTH OF LIGHT TO WHICH THE CONE IS RESPONDING.
A GREEN CONE RESPONDS TO A RANGE OF FREQUENCIES, BUT ITS STRONGEST RESPONSE IS AT 534 NANOMETERS (nm). HOWEVER, IT ALSO RESPONDS WITH VARYING STRENGTH BETWEEN 450 nm AND 600 nm.

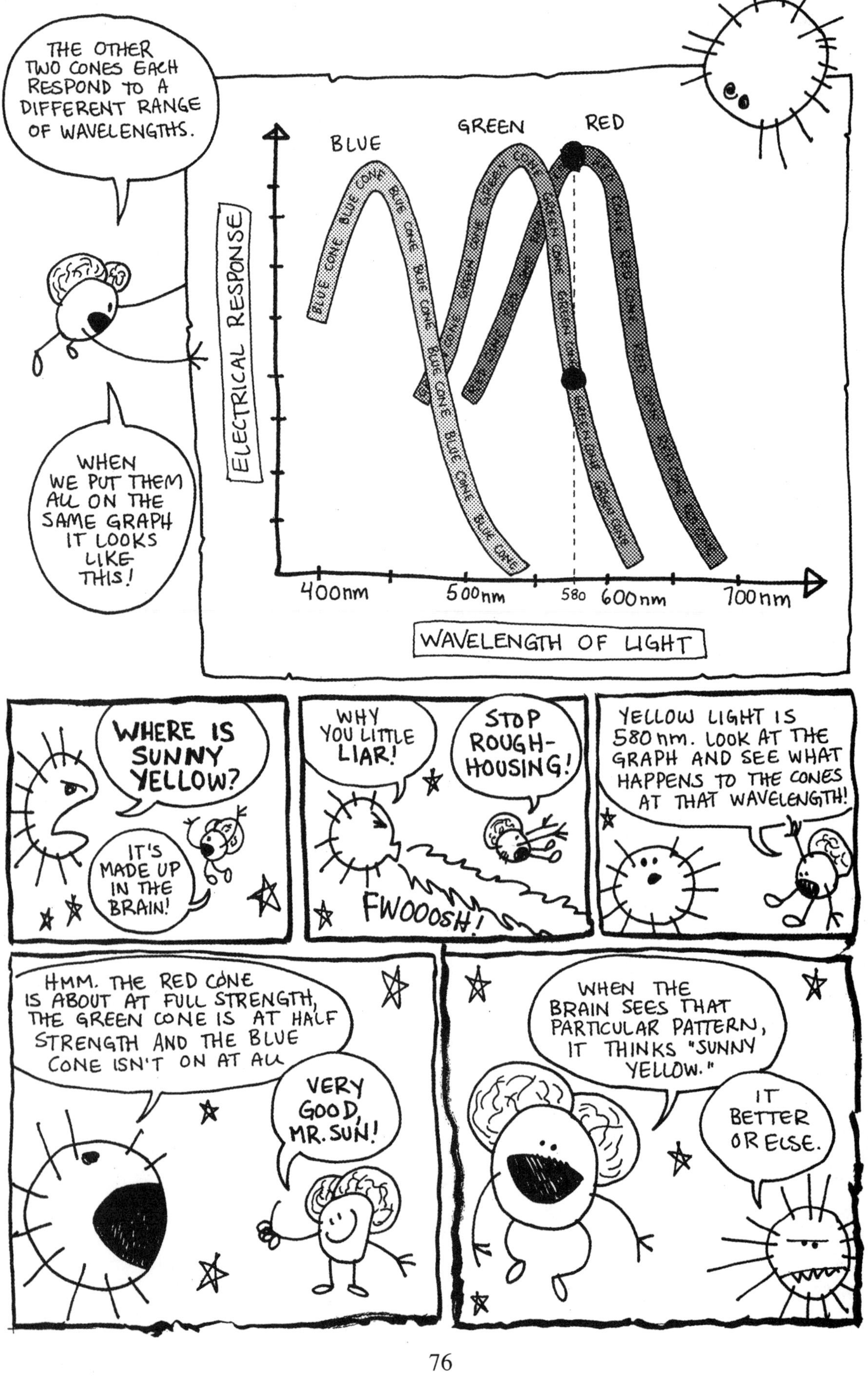
THE OTHER TWO CONES EACH RESPOND TO A DIFFERENT RANGE OF WAVELENGTHS.
BLUE
GREEN
RED
ELECTRICAL RESPONSE
400nm
500nm
580
600nm
700nm
WAVELENGTH OF LIGHT
WHEN WE PUT THEM ALL ON THE SAME GRAPH IT LOOKS LIKE THIS!
WHERE IS SUNNY YELLOW?
IT'S MADE UP IN THE BRAIN!
WHY YOU LITTLE LIAR!
STOP ROUGH-HOUSING!
FWOOOSH!
YELLOW LIGHT IS 580 nm. LOOK AT THE GRAPH AND SEE WHAT HAPPENS TO THE CONES AT THAT WAVELENGTH!
HMM. THE RED CONE IS ABOUT AT FULL STRENGTH, THE GREEN CONE IS AT HALF STRENGTH AND THE BLUE CONE ISN'T ON AT ALL
VERY GOOD, MR. SUN!
WHEN THE BRAIN SEES THAT PARTICULAR PATTERN, IT THINKS "SUNNY YELLOW."
IT BETTER OR ELSE.

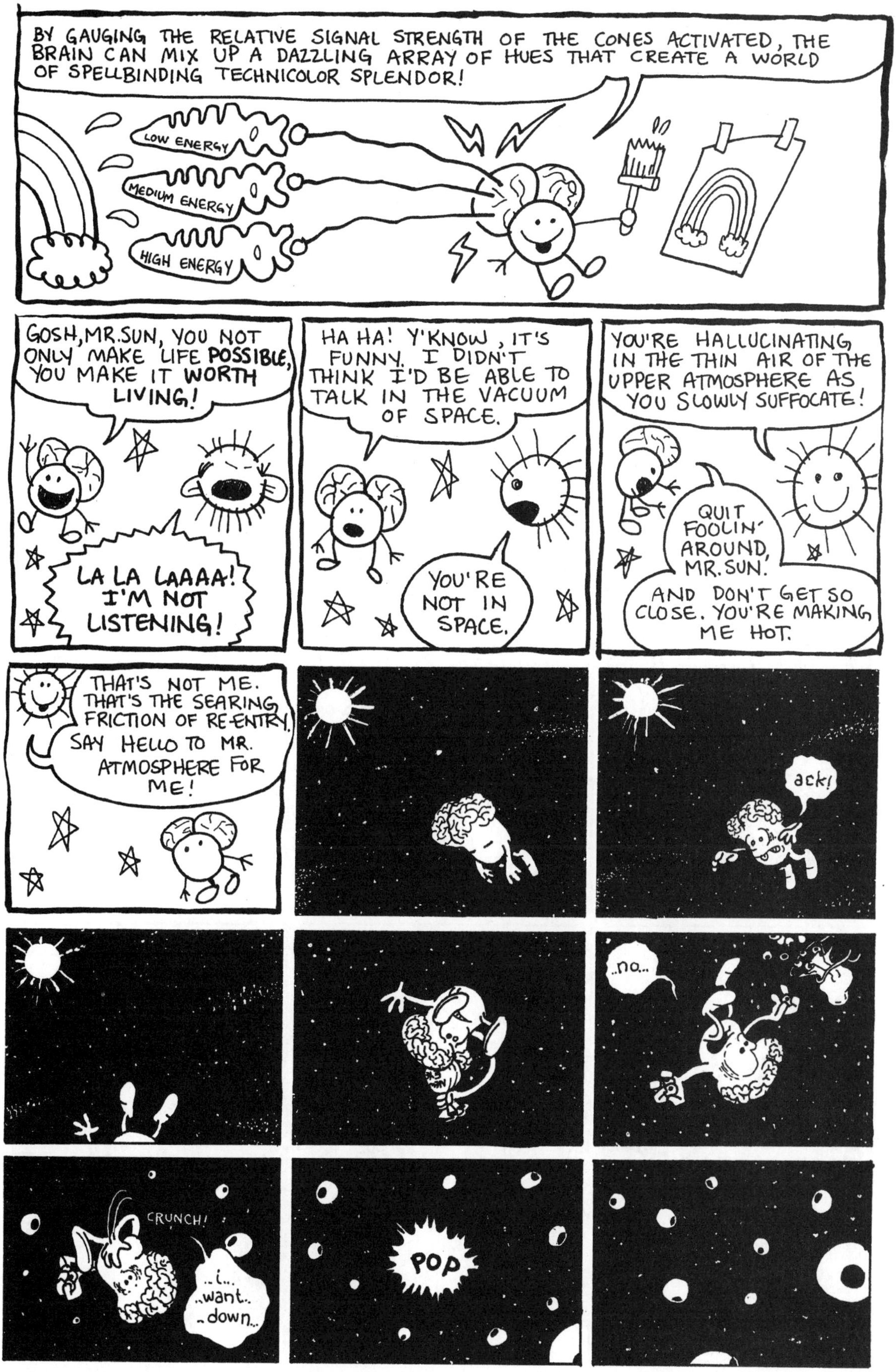
BY GAUGING THE RELATIVE SIGNAL STRENGTH OF THE CONES ACTIVATED, THE BRAIN CAN MIX UP A DAZZLING ARRAY OF HUES THAT CREATE A WORLD OF SPELLBINDING TECHNICOLOR SPLENDOR!
LOW ENERGY
MEDIUM ENERGY
HIGH ENERGY
GOSH, MR. SUN, YOU NOT ONLY MAKE LIFE **POSSIBLE**, YOU MAKE IT **WORTH LIVING**!
LA LA LAAAA! I'M NOT LISTENING!
HA HA! Y'KNOW, IT'S FUNNY. I DIDN'T THINK I'D BE ABLE TO TALK IN THE VACUUM OF SPACE.
YOU'RE NOT IN SPACE.
YOU'RE HALLUCINATING IN THE THIN AIR OF THE UPPER ATMOSPHERE AS YOU SLOWLY SUFFOCATE!
QUIT FOOLIN' AROUND, MR. SUN.
AND DON'T GET SO CLOSE. YOU'RE MAKING ME HOT.
THAT'S NOT ME. THAT'S THE SEARING FRICTION OF RE-ENTRY.
SAY HELLO TO MR. ATMOSPHERE FOR ME!
ack!
..no..
CRUNCH!
..i.. ..want.. ..down..
POP

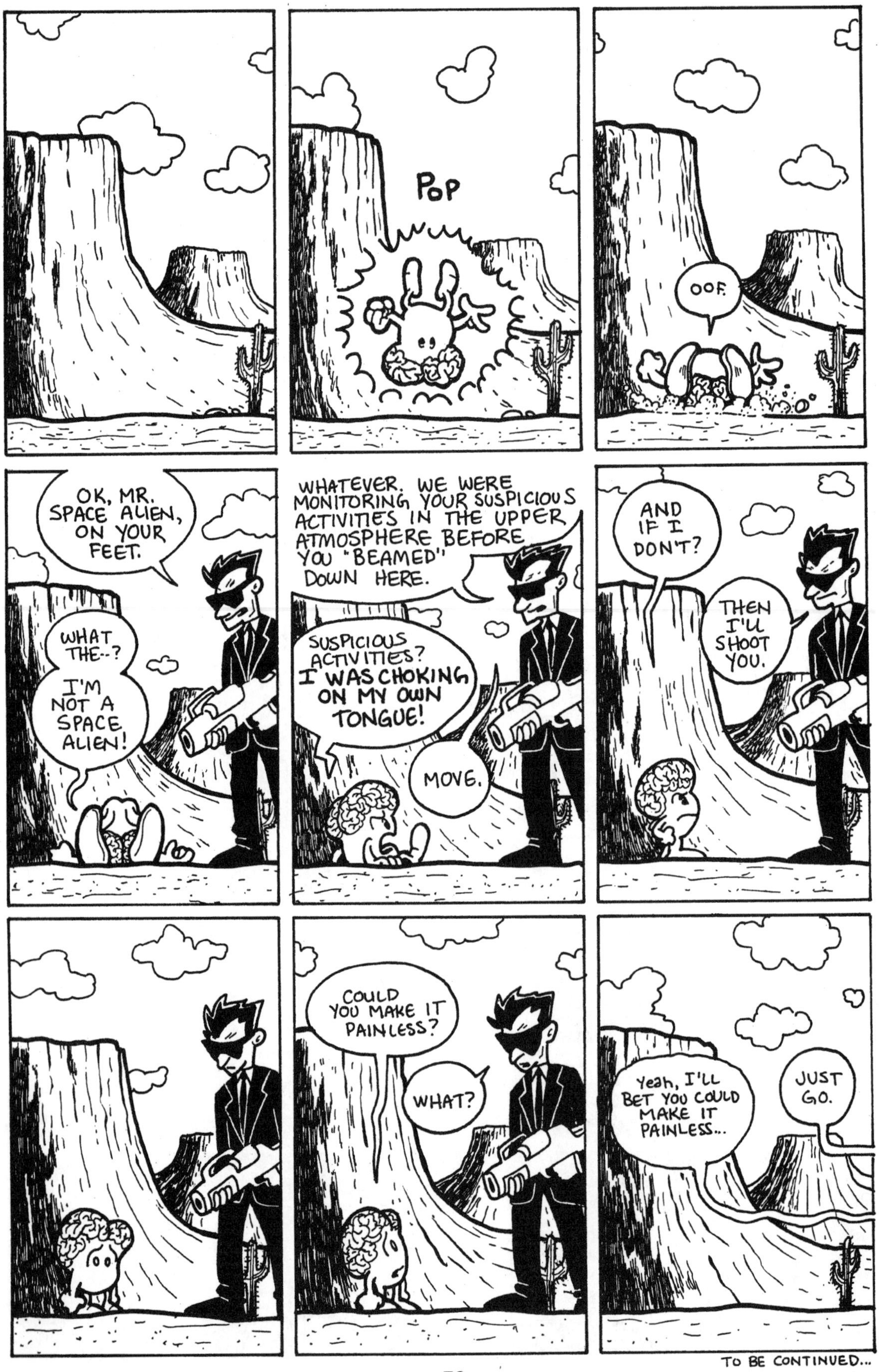
POP
OOF.
OK, MR. SPACE ALIEN, ON YOUR FEET.
WHAT THE--?
I'M NOT A SPACE ALIEN!
WHATEVER. WE WERE MONITORING YOUR SUSPICIOUS ACTIVITIES IN THE UPPER ATMOSPHERE BEFORE YOU "BEAMED" DOWN HERE.
SUSPICIOUS ACTIVITIES? I WAS CHOKING ON MY OWN TONGUE!
MOVE.
AND IF I DON'T?
THEN I'LL SHOOT YOU.
COULD YOU MAKE IT PAINLESS?
WHAT?
Yeah, I'LL BET YOU COULD MAKE IT PAINLESS...
JUST GO.

TO BE CONTINUED...

Seeing the Electromagnetic Rainbow

Seeing the Light Without Eyes

Have you ever noticed that plants sitting on a sill will grow toward the light coming through the window? This tendency of plants to bend toward light is called **phototropism**. Plants exhibit phototropism because they utilize sunlight to turn water and carbon dioxide into the sugars that they (and we) need to survive. The utility of phototropism is clear. But how do plants know where the light is?

All the Colors of the Rainbow

The visible light that plants and animals sense is part of a larger spectrum of **electromagnetic (EM) radiation**. In addition to light, this spectrum includes several other familiar types of radiation: radio waves, microwaves, ultraviolet radiation, X-rays and gamma rays. As Figure 6.1 demonstrates, these forms of radiation exist in a continuum, one blending into the next. So, what distinguishes one type of radiation from another? Why do you need to wear a heavy lead apron when getting an X-ray, but you can be bathed in radio waves all day long without similar protection? To determine what makes them different, we first need to consider some of the fundamental properties all forms of electromagnetic radiation share. Let's begin with a question about the nature of electromagnetic radiation: Does it travel as waves or particles? The answer is a resounding, "It depends!"

The Electromagnetic Spectrum
Red
Orange
Yellow
Green
B.G.
Blue
Indigo
Violet
(0.7×10^{-6} - 0.4×10^{-6} m)
Visible
Wavelength (meters)
Radio
(10^{3} - 10^{-1} m)
Microwave
(10^{-1} - 10^{-4} m)
Infrared
(10^{-4} - 10^{-6} m)
Ultraviolet
(10^{-6} - 10^{-8} m)
X-ray
(10^{-8} - 10^{-10} m)
Gamma Ray
(10^{-11} - 10^{-12} m)
Radiation exists as a continuum and wavelengths change gradually as you move from one end of the spectrum to the other.
The images below are for scale. Wavelengths range from the size of buildings (radio waves) to atomic nuclei (gamma rays).
building
Darwin and Wrinkles
honey bee
pinpoint
amoeba and paramecium
molecules
atoms
atomic nuclei

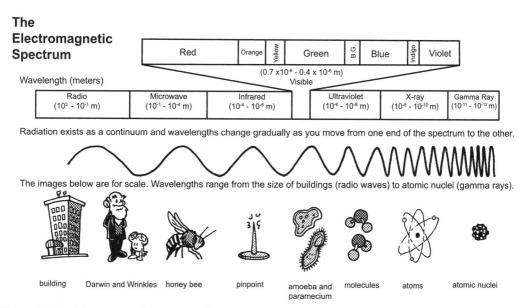

Figure 6.1 The Electromagnetic spectrum. The electromagnetic spectrum comprises a continuum of different types of radiation. At one end are low-energy radio waves. Radio waves are about as long as a building is tall. High energy gamma rays sit at the opposite end of the spectrum and have wavelengths on the scale of atomic nuclei. This figure was modified and redrawn with permission from a diagram available at My NASA Data. (mynasadata.larc.nasa.gov).

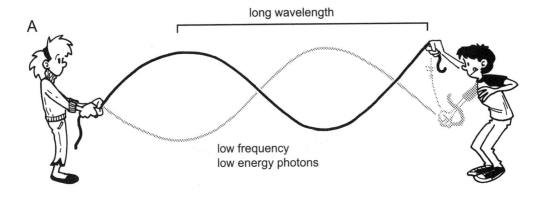

long wavelength

A

low frequency
low energy photons

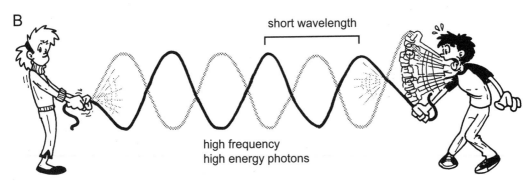

short wavelength

B

high frequency
high energy photons

Figure 6.2. The jump rope/radiation analogy. A) Low energy waves have a long wavelength and low frequency while B) high energy waves have short wavelengths and higher frequencies.

It Depends on How You Look at It

Does light (and other EM radiation) move like a particle or a wave? This conundrum, known as the Wave/Particle duality, is one of the great puzzles of physics. When you run certain types of experiments, light behaves like a wave. To visualize waves, imagine yourself and a friend holding the ends of a long rope. While your friend holds her end still, you raise and lower yours. If you do this slowly, you create a single long wave in the rope (Fig. 6.2A). However, if you pump your arm rapidly, you generate several smaller waves (Fig. 6.2B). In the second case, you have shortened the wavelength and increased the frequency of the waves. The **wavelength** is the distance between the peaks of two successive waves. X-rays have shorter wavelengths than radio waves and, as a result, they also have a higher **frequency**, or number of waves over a given period of time.

When viewed through a different set of experiments, light behaves like it is composed of little packets of energy called **photons**. These photons are discrete particles that can collide with and be absorbed by objects.

Answer the Question Already!

So, why are X-rays potentially hazardous to your health while radio waves are fairly benign? The answer is that X-ray photons have more energy. Imagine the difference between a suitor gently tossing a pebble at your window or firing the same pebble from a bazooka. The latter pebble has more energy and consequently can do more damage. Likewise, when your cells are bombarded by X-ray photons, the DNA and proteins are getting hit with high-energy photons that have the potential to do a lot of damage.

In our discussion of light and vision, we will move between the wave and particle descriptions of light. When discussing light and color, we will talk about wavelengths and frequencies of light. When we later discuss how light is absorbed in the eye, we will talk about how photopigments absorb photons of light. For our purposes, we can reconcile the Wave/Particle duality by saying that a photon's energy is directly proportional to its frequency. In other words, the more energy a photon of a particular type of radiation has, the higher its frequency (Fig. 6.1). Thus, X-ray photons are more energetic than radio photons, and X-ray waves have a higher frequency than radio waves.

See What I Mean?

Visible light sits sandwiched between X-rays and radio waves on the electromagnetic spectrum. It has more energy than radio waves but less than X-rays. Visible light can interact with molecules in our cells, but unlike X-rays, it typically can do so without doing damage (although, if you make it bright enough, it can still blind you, so no staring at the sun). Although it represents only a sliver of the electromagnetic spectrum, visible light can be further subdivided by passing it through a prism. It emerges as a spectrum of colors (or a rainbow, if you prefer). The different colors in the spectrum represent visible light of slightly different energies. Violet light is the most energetic with a wavelength of approximately 400 nanometers (nm; one billionth of a meter), and red light falls at the less energetic end of the spectrum at 700 nm.

Why Growing Plants Have the Blues

At the age of 72, Charles Darwin conducted a series of experiments with his son Francis on the movement of plants (eventually published in *The Power of Movement in Plants*, 1880). In one set of experiments, they examined phototropism in reed canary grass. They grew grass next to several different colored lights and found that only shoots growing next to the blue light exhibited phototropism. The other colored lights had no effect on the grass shoots. Thus, the plants weren't just sensing light, they were sensing a particular *part* of the light.

We now know that plants, just like animals' eyes, contain light-absorbing molecules known as **photopigments**. There are several different types of photopigments found in nature, and each type tends to be tuned to a specific range of the visible-light spectrum. In the Darwins' experiment, phototropism in reed canary grass is triggered when photopigments absorb blue wavelengths of light (450 nm - 500 nm). But, if photopigments only respond to specific chunks of the rainbow, how many different types do we need in order to see the breathtakingly subtle hues of a sunset? Turns out, for humans, the magic number is three.

A Pigment of Your Imagination

Photopigments allow plants, animals and some microorganisms to perceive and respond to light. In the case of plants and animals like flatworms, simple sets of light sensitive cells are adequate. These organisms just need to know if the lights are on or off. But, as we have seen, some animals have evolved eye structures around the cells that contain their photopigments. Eyes manipulate the light to varying degrees so that an image of the environment is formed. Depending on the environment and lifestyle of a species, that image may be monochromatic (black, white and shades of gray) or very colorful. Nocturnal animals, for example, tend to possess a single type of photopigment and have monochromatic vision.

Humans also have monochromatic vision at night. Everything appears in shades of gray as we stumble through the dark on our way to the bathroom. The photopigment at work in our eyes at this time is called **rhodopsin,** and it is very sensitive to low levels of light. But, if you turn on the bathroom lights, the rhodopsin becomes overwhelmed by the brightness and shuts down completely. So how is it that you can still see to check if the toilet seat is down?

One for All and All for One Color

Day vision is handled by a trio of photopigments. These pigments are distributed in three different types of cone cells in the retina: the **S-Cone** preferentially responds to the short wavelengths of light at the blue end of the spectrum, the **M-cone** responds to green light of medium wavelength and the **L-cone** responds to long wavelengths of light at the red end of the spectrum. But we live in a world painted in far subtler hues than just blue, green and red. How do three photopigments generate the myriad colors we see everyday? This is possible because 1) the photopigments in each cone are tuned to a *range* of wavelengths and 2) their response ranges overlap (see the graph on pg. 76). Thus, light of any given wavelength may stimulate more than one type of cone. For example, light with a wavelength of 525 nm will activate all three cones. The M-cone will be strongly activated, the S-cone will be weakly activated and the L-cone will be activated at some intermediate value. When the brain receives the information from the cones, it pays attention to the strengths of the three signals relative to each other. When it registers the relative activity levels described above, it decodes the signal as the color greenish-yellow.

Stranger Than You Can Imagine

The implications of this system are clear: Color is all in your head. The writer Flannery O'Connor wrote, *"The beginning of human knowledge is through the senses...."* It is absolutely true that what we perceive as reality is in large part determined by the nature of our sensory systems. And, in turn, the nature of our sensory systems is a product of our evolutionary history.

Other species have different needs and thus different sensory systems. For example, honey bees have a visual spectrum that is shifted relative to ours. They do not see red as we do, but they do see the ultraviolet colors of the flowers they pollinate. (We need a black light to do that.) In fact, there is a whole world of sensory stimuli that are beyond our capacity to perceive. Plants sense chemicals in the soil, sharks sense the minute electrical signals of their prey's nervous system and sea turtles navigate using magnetic fields. It makes us reconsider what we define as reality and brings to mind the words of the astronomer Sir Arthur Stanley Eddington, "Not only is the universe stranger than we imagine, it is stranger than we **can** imagine."

For Your Consideration

1. What follow-up experiments could you design to explore phototropism more fully?

2. When attempting to spot a very dim star, it's often helpful to look at it out of the corner of one's eye, instead of head on. How might this phenomenon be related to the distribution of rhodopsin in our retina? How might Figure 3.3 (pg. 41) be related to this question?

3. Explain the relationship between wavelength and frequency.

4. Over 200 years ago in 1801, Thomas Young deduced that there were only three types of cones. (He called them color receptors.) He did so without the benefit of a microscope or molecular biology. How could you do the same? How might you use the fact that we can see just fine under monochromatic light (like a red light in a photographic dark room)? How would the primary colors figure into your argument?

Chapter Seven: Curse of the Were-Protein

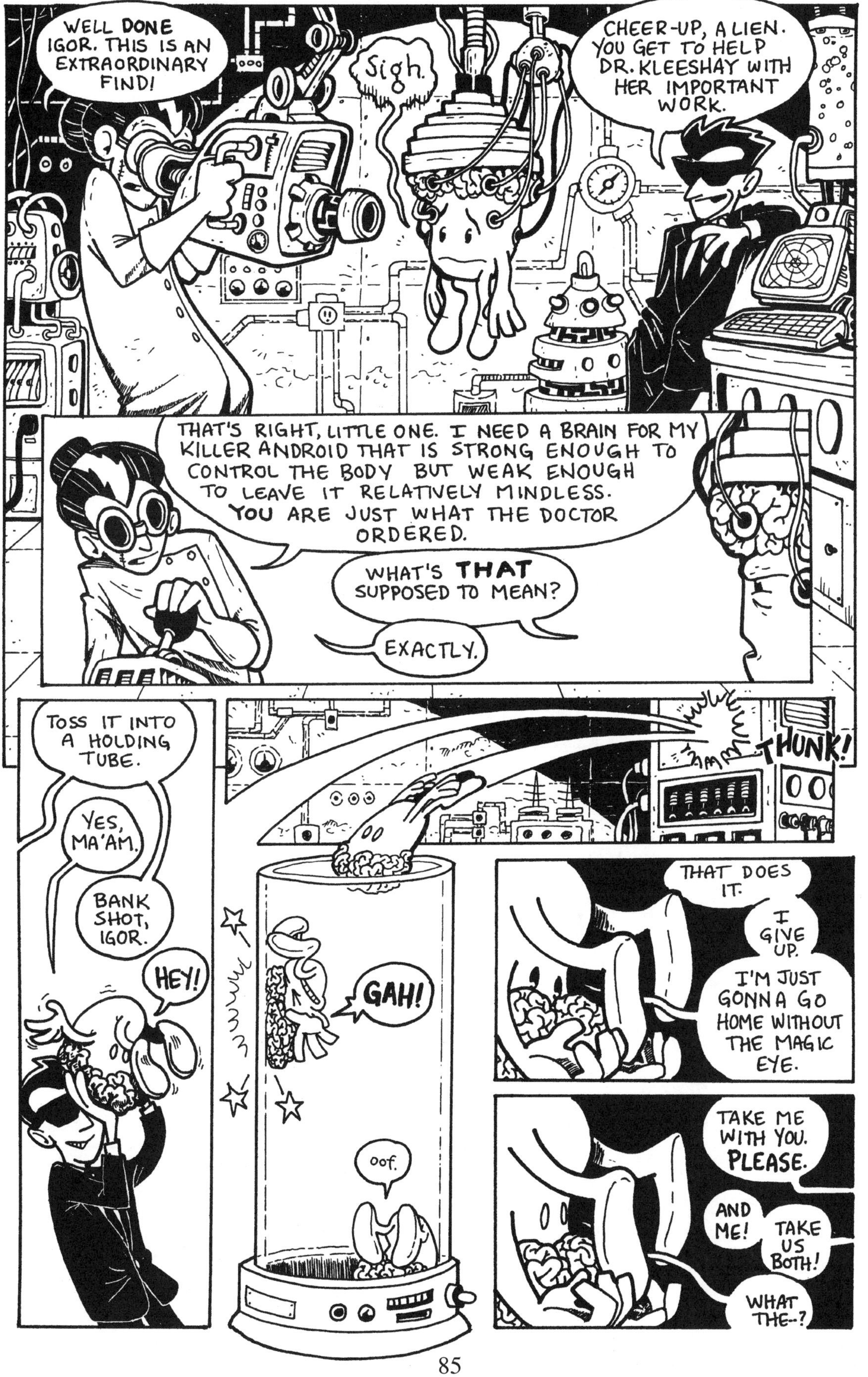

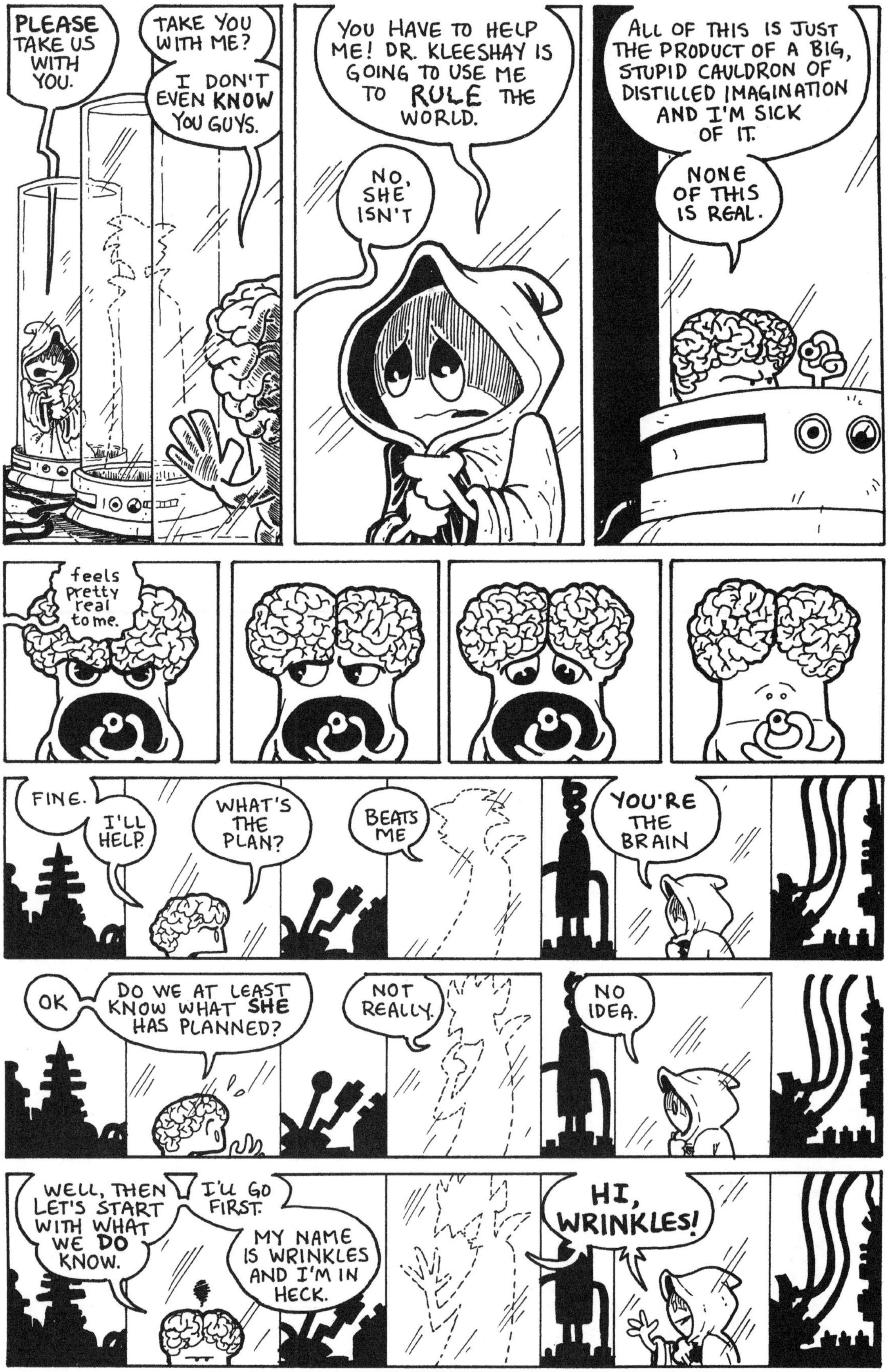
PLEASE TAKE US WITH YOU.
TAKE YOU WITH ME?
I DON'T EVEN KNOW YOU GUYS.
YOU HAVE TO HELP ME! DR. KLEESHAY IS GOING TO USE ME TO RULE THE WORLD.
NO, SHE ISN'T
ALL OF THIS IS JUST THE PRODUCT OF A BIG, STUPID CAULDRON OF DISTILLED IMAGINATION AND I'M SICK OF IT.
NONE OF THIS IS REAL.
feels pretty real to me.
FINE.
I'LL HELP.
WHAT'S THE PLAN?
BEATS ME
YOU'RE THE BRAIN
OK
DO WE AT LEAST KNOW WHAT SHE HAS PLANNED?
NOT REALLY.
NO IDEA.
WELL, THEN LET'S START WITH WHAT WE DO KNOW.
I'LL GO FIRST.
MY NAME IS WRINKLES AND I'M IN HECK.
HI, WRINKLES!

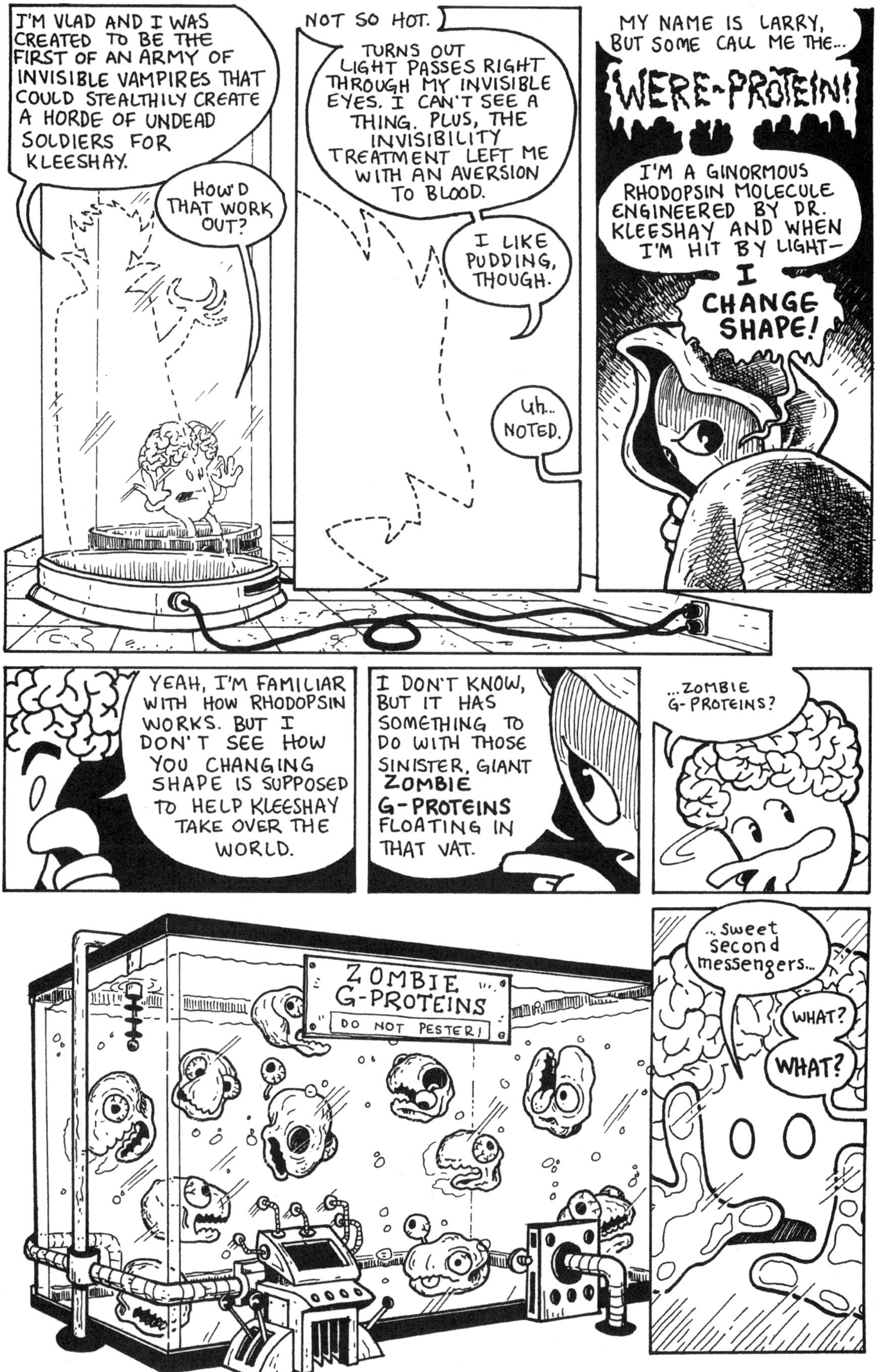
I'M VLAD AND I WAS CREATED TO BE THE FIRST OF AN ARMY OF INVISIBLE VAMPIRES THAT COULD STEALTHILY CREATE A HORDE OF UNDEAD SOLDIERS FOR KLEESHAY.
HOW'D THAT WORK OUT?
NOT SO HOT.
TURNS OUT LIGHT PASSES RIGHT THROUGH MY INVISIBLE EYES. I CAN'T SEE A THING. PLUS, THE INVISIBILITY TREATMENT LEFT ME WITH AN AVERSION TO BLOOD.
I LIKE PUDDING, THOUGH.
Uh... NOTED.
MY NAME IS LARRY, BUT SOME CALL ME THE...
WERE-PROTEIN!
I'M A GINORMOUS RHODOPSIN MOLECULE ENGINEERED BY DR. KLEESHAY AND WHEN I'M HIT BY LIGHT—
I CHANGE SHAPE!
YEAH, I'M FAMILIAR WITH HOW RHODOPSIN WORKS. BUT I DON'T SEE HOW YOU CHANGING SHAPE IS SUPPOSED TO HELP KLEESHAY TAKE OVER THE WORLD.
I DON'T KNOW, BUT IT HAS SOMETHING TO DO WITH THOSE SINISTER, GIANT ZOMBIE G-PROTEINS FLOATING IN THAT VAT.
...ZOMBIE G-PROTEINS?
ZOMBIE G-PROTEINS
DO NOT PESTER!
..Sweet second messengers...
WHAT?
WHAT?

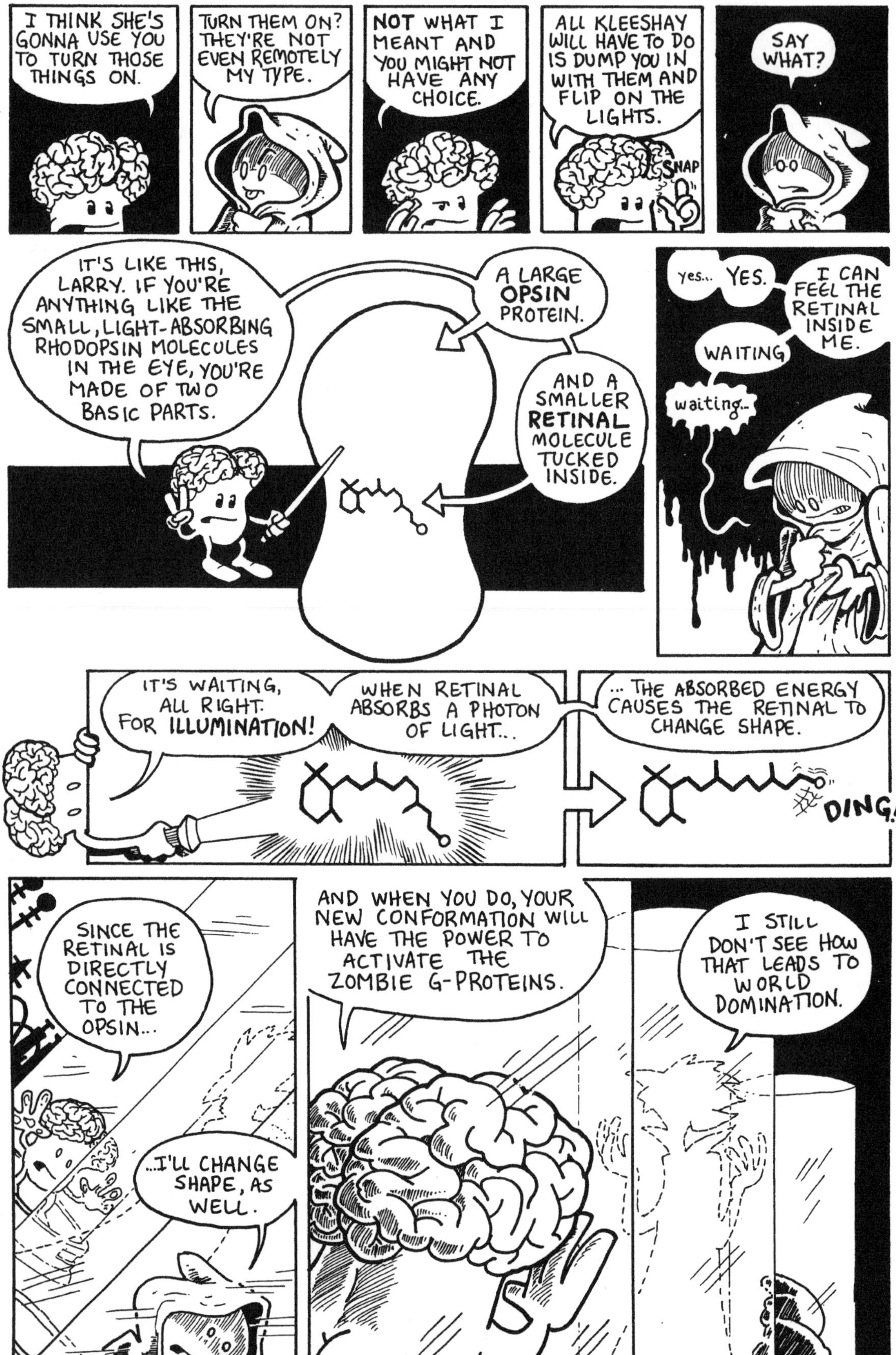
I THINK SHE'S GONNA USE YOU TO TURN THOSE THINGS ON.
TURN THEM ON? THEY'RE NOT EVEN REMOTELY MY TYPE.
NOT WHAT I MEANT AND YOU MIGHT NOT HAVE ANY CHOICE.
ALL KLEESHAY WILL HAVE TO DO IS DUMP YOU IN WITH THEM AND FLIP ON THE LIGHTS.
SNAP
SAY WHAT?
IT'S LIKE THIS, LARRY. IF YOU'RE ANYTHING LIKE THE SMALL, LIGHT-ABSORBING RHODOPSIN MOLECULES IN THE EYE, YOU'RE MADE OF TWO BASIC PARTS.
A LARGE OPSIN PROTEIN.
AND A SMALLER RETINAL MOLECULE TUCKED INSIDE.
yes... YES.
I CAN FEEL THE RETINAL INSIDE ME.
WAITING
waiting...
IT'S WAITING, ALL RIGHT. FOR ILLUMINATION!
WHEN RETINAL ABSORBS A PHOTON OF LIGHT...
... THE ABSORBED ENERGY CAUSES THE RETINAL TO CHANGE SHAPE.
DING!
SINCE THE RETINAL IS DIRECTLY CONNECTED TO THE OPSIN...
...I'LL CHANGE SHAPE, AS WELL.
AND WHEN YOU DO, YOUR NEW CONFORMATION WILL HAVE THE POWER TO ACTIVATE THE ZOMBIE G-PROTEINS.
I STILL DON'T SEE HOW THAT LEADS TO WORLD DOMINATION.

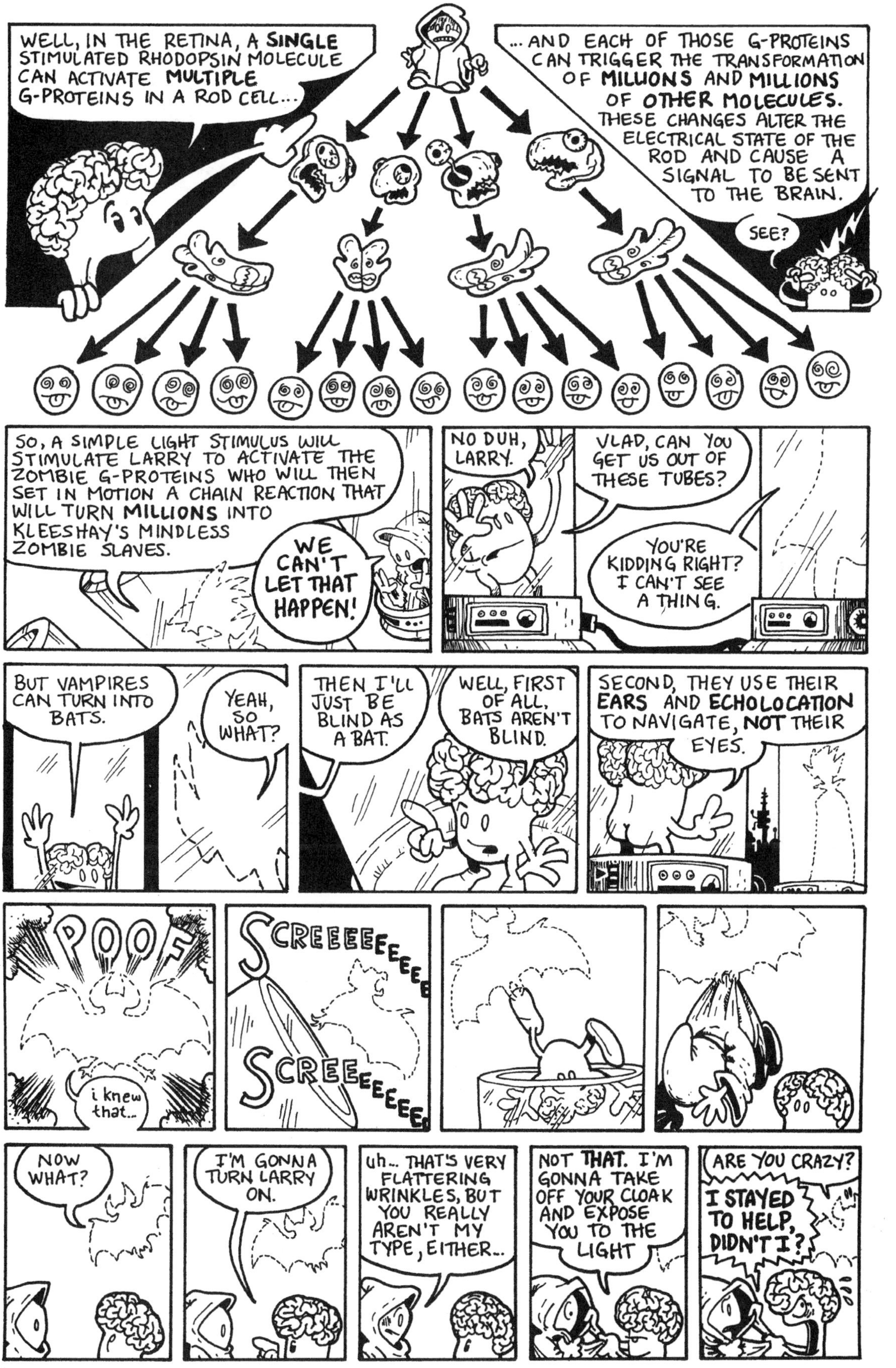
WELL, IN THE RETINA, A SINGLE STIMULATED RHODOPSIN MOLECULE CAN ACTIVATE MULTIPLE G-PROTEINS IN A ROD CELL...
...AND EACH OF THOSE G-PROTEINS CAN TRIGGER THE TRANSFORMATION OF MILLIONS AND MILLIONS OF OTHER MOLECULES. THESE CHANGES ALTER THE ELECTRICAL STATE OF THE ROD AND CAUSE A SIGNAL TO BE SENT TO THE BRAIN.
SEE?
SO, A SIMPLE LIGHT STIMULUS WILL STIMULATE LARRY TO ACTIVATE THE ZOMBIE G-PROTEINS WHO WILL THEN SET IN MOTION A CHAIN REACTION THAT WILL TURN MILLIONS INTO KLEESHAY'S MINDLESS ZOMBIE SLAVES.
WE CAN'T LET THAT HAPPEN!
NO DUH, LARRY.
VLAD, CAN YOU GET US OUT OF THESE TUBES?
YOU'RE KIDDING RIGHT? I CAN'T SEE A THING.
BUT VAMPIRES CAN TURN INTO BATS.
YEAH, SO WHAT?
THEN I'LL JUST BE BLIND AS A BAT.
WELL, FIRST OF ALL, BATS AREN'T BLIND.
SECOND, THEY USE THEIR EARS AND ECHOLOCATION TO NAVIGATE, NOT THEIR EYES.
POOF
i knew that...
SCREEEEEEEEE
SCREEEEEEEE
NOW WHAT?
I'M GONNA TURN LARRY ON.
uh... THAT'S VERY FLATTERING WRINKLES, BUT YOU REALLY AREN'T MY TYPE, EITHER...
NOT THAT. I'M GONNA TAKE OFF YOUR CLOAK AND EXPOSE YOU TO THE LIGHT
ARE YOU CRAZY?
I STAYED TO HELP, DIDN'T I?

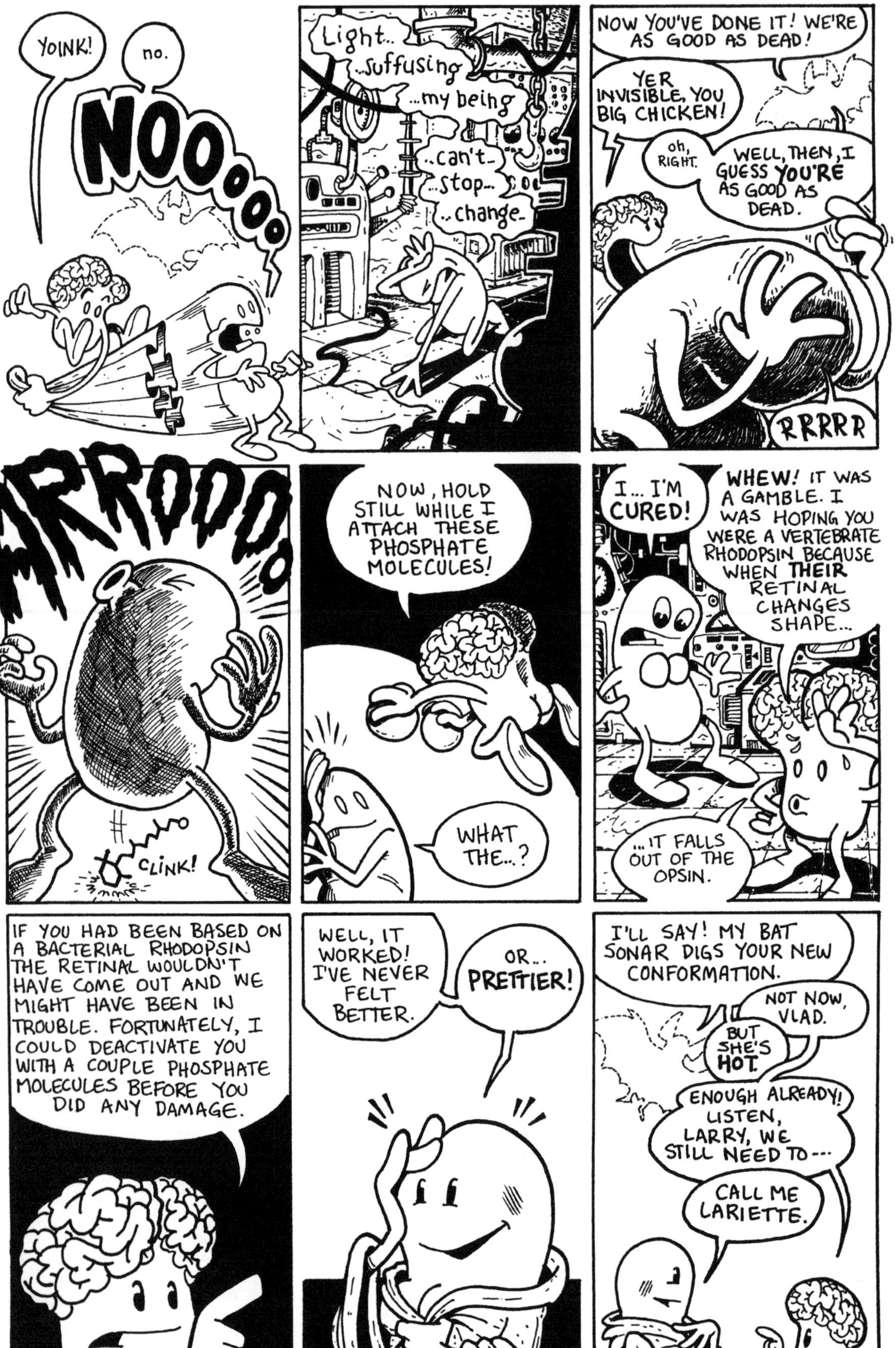
YOINK!
no.
NOOoooo
Light..
..suffusing
...my being
..can't..
...stop...
..change..
NOW YOU'VE DONE IT! WE'RE AS GOOD AS DEAD!
YER INVISIBLE, YOU BIG CHICKEN!
oh, RIGHT.
WELL, THEN, I GUESS YOU'RE AS GOOD AS DEAD.
RRRRR
ARROOOO
CLINK!
NOW, HOLD STILL WHILE I ATTACH THESE PHOSPHATE MOLECULES!
WHAT THE...?
I... I'M CURED!
WHEW! IT WAS A GAMBLE. I WAS HOPING YOU WERE A VERTEBRATE RHODOPSIN BECAUSE WHEN THEIR RETINAL CHANGES SHAPE...
...IT FALLS OUT OF THE OPSIN.
IF YOU HAD BEEN BASED ON A BACTERIAL RHODOPSIN THE RETINAL WOULDN'T HAVE COME OUT AND WE MIGHT HAVE BEEN IN TROUBLE. FORTUNATELY, I COULD DEACTIVATE YOU WITH A COUPLE PHOSPHATE MOLECULES BEFORE YOU DID ANY DAMAGE.
WELL, IT WORKED! I'VE NEVER FELT BETTER.
OR... PRETTIER!
I'LL SAY! MY BAT SONAR DIGS YOUR NEW CONFORMATION.
NOT NOW, VLAD.
BUT SHE'S HOT.
ENOUGH ALREADY! LISTEN, LARRY, WE STILL NEED TO---
CALL ME LARIETTE.

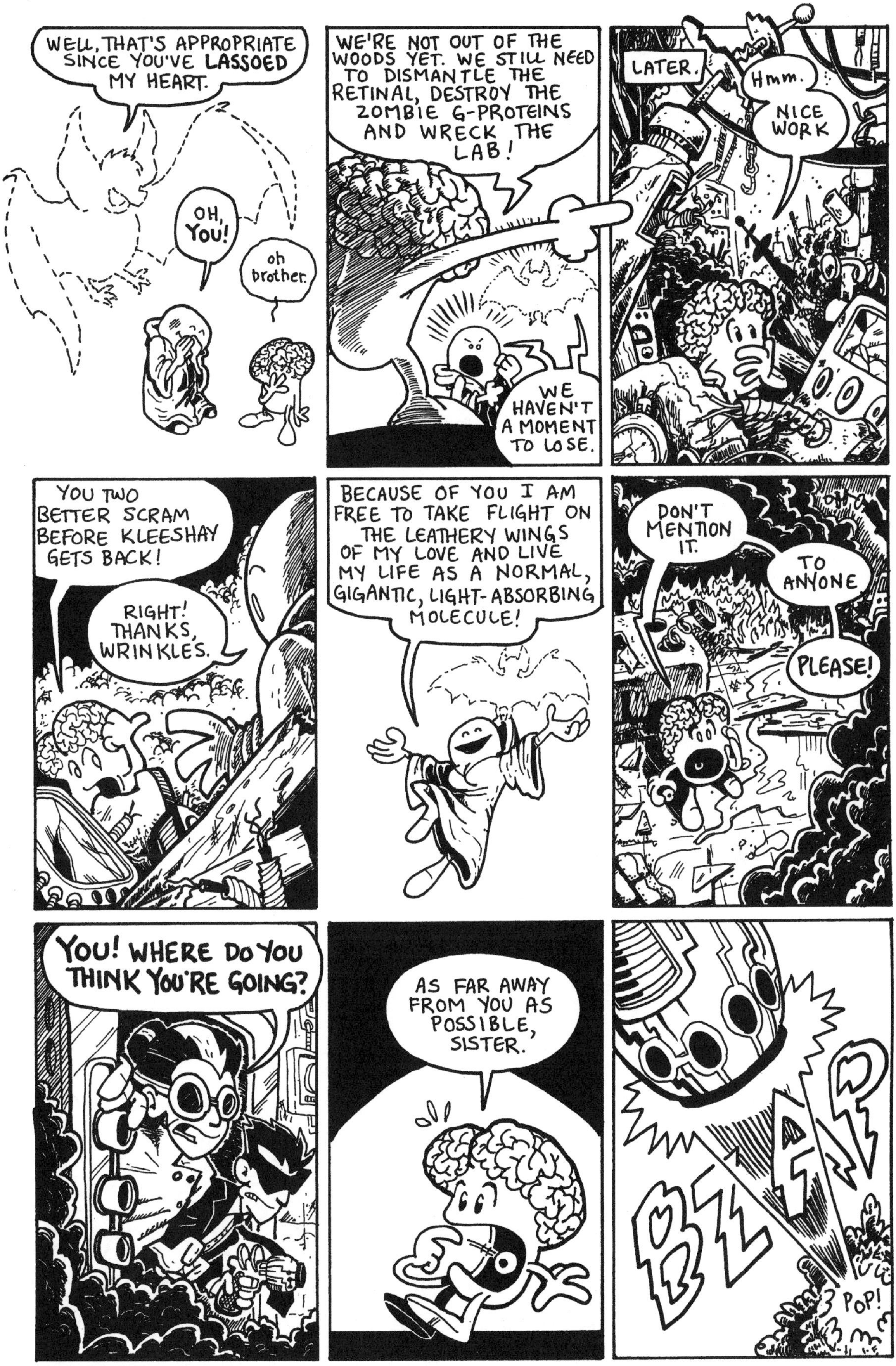
WELL, THAT'S APPROPRIATE SINCE YOU'VE LASSOED MY HEART.
OH, YOU!
oh brother.
WE'RE NOT OUT OF THE WOODS YET. WE STILL NEED TO DISMANTLE THE RETINAL, DESTROY THE ZOMBIE G-PROTEINS AND WRECK THE LAB!
WE HAVEN'T A MOMENT TO LOSE.
LATER.
Hmm.
NICE WORK
YOU TWO BETTER SCRAM BEFORE KLEESHAY GETS BACK!
RIGHT! THANKS, WRINKLES.
BECAUSE OF YOU I AM FREE TO TAKE FLIGHT ON THE LEATHERY WINGS OF MY LOVE AND LIVE MY LIFE AS A NORMAL, GIGANTIC, LIGHT-ABSORBING MOLECULE!
DON'T MENTION IT.
TO ANYONE.
PLEASE!
YOU! WHERE DO YOU THINK YOU'RE GOING?
AS FAR AWAY FROM YOU AS POSSIBLE, SISTER.
BZZAP
POP!

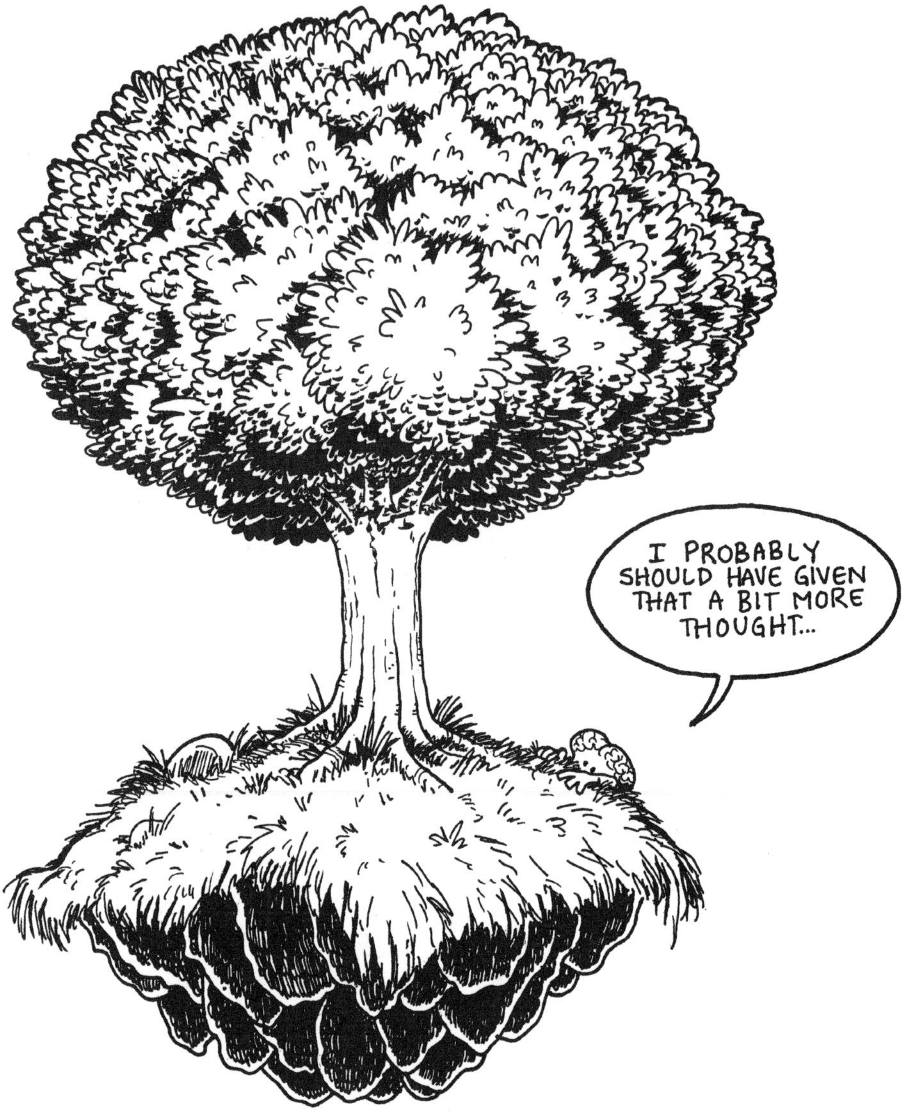
I PROBABLY SHOULD HAVE GIVEN THAT A BIT MORE THOUGHT...

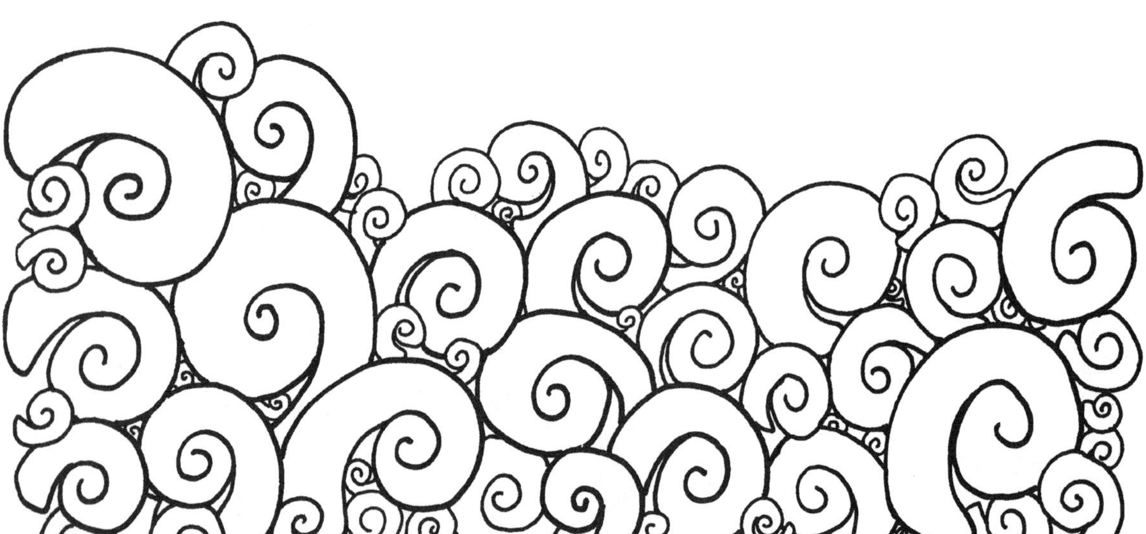

Proteins See the Light

Sensory Transduction

Our eyes act as intermediaries between the electromagnetic radiation all around us and our brains. In order to "see" something, our eyes must convert visible light into a language the brain can understand. In this case, light cues must somehow be converted into the bioelectric pulses (called **action potentials**) that the brain can decode. The process of converting external stimuli into bioelectric signals is called **sensory transduction**. In the human eye, the transduction of light begins when a photon is absorbed by the photopigment **rhodopsin** in rods or by one of the three different photopigments found in the cones. Since rhodopsin is a ubiquitous light-sensing molecule in nature, we will focus our discussion on how it works.

A

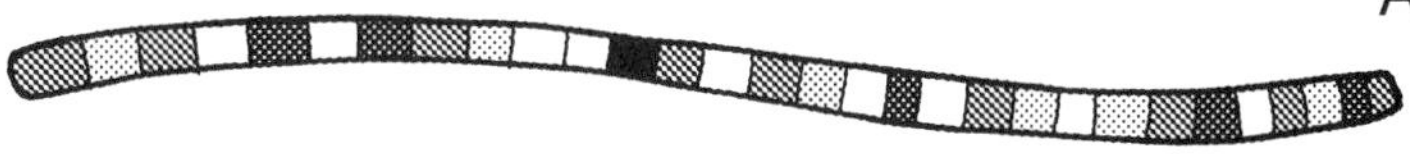

Rhodopsin

A molecule of rhodopsin is composed of two parts: a large opsin protein and a smaller retinal molecule. Like all proteins, the opsin is composed of amino acids. Those amino acids are strung together in a specific sequence called the protein's **primary structure** (Fig. 7.1A). In the case of bovine rhodopsin, the primary structure of the opsin is a string of 348 amino acids. But proteins don't exist as nice neat strings. Once a protein's amino acids are assembled, they begin to interact with each other in specific ways, and these interactions cause the long protein string to start folding up on itself.

A protein folds in many ways. There can be small regional changes in a protein that only affect a handful of the amino acids. These cause some parts of the protein to coil into a spring-like **alpha-helix** or perhaps fold into a corrugated **beta-pleated** sheet. These regional changes in a protein are called the **secondary structure** (Fig. 7.1B). Eventually, the entire protein, with all its secondary structures, folds in on itself. This overall shape of the protein is called its **tertiary structure** (Fig. 7.1C). In some cases, a protein joins with other proteins to form a larger protein molecule (sort of like how Moe, Larry and Curly came together to form the Three Stooges). In this case, each separate protein is considered a **subunit** of the larger protein. The shape of this amalgam of protein subunits is referred to as the protein's **quaternary structure** (Fig. 7.1D). The final shape a protein takes determines how it works in the body.

The final folding of the protein is due in part to the interactions of the various amino acids, but it is also a result of the protein's interactions with the water surrounding it. When is comes to water, amino acids can have slightly different personalities. Some are **hydrophilic** (they love water) and some are **hydrophobic** (they prefer not to interact with water). During the folding process, water forces regions of the protein with lots of hydrophobic amino acids to be tucked to the inside of the protein molecule, while regions with

B
alpha helix
beta-pleated sheet
C
D

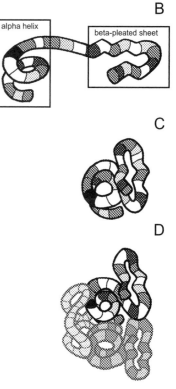

Figure 7.1 Folding of a fictitious protein showing primary (A), secondary (B), tertiary (C) and quaternary (D) structures. Amino Acids are represented in different shades of gray in the protein. See text for further explanation.

hydrophilic amino acids are rotated to the outside.

Once it has assumed its final shape, rhodopsin is inserted into the lipid membrane of a rod cell's disk (Figs. 3.2C and 7.3). Rhodopsin is bigger than the width of the membrane and as a result it sticks out on either side (Fig.7.3). Because of this, we say that rhodopsin is a **transmembrane protein**. The opsin is stable in the membrane because of the specific arrangement of the protein's hydrophilic and hydrophobic amino acids. The inside of the membrane is composed of highly hydrophobic lipids (fats). Thus, the regions of the opsin imbedded in the membrane are also composed of primarily hydrophobic amino acids. The portions that extend outside the membrane into the watery cytoplasm of the cell consist primarily of hydrophilic amino acids.

Why Bugs Bunny Doesn't Need Glasses.

The ability of rhodopsin to sense light depends on the small retinal molecule tucked inside the larger opsin. Retinal is a chemically-modified version of Vitamin A. Although most invertebrates can make it, vertebrates cannot and must import the raw materials. We synthesize retinal from the Beta-carotene in our diet (of which carrots are a great source). One important note before you run out and try the Bugs Bunny celebrity diet: assuming you already eat a balanced diet, chowing down on a bunch of extra carrots will not improve your vision.

Transducing Light

The transduction of light into a biological signal begins when the retinal molecule in rhodopsin absorbs a photon of light. The energy of the photon causes the retinal molecule to undergo a change in shape. The retinal shifts from its 11-cis retinal form (Fig. 7.2A) to its all-trans retinal form (Fig. 7.2B). Recall that the retinal is inside the opsin. When it changes shape, the retinal straightens out and pushes on the inside of the opsin. Much like a sleeping pregnant woman may assume a new position when her restless baby changes position, the opsin changes shape to accommodate retinal's new conformation. As we mentioned earlier, a protein's shape determines its function. When the opsin changes shape in response to the retinal, its function changes. It now has the ability to interact with special proteins known as G-proteins.

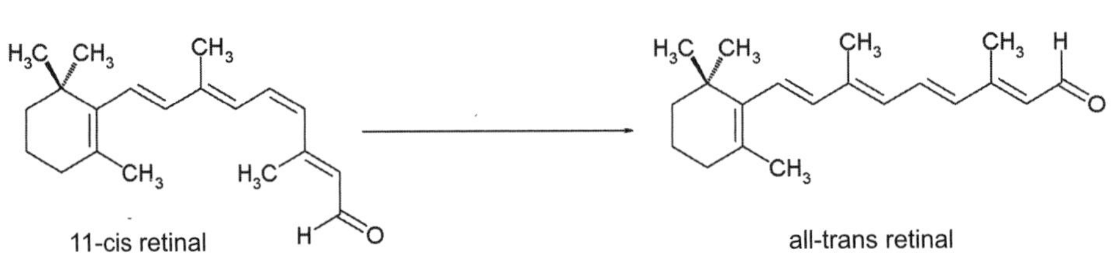
H3C CH3
CH3
CH3
H3C
H
O
11-cis retinal
H3C CH3
CH3
CH3
H
O
CH3
all-trans retinal

Figure 7.2 The conversion of 11-cis retinal to all-trans retinal by the absorption of a photon of light.

disk plasma membrane
rhodopsin
open sodium channel
transducin
PDE
Na+
cGMP
light
cGMP
5' GMP
closed sodium channel

Figure 7.3 The transducin photocascade. A photon of light stimulates a rhodopsin molecule that changes shape and activates a G-protein called trandsducin. Transducin activates phosphodiesterase which converts cGMP to 5'GMP. The loss of cGMP causes cGMP-gated sodium channels to close and cancels the sodium current flowing into the rod.

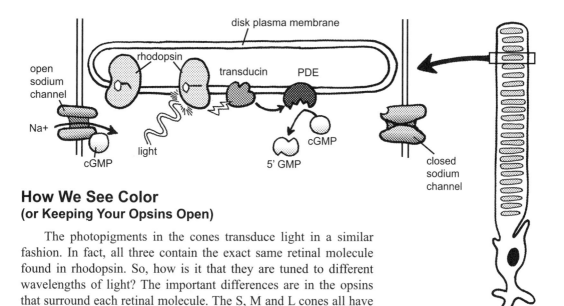

How We See Color
(or Keeping Your Opsins Open)

The photopigments in the cones transduce light in a similar fashion. In fact, all three contain the exact same retinal molecule found in rhodopsin. So, how is it that they are tuned to different wavelengths of light? The important differences are in the opsins that surround each retinal molecule. The S, M and L cones all have opsins with slightly different primary structures than the rhodopsin opsin. The difference is only a few amino acids out of hundreds, but the effect on spectral sensitivity is profound.

G-proteins

Rhodopsin clearly plays an important role in absorbing photons, but how does it tell the rest of the cell that the lights are on? It's the messenger, but it's also trapped in the membrane. To spread the word, it needs a **second messenger** molecule to carry the signal from the membrane to the rest of the cell. In the visual system, this role is played by a G-protein known as **transducin**. **G-proteins** are a special class of proteins that are activated by receptors in the cell membrane and go on to activate proteins elsewhere in the cell. Once stimulated by a single photon of light, one rhodopsin can activate approximately 500 transducin molecules. (See Fig. 7.3 for details of the following reactions.) This represents a tremendous amplification of the signal! Each of the activated 500 transducin molecules can then activate one molecule of the enzyme phosphodiesterase (PDE). But before we discuss the significance of PDE, we need to turn our attention to another aspect of this signal cascade.

Beware the Dark Current

The cascade of chemical reactions kicked off when a photon is absorbed eventually changes the electrical current flowing across the membrane of the rod or cone. An **electrical current** is defined as the flow of charged particles. When we think of electrical current flowing though a light bulb, we are talking about the flow of negatively-charged particles called **electrons**. In nerve cells, current is generated by the flow of charged particles called **ions**, like sodium (Na^+), potassium (K^+) and chloride (Cl^-).

Ions flow across the cell membrane of rods and cones through

protein channels. **Protein channels** are transmembrane proteins that act as gated pores in the cell membrane. These channels allow charged ions to flow into and out of the cell. When a rod's rhodopsin is unstimulated, the sodium channels are open, which means sodium (and consequently positive electrical current) is flowing into the cell. This current, which is flowing into the cell when the lights are off, is called the **dark current**. This is an unusual situation. Normally, electrical current flows in a nerve when it is stimulated, not when it is NOT being stimulated.

Okay, now back to PDE. The sodium channels in the rod are held open by small molecules called cyclic GMP (or cGMP, for short). When PDE is activated by transducin, it begins turning off cGMP. When that happens, cGMP levels in the cell decline and the sodium channels close. This terminates the dark current and the rod turns off. Yes, you read that correctly. You can see things because when light hits your rods and cones, the cells *turn off*.

Catching Some Rays

In Chapter 6 we mentioned that plants are phototrophic. They often bend toward the light to promote a process called photosynthesis. As the names suggests, **photosynthesis** is the process by which a plant uses the energy of a *photon* to *synthesize* something (in this case, sugar). In plants, photons are absorbed by a photopigment known as **chlorophyll** and the photon's energy is channeled into a system that uses it to turn water and carbon dioxide into sugar.

Photosynthesis takes place in a small sub-compartment of the plant cell called a **chloroplast** (Fig. 7.4). Inside the chloroplast is a network of membranes called the **thylakoid membranes**. These thylakoid membranes are arranged as stacks of disks called **grana** (a single disk is called a granum) and the membranes are studded with the chlorophyll pigments that absorb light. Although the plant doesn't use the photosynthetic apparatus to "see," this set-up is very

plasma membrane
cytoplasm
cell wall
vacuole
ribosome
mitochondria
DNA
Golgi apparatus
endoplasmic reticulum
nucleus
chloroplast
thylacoid membrane
chlorophyll
grana

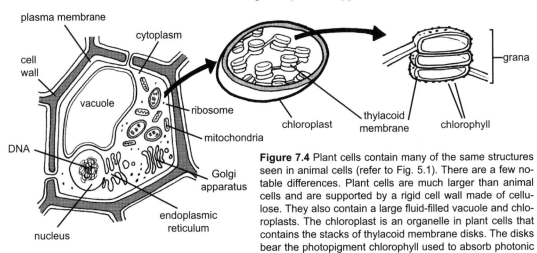

Figure 7.4 Plant cells contain many of the same structures seen in animal cells (refer to Fig. 5.1). There are a few notable differences. Plant cells are much larger than animal cells and are supported by a rigid cell wall made of cellulose. They also contain a large fluid-filled vacuole and chloroplasts. The chloroplast is an organelle in plant cells that contains the stacks of thylacoid membrane disks. The disks bear the photopigment chlorophyll used to absorb photonic energy for photosynthesis.

reminiscent of how photopigments are arranged in the rods of the retina. Pretty cool.

(I told you this so you could answer question #3).

For Your Consideration

1. All of an organism's sensory systems ultimately transduce external stimuli into action potentials. But, what if your nose and eyes are both sending action potentials to the brain? How do you suppose the brain can tell them apart?

2. The sodium channels in Figure 7.3 are transmembrane proteins made of amino acids. Where do you suppose the hydrophobic and hydrophilic amino acids are located in the protein? Which type of amino acid (hydrophilic/hydrophobic) do you suppose line the pore of the channel? Why?

3. Rods are cells that contain stacks of membrane disks containing the photopigment rhodopsin. Their organization is reminiscent of that seen in the thylakoid membranes of plant cells. Thylakoid membranes are composed of stacks of membrane disks (called grana) that contain the photopigments required for photosynthesis. What do you suppose was the shared evolutionary pressure that drove the independent evolution of these structures? Why use stacks of disks and not just one disk?

4. Where is the second messenger cascade in the preceding Wrinkles story? In that image, identify the G-proteins, phosphodiesterase (PDE) and cGMP. Where are the points of amplification in this cascade?

5. If retinal is made from beta-carotene in carrots, why wouldn't eating lots of carrots improve the vision of someone who wears glasses? *Hint: you need to find out why people need glasses in the first place.*

6. Compare and contrast the structures of the plant cell in Figure 7.4 and the animal cell in Figure 5.1.

Chapter Eight: Up a tree

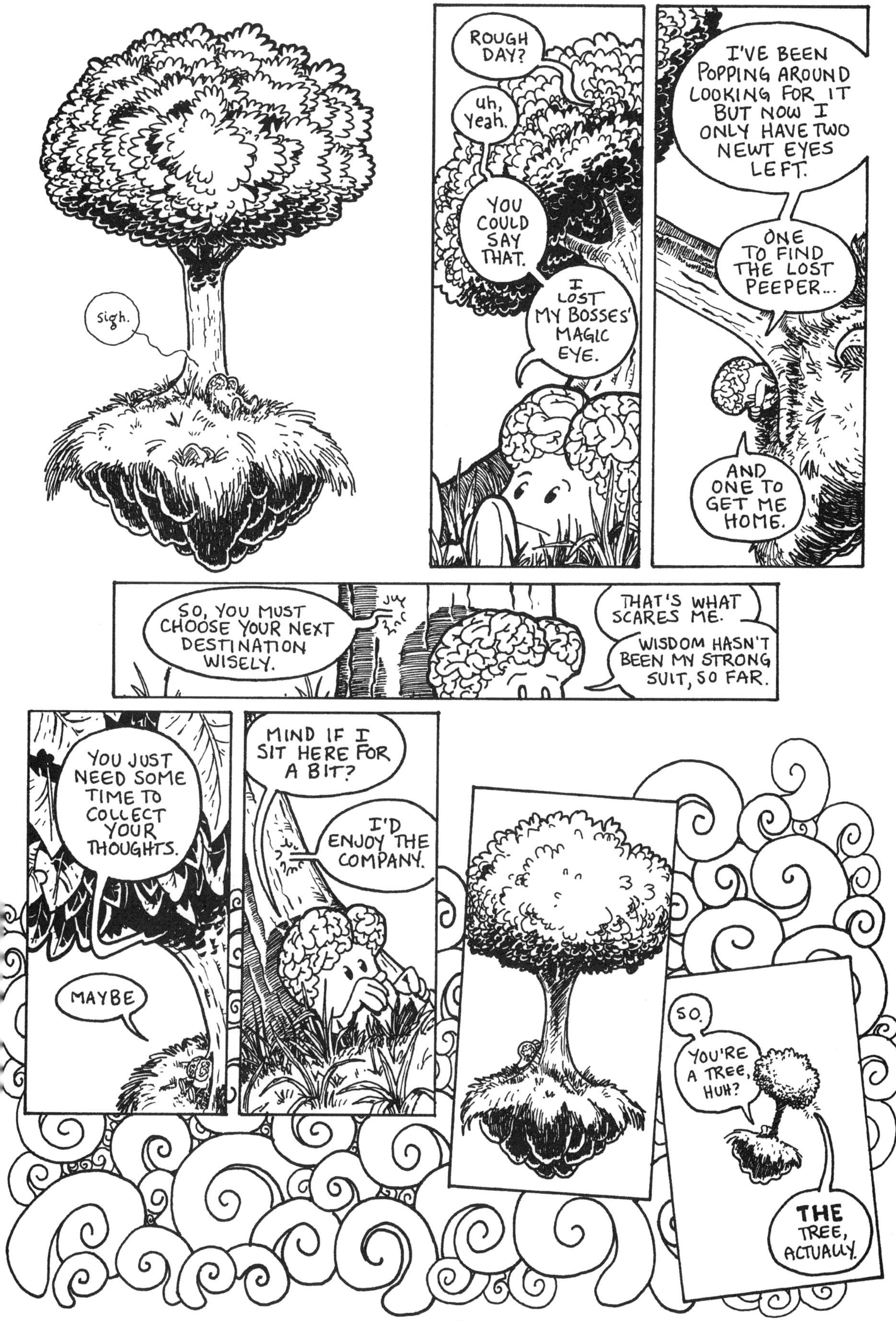

Sigh.
ROUGH DAY?
uh, Yeah.
YOU COULD SAY THAT.
I LOST MY BOSSES' MAGIC EYE.
I'VE BEEN POPPING AROUND LOOKING FOR IT BUT NOW I ONLY HAVE TWO NEWT EYES LEFT.
ONE TO FIND THE LOST PEEPER...
AND ONE TO GET ME HOME.
SO, YOU MUST CHOOSE YOUR NEXT DESTINATION WISELY.
THAT'S WHAT SCARES ME.
WISDOM HASN'T BEEN MY STRONG SUIT, SO FAR.
YOU JUST NEED SOME TIME TO COLLECT YOUR THOUGHTS.
MAYBE
MIND IF I SIT HERE FOR A BIT?
I'D ENJOY THE COMPANY.
SO.
YOU'RE A TREE, HUH?
THE TREE, ACTUALLY.

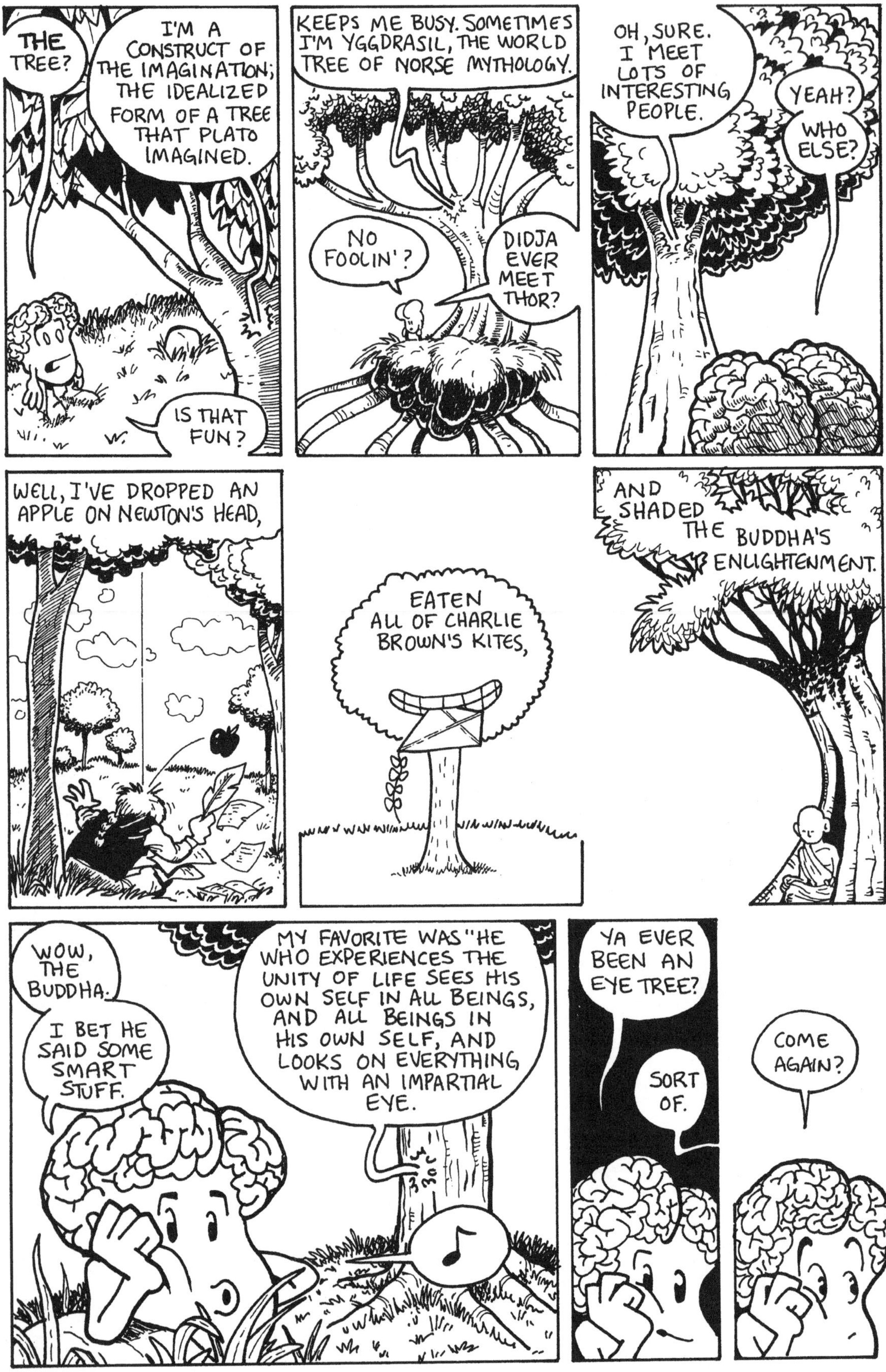
THE TREE?
I'M A CONSTRUCT OF THE IMAGINATION; THE IDEALIZED FORM OF A TREE THAT PLATO IMAGINED.
IS THAT FUN?
KEEPS ME BUSY. SOMETIMES I'M YGGDRASIL, THE WORLD TREE OF NORSE MYTHOLOGY.
NO FOOLIN'?
DIDJA EVER MEET THOR?
OH, SURE. I MEET LOTS OF INTERESTING PEOPLE.
YEAH?
WHO ELSE?
WELL, I'VE DROPPED AN APPLE ON NEWTON'S HEAD,
EATEN ALL OF CHARLIE BROWN'S KITES,
AND SHADED THE BUDDHA'S ENLIGHTENMENT.
WOW, THE BUDDHA.
I BET HE SAID SOME SMART STUFF.
MY FAVORITE WAS "HE WHO EXPERIENCES THE UNITY OF LIFE SEES HIS OWN SELF IN ALL BEINGS, AND ALL BEINGS IN HIS OWN SELF, AND LOOKS ON EVERYTHING WITH AN IMPARTIAL EYE.
YA EVER BEEN AN EYE TREE?
SORT OF.
COME AGAIN?

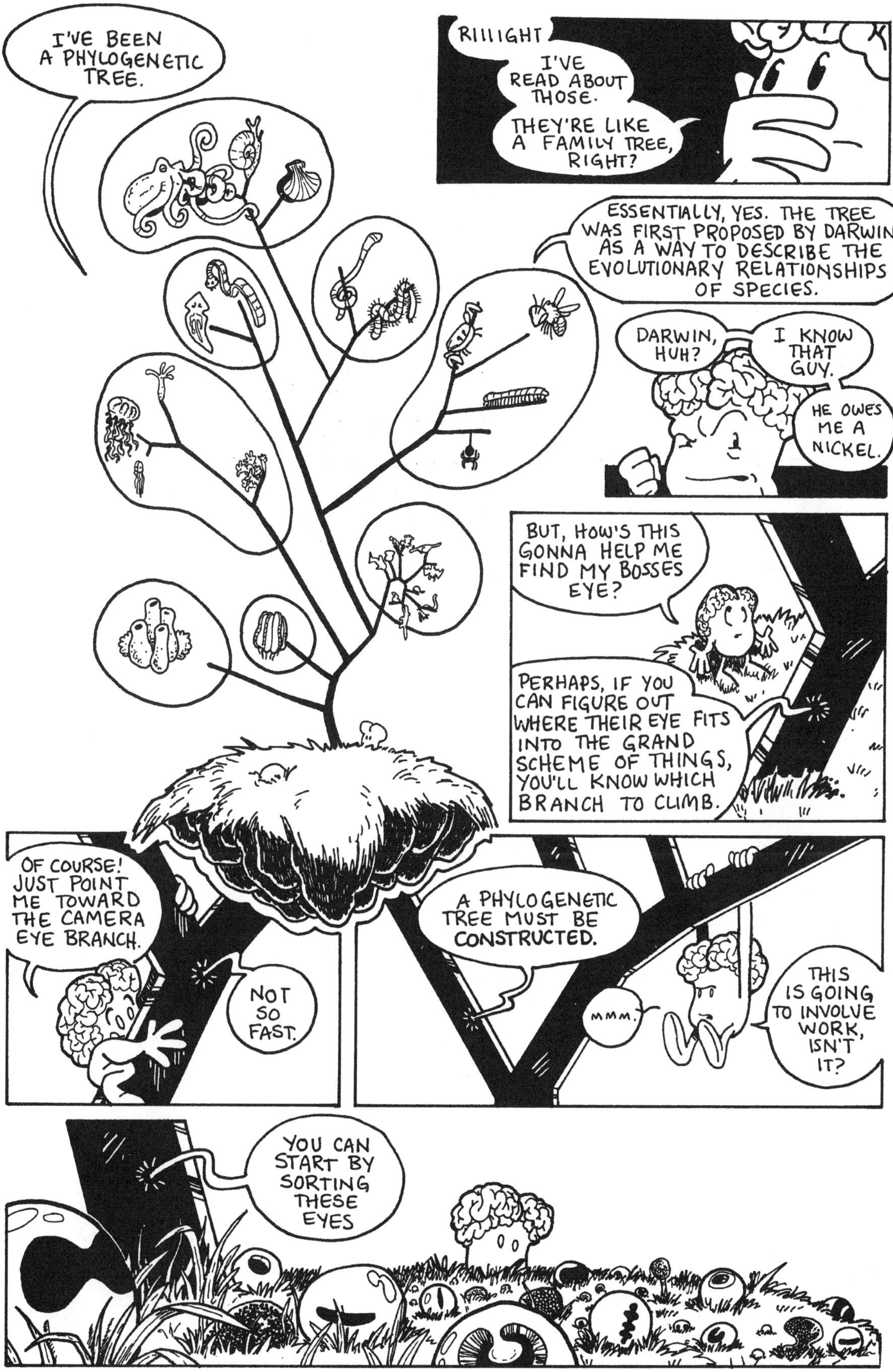
I'VE BEEN A PHYLOGENETIC TREE.
RIIIIGHT
I'VE READ ABOUT THOSE.
THEY'RE LIKE A FAMILY TREE, RIGHT?
ESSENTIALLY, YES. THE TREE WAS FIRST PROPOSED BY DARWIN AS A WAY TO DESCRIBE THE EVOLUTIONARY RELATIONSHIPS OF SPECIES.
DARWIN, HUH?
I KNOW THAT GUY.
HE OWES ME A NICKEL.
BUT, HOW'S THIS GONNA HELP ME FIND MY BOSSES EYE?
PERHAPS, IF YOU CAN FIGURE OUT WHERE THEIR EYE FITS INTO THE GRAND SCHEME OF THINGS, YOU'LL KNOW WHICH BRANCH TO CLIMB.
OF COURSE! JUST POINT ME TOWARD THE CAMERA EYE BRANCH.
NOT SO FAST.
A PHYLOGENETIC TREE MUST BE CONSTRUCTED.
MMM.
THIS IS GOING TO INVOLVE WORK, ISN'T IT?
YOU CAN START BY SORTING THESE EYES

LATER

DONE. NOW WHAT?

PLACE THEM ON THE CORRECT BRANCHES.

CAMERA EYES

MISC

COMPOUND EYES

I'LL START WITH THE CAMERA EYES.

CAMERA EYES

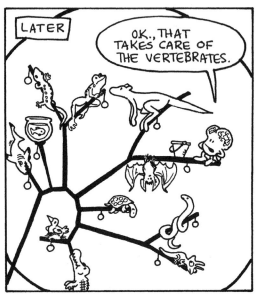

LATER

OK., THAT TAKES CARE OF THE VERTEBRATES.

HUH. I'VE GOT SOME LEFT OVER.

CAMERA EYES

THOSE ARE FOR THE SQUID, OCTOPUSES AND SOME OF THE JELLYFISH.

BUT THEY'RE "LOWER" ANIMALS.

HURK!

Y'KNOW THEY REALLY HATE COMMENTS LIKE THAT.

THERE'S NO "HIGHER" OR "LOWER" IN A PHYLOGENETIC TREE ; ONLY EVOLUTIONARY SURVIVORS. BESIDES, AN OCTOPUS EYE DOESN'T HAVE A BLIND SPOT. IN THAT RESPECT, THEIR EYE IS BETTER THAN YOURS.

my bad.

SO, HOW'D WE GET SIMILAR EYES?

CONVERGENT EVOLUTION.

OCTOPUSES ARE FAST MOVING, INTELLIGENT PREDATORS.

SOUND FAMILIAR?

BEING ABLE TO FOCUS LIGHT AND FORM AN IMAGE IS JUST AS MUCH AN ADVANTAGE FOR THEM AS YOU.

OVER EVOLUTIONARY TIME, YOUR RESPECTIVE LINES HAVE INDEPENDENTLY **CONVERGED** ON A SIMILAR SOLUTION.

sigh. hickees...

WELL SHOOT. THIS IS GONNA BE HARDER THAN I THOUGHT.

I SUPPOSE I COULD CONSIDER GENETIC DIFFERENCES AS WELL.

MOST PHYLOGENETIC TREES **DO** INCORPORATE BOTH ANATOMICAL AND GENETIC INFORMATION.

OF COURSE, AT ONE LEVEL GENETICALLY, ALL EYES ARE BASICALLY THE SAME

OH, C'MON.

SERIOUSLY. THE **PAX** GENE GUIDES THE DEVELOPMENT OF ALL ANIMALS EYES.

MY EYE IS BUILT BY THE SAME GENE THAT BUILT THE EYES OF THIS FOUR-EYED FISH?

YES.

ARE YOU **SURE**? I MEAN, LOOK AT THIS THING. EACH OF ITS EYES HAS TWO PUPILS AND TWO RETINAS: ONE SET FOR SEEING **ABOVE** THE WATER AND THE OTHER FOR SEEING **BELOW**.

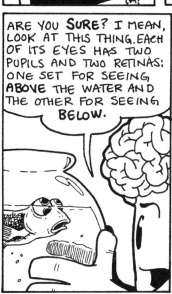

COMPARE THE PROTEIN SEQUENCE OF EACH OF YOU PAX GENES.

MY WORD! THIS LOOKS JUST LIKE MINE!

WHICH I MEMORIZED EARLIER.

IT TAKES A LOT OF DIFFERENT GENES TO MAKE AN EYE AND THEY HAVE TO TURN ON AND OFF AT SPECIFIC TIMES FOR THE EYE TO DEVELOP PROPERLY. **PAX** IS THE GENE THAT COORDINATES THEIR ACTIVITY.

BUT THIS SIMILARITY IS JUST BECAUSE THE FISH AND I SHARE A COMMON VERTEBRATE ANCESTOR THAT HAD A CAMERA EYE. OUR DIFFERENCES ARE JUST VARIATIONS ON A THEME.

BUT IT'S **GOTTA** BE DIFFERENT FOR OCTOPUSES.

AND WHAT ABOUT **INSECTS?**

A COMPOUND EYE WITH ALL OF IT'S LITTLE FACETS IS FUNDAMENTALLY DIFFERENT THAN A CAMERA EYE.

SEE FOR YOURSELF.

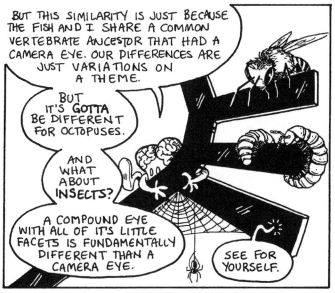

OK, THEY **ARE** VERY SIMILAR, BUT **NOT** IDENTICAL.

THOSE DIFFERENCES ARE HARMLESS TYPOS THAT HAVE ACCUMULATED OVER EVOLUTIONARY TIME. THEY DON'T AFFECT PAX'S FUNCTION.

HOW CAN YOU KNOW **THAT?**

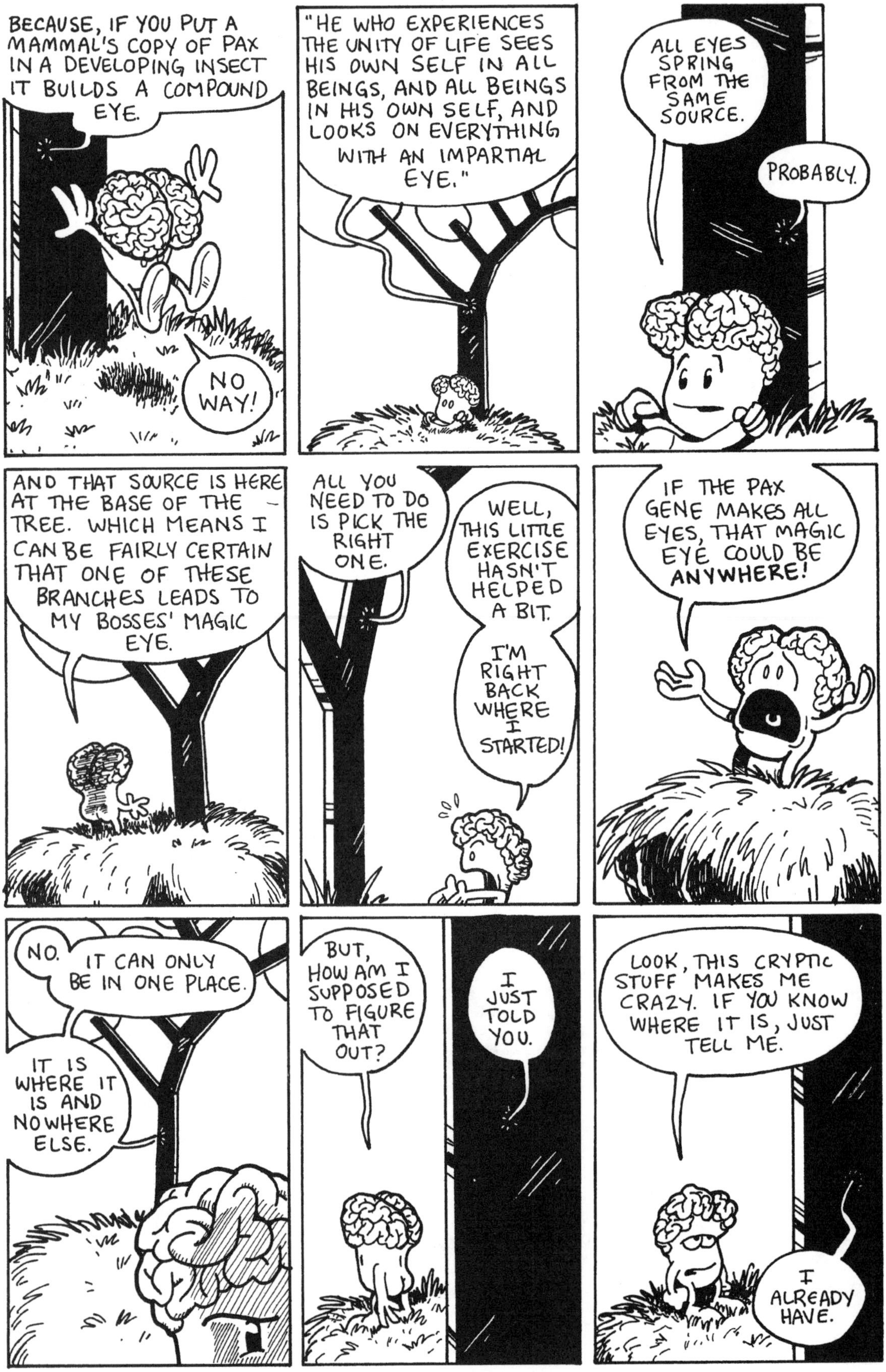
BECAUSE, IF YOU PUT A MAMMAL'S COPY OF PAX IN A DEVELOPING INSECT IT BUILDS A COMPOUND EYE.
NO WAY!
"HE WHO EXPERIENCES THE UNITY OF LIFE SEES HIS OWN SELF IN ALL BEINGS, AND ALL BEINGS IN HIS OWN SELF, AND LOOKS ON EVERYTHING WITH AN IMPARTIAL EYE."
ALL EYES SPRING FROM THE SAME SOURCE.
PROBABLY.
AND THAT SOURCE IS HERE AT THE BASE OF THE TREE. WHICH MEANS I CAN BE FAIRLY CERTAIN THAT ONE OF THESE BRANCHES LEADS TO MY BOSSES' MAGIC EYE.
ALL YOU NEED TO DO IS PICK THE RIGHT ONE.
WELL, THIS LITTLE EXERCISE HASN'T HELPED A BIT.
I'M RIGHT BACK WHERE I STARTED!
IF THE PAX GENE MAKES ALL EYES, THAT MAGIC EYE COULD BE **ANYWHERE!**
NO.
IT CAN ONLY BE IN ONE PLACE.
IT IS WHERE IT IS AND NOWHERE ELSE.
BUT, HOW AM I SUPPOSED TO FIGURE THAT OUT?
I JUST TOLD YOU.
LOOK, THIS CRYPTIC STUFF MAKES ME CRAZY. IF YOU KNOW WHERE IT IS, JUST TELL ME.
I ALREADY HAVE.

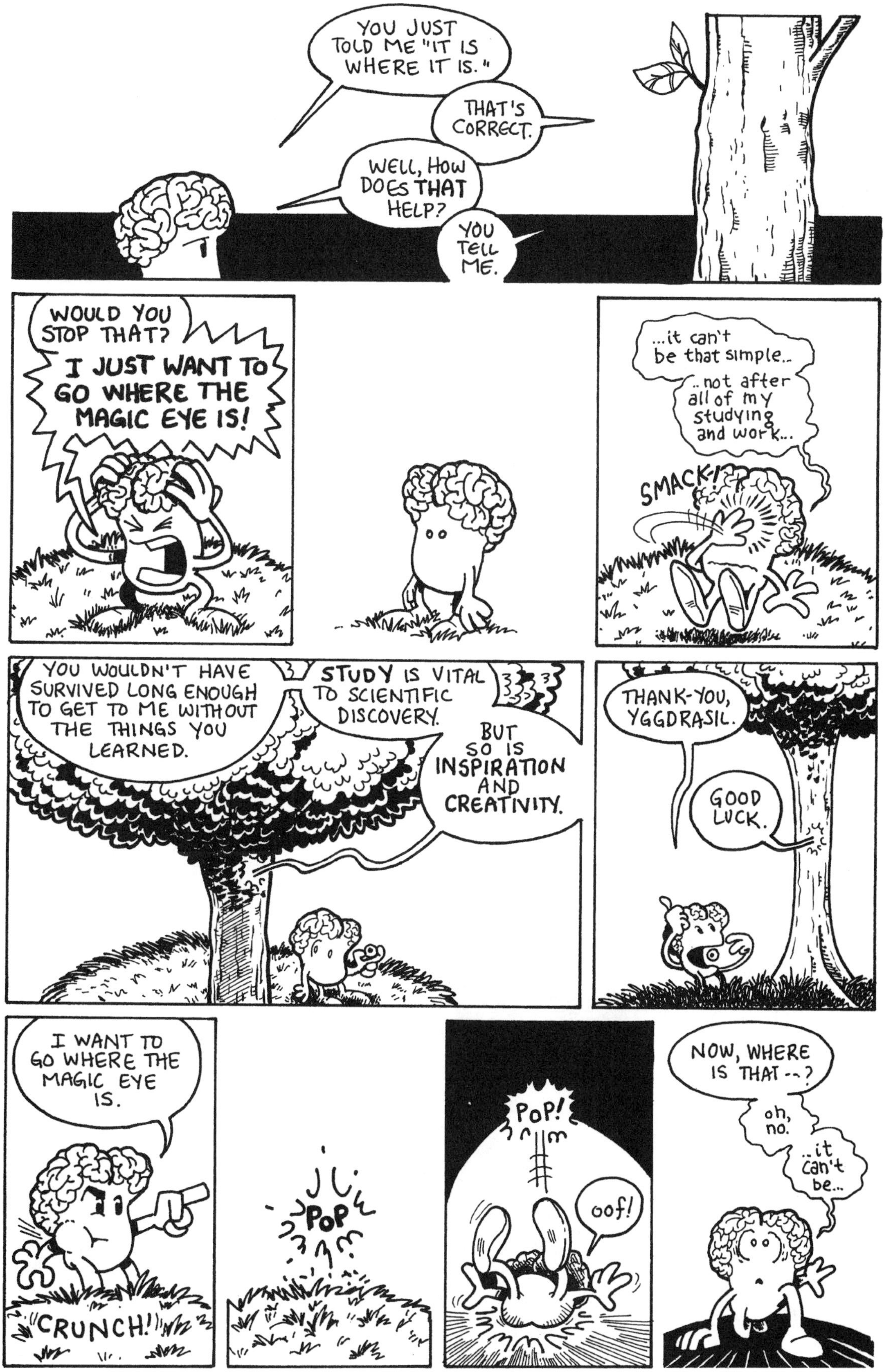
YOU JUST TOLD ME "IT IS WHERE IT IS."
THAT'S CORRECT.
WELL, HOW DOES THAT HELP?
YOU TELL ME.
WOULD YOU STOP THAT?
I JUST WANT TO GO WHERE THE MAGIC EYE IS!
...it can't be that simple..
..not after all of my studying and work...
SMACK!
YOU WOULDN'T HAVE SURVIVED LONG ENOUGH TO GET TO ME WITHOUT THE THINGS YOU LEARNED.
STUDY IS VITAL TO SCIENTIFIC DISCOVERY.
BUT SO IS INSPIRATION AND CREATIVITY.
THANK-YOU, YGGDRASIL.
GOOD LUCK.
I WANT TO GO WHERE THE MAGIC EYE IS.
CRUNCH!
POP
POP!
oof!
NOW, WHERE IS THAT --?
oh, no.
..it can't be...

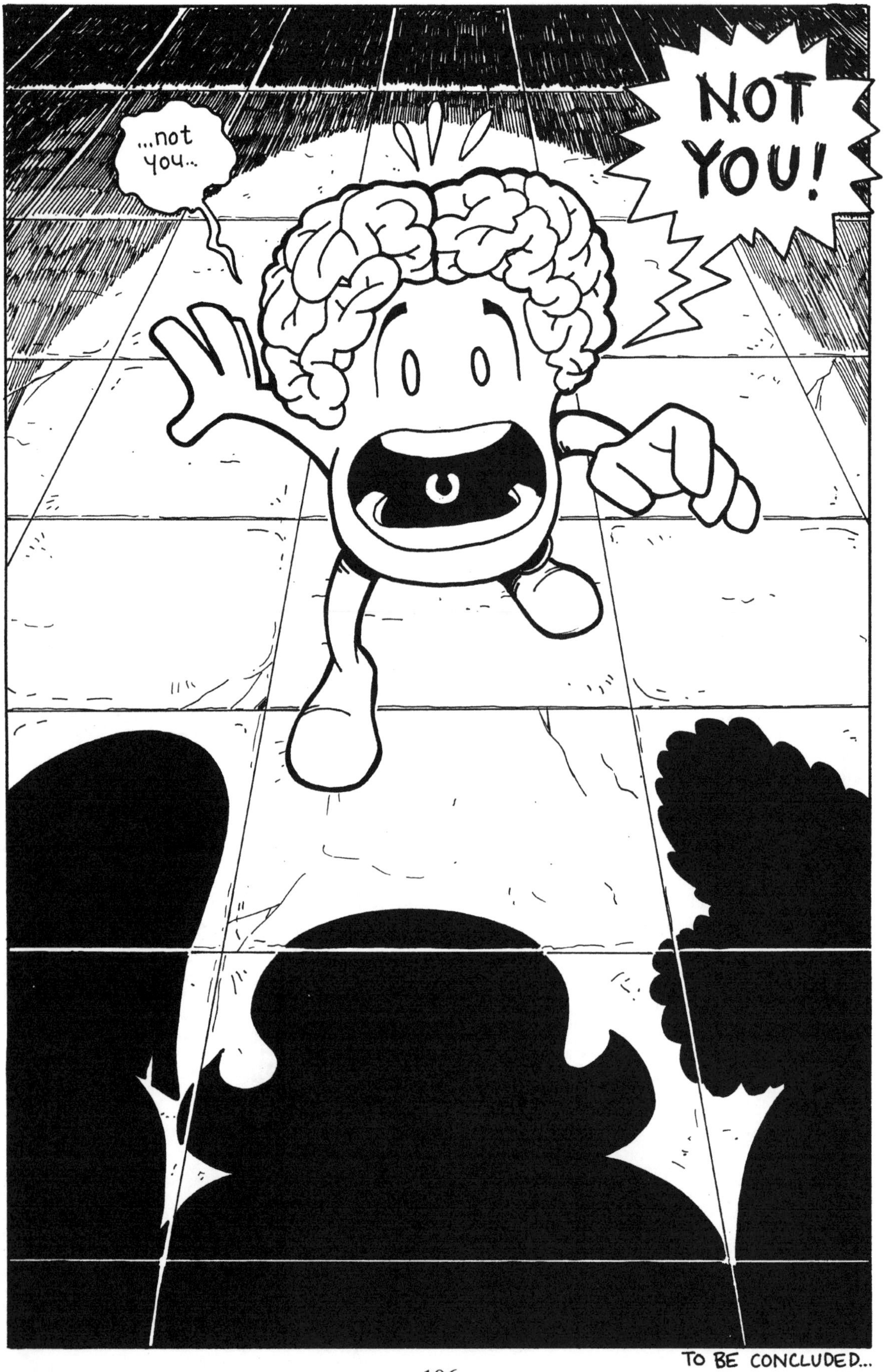

...not you...
NOT YOU!

TO BE CONCLUDED...

Branching Out

The Tree of Life

One of the things scientists like to do is collect, count and sort. For evolutionary biologists, sorting species into meaningful categories requires a basic understanding of how closely or distantly species are related. These relationships are often represented as a branching phylogenetic tree, a convention started by Darwin when he was formulating his theory of natural selection (Fig. 8.1). **Phylogenetic trees** are maps of the evolutionary patterns and histories of species. Biologists use several different lines of evidence to infer evolutionary relationships when building a tree, including genetic differences among species, comparisons of how the embryos of various species develop, comparisons of the bodies of various species and the fossil record.

While phylogenetic trees are essential tools for our understanding of the history of life, in a few rare cases they can even be a matter of life and death. In 2006, an international team of health workers consisting of five Bulgarian nurses and one Palestinian doctor were accused of intentionally infecting 400 Libyan children with HIV in a Tripoli hospital in 1998. HIV is a rapidly-mutating virus and consequently can generate several different strains in a relatively short period of time. When molecular biologists from Oxford and Rome built a phylogenetic tree of the HIV strain infecting the children, they discovered that it was most closely related to HIV strains that had been in Libya since the mid 1990s, long before the arrival of the health workers. This evidence, along with intense international political pressure, eventually helped win the release of the health workers.

To get a very basic understanding of how trees are built, let's consider a less harrowing example using a squid, a sloth, a butterfly, a hummingbird and sponge.

The Sorting Hat

So, you put on your sorting hat and begin organizing the critters in Figure 8.2 based on their evolutionary relationships. Where do you start? When evolutionary biologists start sorting, they begin with the assumption that all life on earth started with a common ancestor who lived a couple billion years ago.

In our phylogenetic tree, we want to cluster related species together in relatively close branches. To do that, we need to find ways to distinguish between one species and another. In many cases this is easier said than done. Although squid and octopuses have tentacles and are closely related, they are clearly different species. But what specifically makes them different? To answer that question, biologists look to a species unique blend of adaptations as a physical record of a species' evolutionary history.

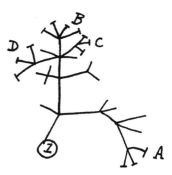

Figure 8.1 Charles Darwin first sketched a tree to represent the evolutionary relationships of species in his *First Notebook on Transmutation of Species* (1837).

Figure 8.2 Stuff to sort, including (clockwise from upper left) a hummingbird, butterfly, sloth, squid and sponge. See text for details.

You Have Your Mother's Eyes...and Arms

We have to start sorting somewhere, so let's pick a trait. Hey! I have an idea. How about eyes? It is readily apparent that four of the five animals to be sorted have eyes, while the sponge does not. Sponges are the simplest multicellular animals on the tree of life. They live their lives as sedentary filter feeders, primarily in marine environments, and their cells are not organized into tissues (like muscles and nerves) or organs (such as eyes). By contrast, the giant squid, hummingbird, butterfly and sloth all have well developed tissues and organ systems. This is a major difference and constitutes an important evolutionary divergence.

About 900 million years ago, an organism with rudimentary organs split from the sponges (Fig. 8.3A). This new species was the ancestor of the evolutionary line that eventually led to squid, sloths, butterflies and hummingbirds. Because these four are all descended from a common ancestor, we say that they comprise a **monophyletic group** (mono = one, phylogeny = evolutionary history). Since members of a monophyletic group share a common ancestor, they also share some homologous traits. A **homologous trait** is a feature that appears similar between two species and is inherited from a common ancestor.

Homologous features can be anatomical, genetic or developmental. A classic example of anatomical homology can be seen in the bones of vertebrate forelimbs. While they vary dramatically in external appearance and perform different functions, the forelimbs of bats, seals and humans all contain the same bone structure (Fig. 8.4).

Fool Me Once, Shame on You...

You can't really sort the remaining four animals based on the presence of tissues and organs because that is a homologous adaptation shared by all four species in this group. But what if you sorted based on the *type* of adaptation, in this case the type of eye? Based on that criterion, two groups are generated: organisms with camera eyes (the giant squid, sloth and hummingbird) and those

A
no tissues
or organs
tissues and organs
B
compound
eyes
camera eyes
?

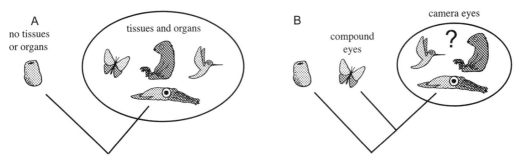

Figure 8.3 Sorting our five animals. A) A simple phlyogenetic tree with animals sorted using the presence of tissues and organs. Two groups are formed, one containing sponges (which lack tissues and organs) and one containing the other four animals. B) Further sorting of the animals with tissues and organs. In this case, the feature used to sort was the presence of camera eyes. This separates the butterfly from the remaining three, but is the group of squid, sloth and hummingbird monophyletic?

with compound eyes (the butterfly). Will that work? Not really.

Not every aspect of an organism that can be used to sort is useful in building a phylogenetic tree. Sorting based on eye type works for butterflies (Fig . 8.3B) because insects evolved compound eyes independently of organisms that evolved camera eyes (see our discussion in Chapter 3). But the important question for our phylogenetic tree becomes, "Is the group that contains the squid, sloth and hummingbird monophyletic based on their type of eye?" In other words, do these three share a common ancestor that had a camera eye? The answer is that they probably did not.

Analogous Traits and Convergent Evolution

One of the trickiest aspects of creating a phylogenetic tree is realizing that adaptations that look like they were inherited from a common ancestor (*i.e.* they are homologous) often are not. Sometimes adaptations are the product of convergent evolution. As the name suggests, **convergent evolution** is the process by which two distantly related species evolve similar features (known as analogous traits) to deal with similar environmental conditions or similar ways of life. Thus, **analogous traits** are traits that perform analogous *functions* but have evolved independently in two species and are not inherited from a common ancestor.

At first blush, the sloth's camera eye and the squid's camera eye look like they might be homologous traits. They are camera eyes, after all. They both have corneas and lenses that focus light. Both eyes form an image and both have retinas full of small photosensitive cells. So, from a functional standpoint, it seems like they were inherited from the same ancestor. But similarity in form and function can be deceiving.

Upon closer inspection, we can identify several important differences that suggest that the two types of camera eyes evolved independently of each other. (Fig. 8.5). In some squid and octopuses, the cornea is actually open to the environment. This means that the front chamber of the eye is filled with sea water. Vertebrate eyes (like that of the sloth and hummingbird) have a closed front chamber filled with aqueous humor. To focus an image, the sloth uses the ciliary muscles to change the shape of the lens. In squid and octopuses, the ciliary muscle moves the lens forward and backward to focus (just as a camera lens is moved to focus). Unlike in the camera eyes of the sloth and hummingbird, the sensory cells of the squid retina point toward the lens and the incoming light; consequently, the axons going to the brain do not need to pass through the retina, as they do in vertebrates. Thus, the squid, unlike the sloth and other vertebrates, doesn't have a blind spot. Finally, the photosensitive cells of the squid retina are called **retinula cells** and are very similar structurally to the retinula cells found in the insect compound eye (Fig. 3.1).

Let's Split

Since squid and sloth camera eyes are the product of convergent evolution, sorting based on eye type does not really help us with the

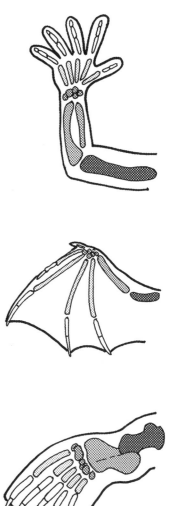

Figure 8.4 Anatomical homology of the mammalian forelimb. Although the forelimbs of humans, bats and seals are highly modified for their respective environments and ways of life, they all share the same basic skeletal components. This shared skeletal structure was inherited from the common ancestor of all mammals.

final four animals. We need to find a homologous feature that will help us establish reliable evolutionary relationships.

Now what? Well, a quick flip back to Chapter 2: *Anatomy of Vision* should give us a good idea. Hummingbirds and sloths are both vertebrates. Their backbones are homologous features inherited from a common fishy ancestor. The squid and butterfly, on the other hand, are invertebrates. Using the adaptations 1) organs and 2) backbones we can build a tree that looks something like Figure 8.6.

It's Not Quite That Easy. (You Know That, Right?)

Constructing the phylogenetic tree above was relatively simple. We lumped species together based on shared anatomical traits. Unfortunately, when dealing with more complex phylogenetic questions, a number of factors can muddy the waters for researchers. Convergent evolution can generate traits that appear to have been inherited from a common ancestor but are not. And sometimes adaptations like eyes can be lost all together, as we've seen in blind cave fishes.

It might be tempting to suggest that we just skip the anatomy and focus on genetics. But DNA sequences aren't perfect records of an organism's evolutionary history either. **Reversals** sometimes occur when a single nucleic acid in a DNA sequence changes and causes the sequence to revert to a more ancient state. Such a reversal can make two closely related species appear distantly related.

For these reasons, relying solely on anatomical or genetic homologies can be problematic. Whenever possible, evolutionary biologists try to utilize a combination of multiple factors (such as embryonic development, genetics, fossils and anatomy) to increase the reliability of their phylogenetic trees.

A.
Pupil
Aqueous
Humor
Cornea
Sclera
Iris
Lens
Ciliary
Muscle
Vitreous
Humor
Optic
Disk
Fovea
Pigmented
Layer
Optic
Nerve
Retina
B.
Pupil
Cornea
Pigmented
Layer
Hole in
cornea
Retina
Iris
Lens
Vitreous
Humor
Optic
lobe
Anterior
Chamber
Ciliary
Muscle

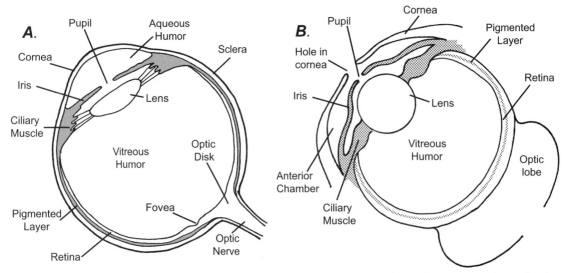

Figure 8.5 The camera eyes of a A) mammal (human) and B) squid. While they perform the same image-forming function for their respective owners, these two camera eyes are the product of convergent evolution. Similar structures like the lenses and retinas are not inherited from a common ancestor and are thus considered analogous traits. See text for further explanantion.

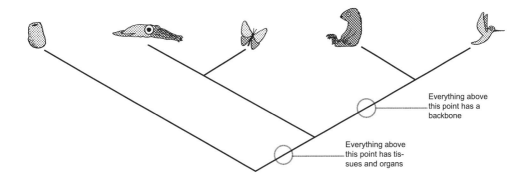

Everything above this point has a backbone

Everything above this point has tissues and organs

Figure 8.6 A proposed phylogenetic tree for a sponge, squid, butterfly, sloth and hummingbird. The point at which two branches diverge is known as a node. The criteria for sorting are indicated at the two major nodes. There are additional nodes at the points where squid diverge from insects and where sloths split from hummingbirds.

An Eye for an Eye

In a letter to Harvard University botanist Asa Grey, Charles Darwin once wrote, "The eye to this day gives me a cold shudder…" Critics of evolution have made a lot of hay from this quote. They like to suggest that Darwin's confidence in his theory was wavering. Of course, they usually fail to note that Darwin continued, "…but when I think of the fine known gradations, my reason tells me I ought to conquer the cold shudder."

The "fine known gradations" to which Darwin was referring are the numerous different types of eyes seen in nature (Fig. 2.2). They range from simple patches of photosensitive cells to elaborate camera eyes. But even more remarkable than their diversity is the fact that these wildly different eyes all share the same developmental guidance from the *hox* gene *pax-6*. Recall from Chapter 5 that *pax-6* is the gene that regulates eye development in everything from people to insects. But does that make the genes interchangeable across species?

Placing the vertebrate *pax-6* gene (called *Aniridia*) in a fruit fly (whose *pax-6* gene is called *eyeless*) sounds like an experiment straight from the script of a monster movie, but that is just what biologist Walter Gehring did. The result? Did inserting the *Aniridia* gene into a developing fruit fly yield freaky camera eyes popping out of the insect? No. (Although that would have been really cool.) Instead, he found that the vertebrate *pax-6* made perfectly good compound eyes when it was in the fly. Such profound evidence for our shared evolutionary history should effectively ward off any more Darwinian shudders.

Eye Did It Myyyyyyyy Waaaaaay

Is the eye a miraculous invention or a logical outcome of the struggle to survive? The ability to perceive light is a tremendous advantage for organisms. It gives them highly reliable information about the world that can facilitate finding food and mates and escaping harm. And, as we have seen, evolving an elaborate image-forming apparatus around the simple light-sensitive cells could have happened extraordinarily quickly (Fig. 2.2) and probably did.

Approximately 550 million years ago at the start of the Cambrian Period, the types of animals found in the fossil record dramatically changed. Animals before this (during a 4 billion year stretch of time called the Precambrian Period) were generally small, soft-bodied animals with no discernible visual apparatus to speak of. However, at the start of the Cambrian there is an explosion of body forms in the fossil record. Animals evolved larger, more heavily-armored bodies and they had well-developed eyes (most of which were of the compound variety).

Several researchers have suggested that the evolution of vision was the driving force for the diversification of life. They argue that if a predator developed the ability to see prey, the prey would need to evolve adaptations to counter the predator's advantage. This evolutionary "arms race" could have driven the evolution of eyes to spot the predators in time to evade consumption. Some of the experiments in vision are unlike anything we see today (Fig. 8.7).

But how could everyone get eyes all at once? Well, everyone probably didn't. Only those with the genetic wherewithal could evolve eyes. Since the *hox* gene *pax-6* is found in all animals, it undoubtedly played a major role in the evolution of vision. Perhaps, as a consequence, it also played a role in evolution's equivalent of the Big Bang, making the Cambrian Explosion, quite literally, an eye-opening event.

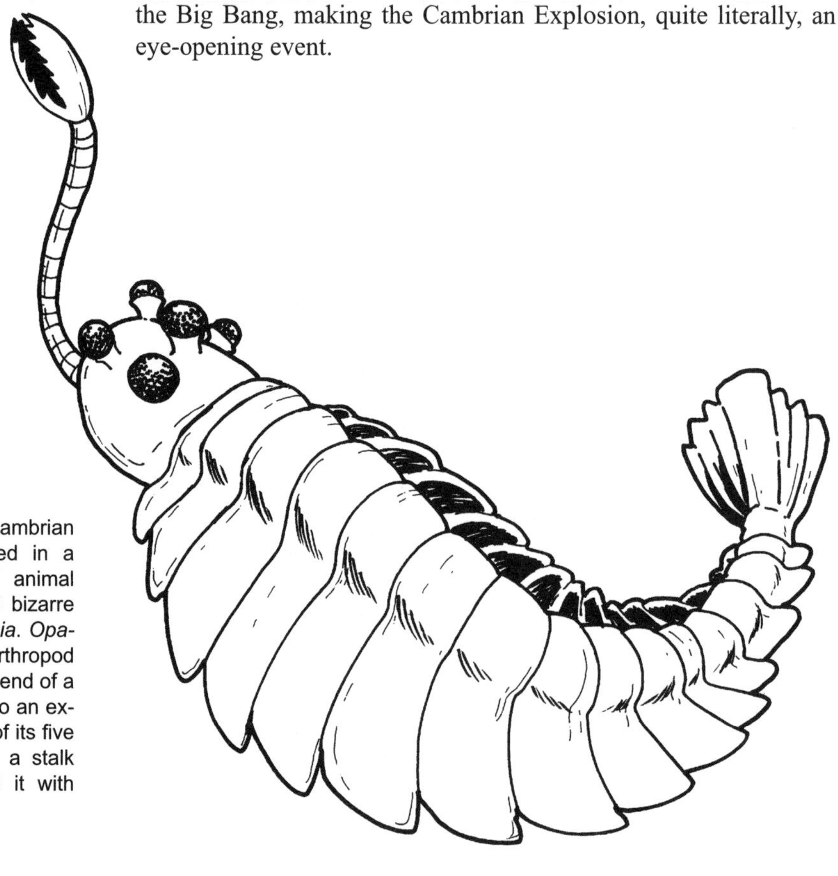

Figure 8.7 During the Cambrian Explosion, life proliferated in a spectacular radiation of animal forms. One of the more bizarre forms was that of *Opabinia*. *Opabinia* was an oddball arthropod whose mouth was on the end of a long proboscis. It was also an experiment in vision. Each of its five compound eyes was on a stalk and may have provided it with 360° vision.

For Your Consideration

1. Why wouldn't it always be possible to use genetic information in reconstructing trees?

2. Define monophyly. Look at Figure 8.4. How many monophyletic groups are there? What adaptations might you use to further distinguish the hummingbird from the sloth on one branch and the squid and butterfly on the other?

3. Construct a phylogenetic tree that includes an eagle, iguana, salamander and trout. What traits did you use to determine points of divergence? How many monophyletic groups did you make? Which traits are shared by the species in each monophyletic group?

4. How many ways can you sort dogs? Are these meaningful distinctions in evolutionary terms? Why or why not?

5. Find an example of convergent evolution in Chapter 7.

6. Not all of the animals in the Cambrian evolved eyes. But those that didn't tended to live in burrows in the ocean floor. How might the presence of these eyeless animals support the "arms race" argument?

Chapter Nine: Lost and Found

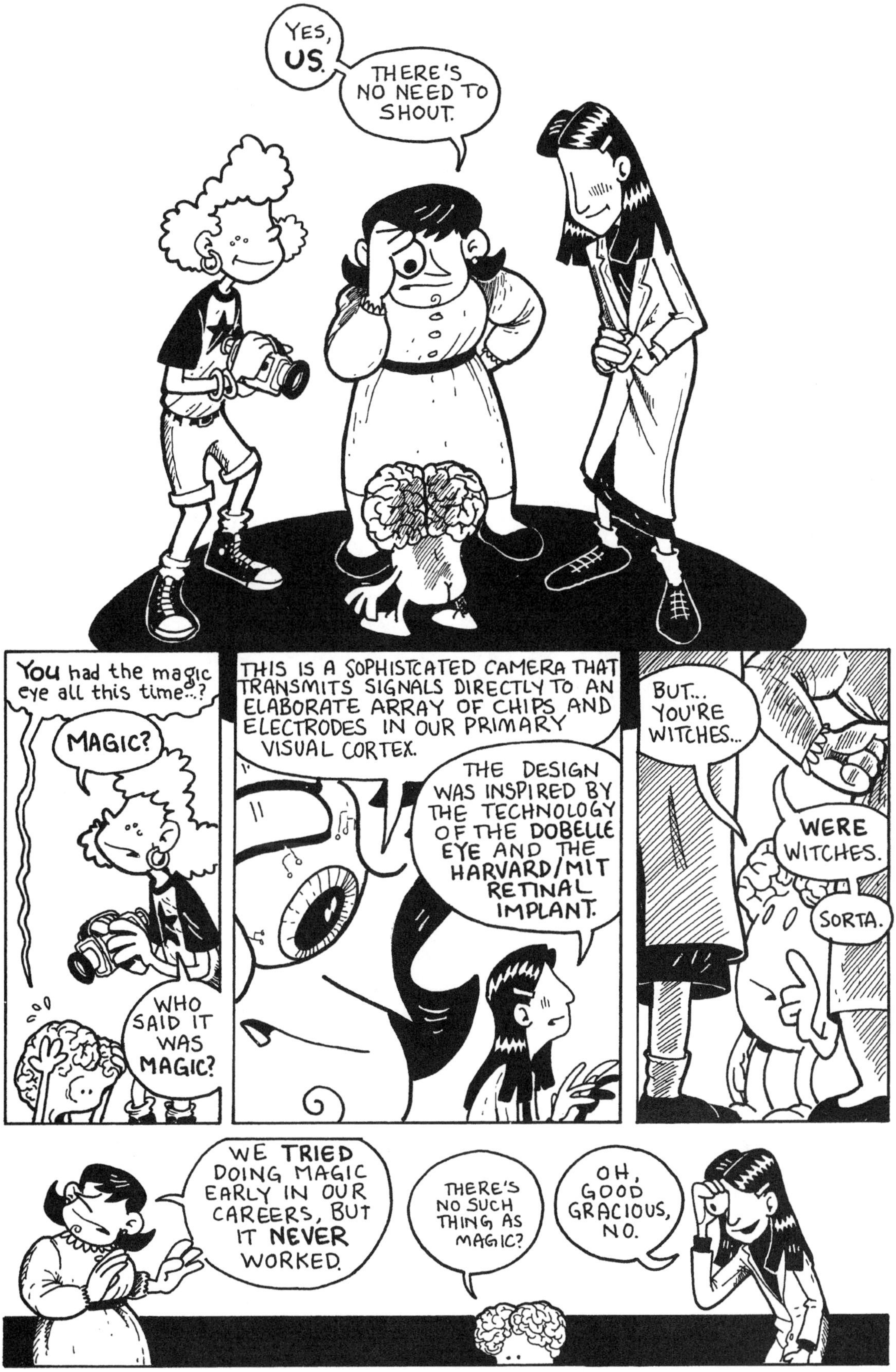
YES, US.
THERE'S NO NEED TO SHOUT.
YOU had the magic eye all this time...?
MAGIC?
WHO SAID IT WAS MAGIC?
THIS IS A SOPHISTCATED CAMERA THAT TRANSMITS SIGNALS DIRECTLY TO AN ELABORATE ARRAY OF CHIPS AND ELECTRODES IN OUR PRIMARY VISUAL CORTEX.
THE DESIGN WAS INSPIRED BY THE TECHNOLOGY OF THE DOBELLE EYE AND THE HARVARD/MIT RETINAL IMPLANT.
BUT... YOU'RE WITCHES...
WERE WITCHES.
SORTA.
WE TRIED DOING MAGIC EARLY IN OUR CAREERS, BUT IT NEVER WORKED.
THERE'S NO SUCH THING AS MAGIC?
OH, GOOD GRACIOUS, NO.

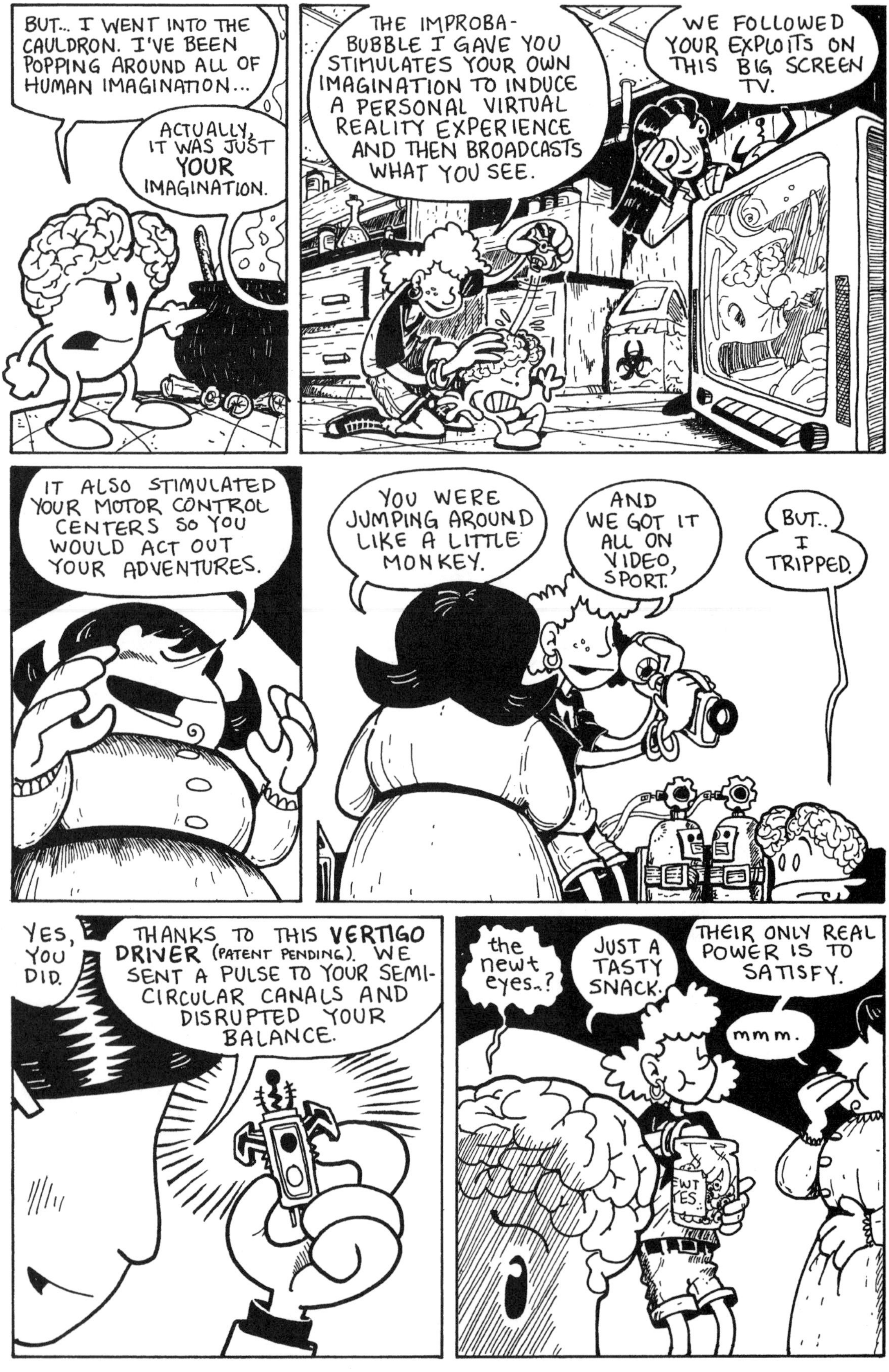
BUT... I WENT INTO THE CAULDRON. I'VE BEEN POPPING AROUND ALL OF HUMAN IMAGINATION...
ACTUALLY, IT WAS JUST YOUR IMAGINATION.
THE IMPROBA-BUBBLE I GAVE YOU STIMULATES YOUR OWN IMAGINATION TO INDUCE A PERSONAL VIRTUAL REALITY EXPERIENCE AND THEN BROADCASTS WHAT YOU SEE.
WE FOLLOWED YOUR EXPLOITS ON THIS BIG SCREEN TV.
IT ALSO STIMULATED YOUR MOTOR CONTROL CENTERS SO YOU WOULD ACT OUT YOUR ADVENTURES.
YOU WERE JUMPING AROUND LIKE A LITTLE MONKEY.
AND WE GOT IT ALL ON VIDEO, SPORT.
BUT.. I TRIPPED.
YES, YOU DID.
THANKS TO THIS VERTIGO DRIVER (PATENT PENDING). WE SENT A PULSE TO YOUR SEMI-CIRCULAR CANALS AND DISRUPTED YOUR BALANCE.
the newt eyes..?
JUST A TASTY SNACK.
THEIR ONLY REAL POWER IS TO SATISFY.
mmm.

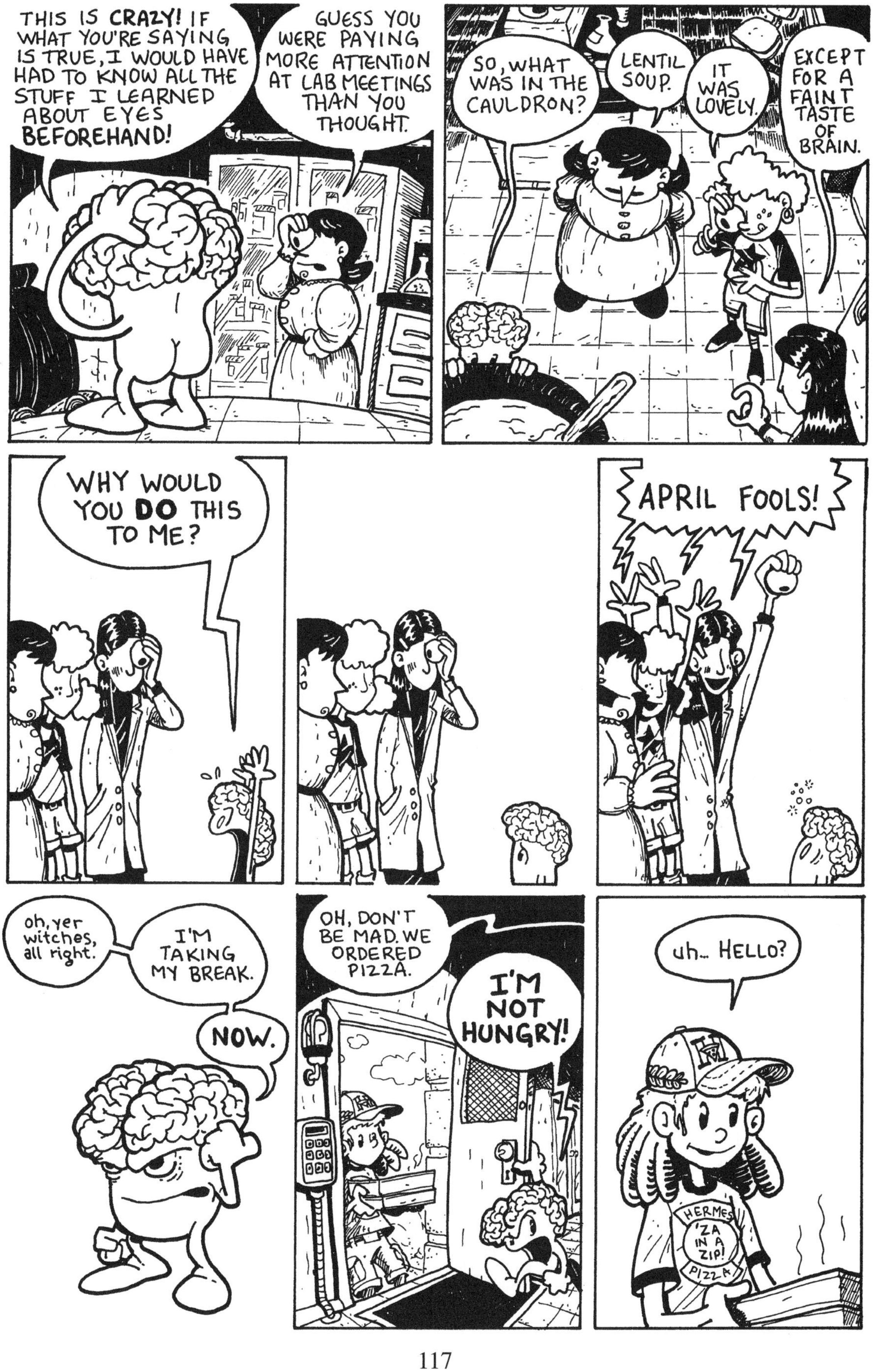

THIS IS CRAZY! IF WHAT YOU'RE SAYING IS TRUE, I WOULD HAVE HAD TO KNOW ALL THE STUFF I LEARNED ABOUT EYES BEFOREHAND!
GUESS YOU WERE PAYING MORE ATTENTION AT LAB MEETINGS THAN YOU THOUGHT.
SO, WHAT WAS IN THE CAULDRON?
LENTIL SOUP.
IT WAS LOVELY.
EXCEPT FOR A FAINT TASTE OF BRAIN.
WHY WOULD YOU DO THIS TO ME?
APRIL FOOLS!
oh, yer witches, all right.
I'M TAKING MY BREAK.
NOW.
OH, DON'T BE MAD. WE ORDERED PIZZA.
I'M NOT HUNGRY!
uh... HELLO?
HERMES 'ZA IN A ZIP! PIZZA

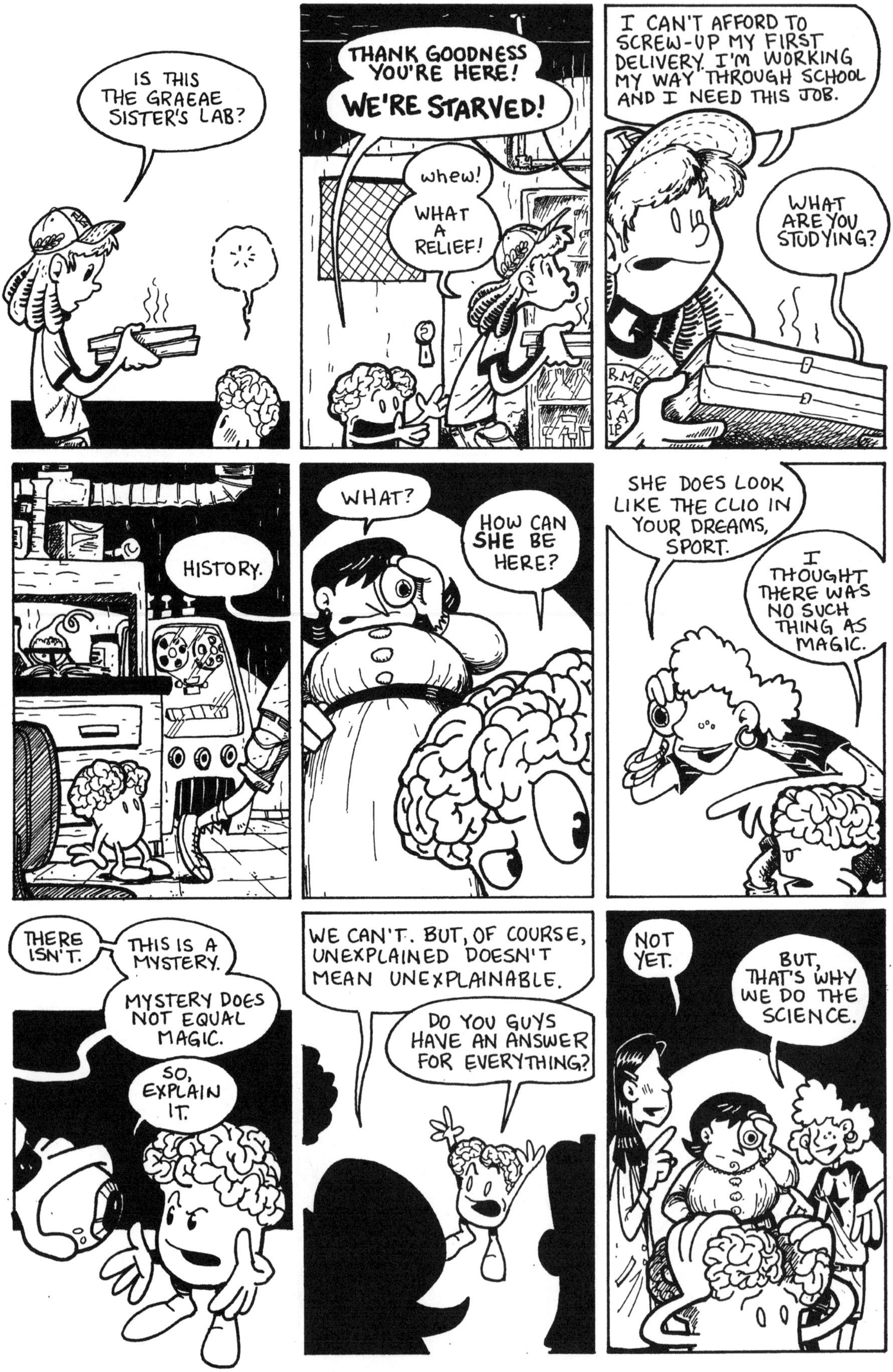
IS THIS THE GRAEAE SISTER'S LAB?
THANK GOODNESS YOU'RE HERE! WE'RE STARVED!
whew!
WHAT A RELIEF!
I CAN'T AFFORD TO SCREW-UP MY FIRST DELIVERY. I'M WORKING MY WAY THROUGH SCHOOL AND I NEED THIS JOB.
WHAT ARE YOU STUDYING?
HISTORY.
WHAT?
HOW CAN SHE BE HERE?
SHE DOES LOOK LIKE THE CLIO IN YOUR DREAMS, SPORT.
I THOUGHT THERE WAS NO SUCH THING AS MAGIC.
THERE ISN'T.
THIS IS A MYSTERY.
MYSTERY DOES NOT EQUAL MAGIC.
SO, EXPLAIN IT.
WE CAN'T. BUT, OF COURSE, UNEXPLAINED DOESN'T MEAN UNEXPLAINABLE.
DO YOU GUYS HAVE AN ANSWER FOR EVERYTHING?
NOT YET.
BUT, THAT'S WHY WE DO THE SCIENCE.

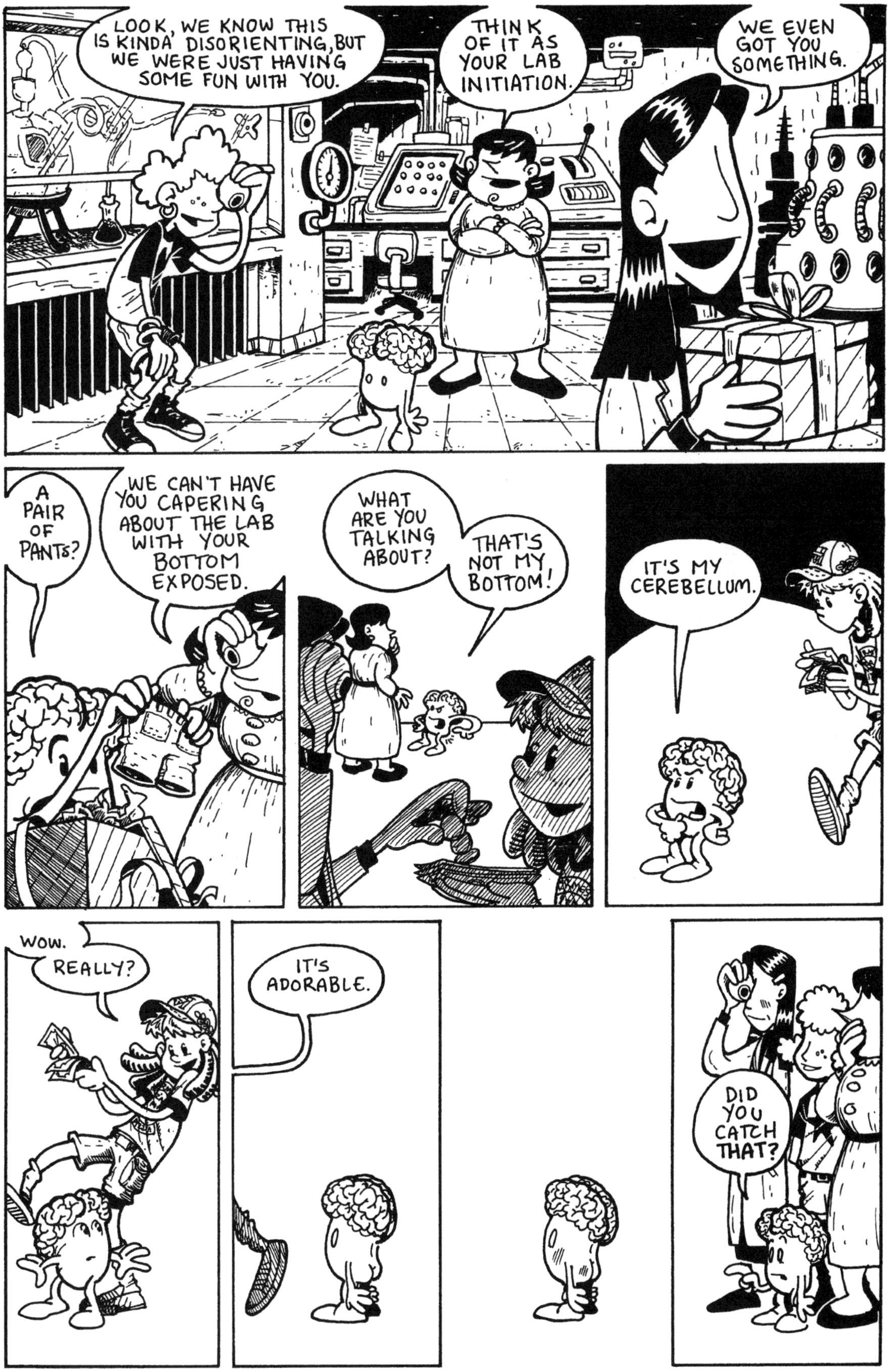
LOOK, WE KNOW THIS IS KINDA' DISORIENTING, BUT WE WERE JUST HAVING SOME FUN WITH YOU.
THINK OF IT AS YOUR LAB INITIATION.
WE EVEN GOT YOU SOMETHING.
A PAIR OF PANTS?
WE CAN'T HAVE YOU CAPERING ABOUT THE LAB WITH YOUR BOTTOM EXPOSED.
WHAT ARE YOU TALKING ABOUT?
THAT'S NOT MY BOTTOM!
IT'S MY CEREBELLUM.
WOW.
REALLY?
IT'S ADORABLE.
DID YOU CATCH THAT?

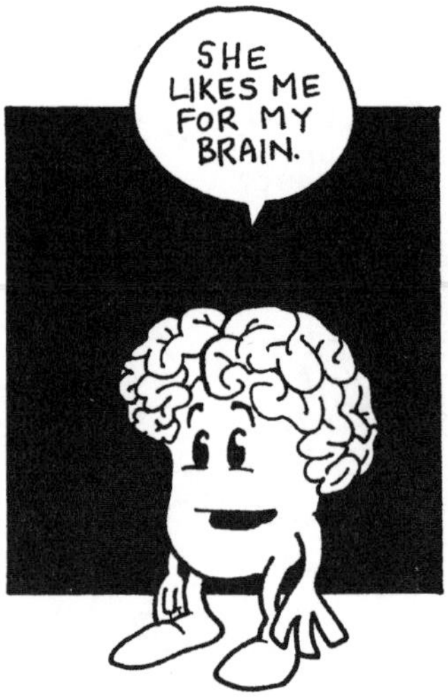
SHE LIKES ME FOR MY BRAIN.

There is no Eye in Team

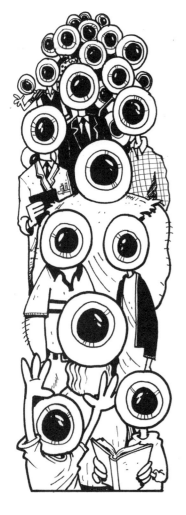

Drafts of this book have passed before several eyes. The first set of peepers belongs to my wife, Lisa. She has an eye (the left one, I think) for good stories. Her right eye is that of a teacher. This book benefited from her unique binocular vision. Add to this the fact that she has a physiological inability to lie and I received the unvarnished truth from multiple directions. She doesn't let me get away with anything.

I am grateful for my sons, Max and Jack. A few seconds wrapped in their arms or listening to them giggle at a silly joke was always enough to replenish me when my energies were ebbing. I am also delighted to present their first published drawings throughout Chapter 6. In the first panel, Max designed Wrinkle's look for the story and Jack gave us the naughty, naughty Mr. Sun. In the last panel on page 74, Jack drew me and Max drew Lisa. They are uncanny likenesses.

Laura White edited everything I wrote and drew. For free. It is a debt I can never repay, but I will continue to try. As a trained biologist and teacher (and master grammarian-is that a word, Laura?), she patiently corrected the same stupid grammatical errors over and over again and held my feet to the fire when I neglected the nuances and complexities of certain biological principles. Her husband Jamie let me know when jokes and images worked and helped me with the physics. I feel very fortunate to have friends so willing to do so much for nothing more in return than an occasional game of euchre.

Thanks to the indefatigable Daryn Guarino at Active Synapse Comics for his tireless promotion of my books. He is a business juggernaut and it is because of his efforts that my books have found an audience. His unwavering support and encouragement have made it possible for me to make comics and I can never thank him enough.

If you noticed the wonderful colors on the cover of this book, you can join me in thanking Troy Cummings. It has been a delight to get to know him during my sabbatical and I'm glad I could enlist his services now, because it won't be long before he will be rich, famous and in demand. I also want to thank my invisible collaborator on this project, KB Boomer. *Optical Allusions* is an educational experiment and KB is the statistician who will be testing its effectiveness in the classroom. It has been fun working with her and I am crossing my fingers about the results. And, of course, thanks go to Chris, John, Adam and Denny at the incomparable Comics Swap in State College, PA.

I am grateful to several friends and fellow comic book creators for their comments on the Wrinkles story. Jim Ottaviani's assistance was invaluable. He caught important things I missed, asked the questions about things I had hoped no one would notice and graciously provided technical guidance as I prepared this book. John Kerschbaum provided comedic inspiration, guidance in helping me navigate tricky storytelling terrain and a steady supply of pictures of his new baby, Norah, to lift my spirits when things got tedious. Zander Cannon said something so inspirational early on that it stuck in my mind the entire time I as working on this book. Kurt Busiek provided encouragement, helpful storytelling hints and mythological insights.

My academic friends and colleagues have offered support, suggestions, critiques and insight into the science and pedagogy of this book. I benefited greatly from the advice of Mike Boyle, Kevin Kinney, Randy Bennet, Craig Nelson, Victor DeCarlo, Alex Komives, Glenn Branch, Dana Dudle, Jim and Belle Tuten, Bill White, David Hsiung, and Richard and Memory Hark.

This book was started at my home institution Juniata College and completed while on sabbatical at DePauw University. I am deeply grateful for the support of my Provost at Juniata, Jim Lakso, the chair of the Biology Department, Jill Keeney, and Juniata College's President, Tom Kepple. I am also grateful for Susan Pierotti's help with the copier (among other things) and for Chris Walls' help ordering books. They have all provided a place to work that exceeds all of my expectations. I am also grateful to the tireless Jon Wall, Juniata's Director of Public Relations, for his efforts to promote my work.

At DePauw, I am indebted to Provost Neal Abraham for providing the sabbatical opportunity and President Robert Bottoms for letting me come back (after a number of…unflattering cartoons I did as an undergraduate). I am also thankful to Jane Griswold, Tavia Pigg, Wade Hazel, Bonnie Bryant, Mary Gardner and Jim Benedix for their help getting the sabbatical set-up and getting my family and I settled in Greencastle.

This work was supported by a grant from the National Science Foundation. My gratitude goes to Jeanne Small at the NSF for encouraging me to submit the grant proposal and Juniata's Grants Officer, Mike Keating, for helping me to hit deadlines and coordinate the myriad pieces that must be assembled for a grant submission. Additionally, I am grateful to my NSF Program Officers Nancy Pelaez, Nancy Pruitt and Terry Woodlin for their help in securing funding and navigating the bureaucracy. Thanks to Juniata's John Alfano for managing the budget.

Finally, I offer a special thanks to Tonia Lawson, Michelle Jeffers, Tim Scarbrough and Mike Goodale and the other folks at Malloy Printing. They are wonderful to work with and have made the process of putting this book much easier.

Bibliography

General Reference

Carrol, S.B. (2005). *Endless Forms Most Beautiful*. New York, London: W.W. Norton & Company.

Darwin, C. (1993) *The Origin of Species* (6th ed.). New York: Random House, Inc.

Evans, A.V., & Bellamy, C.L. (1996). *An Inordinate Fondness for Beetles*. New York: Henry Holt & Company.

Freeman, S. (2005). *Biological Science* (2nd ed.). Upper Saddle River, NJ: Pearson Prentice Hall.

Freeman, S., & Herron, J.C. (2007). *Evolutionary Analysis* (4th ed.). Upper Saddle River, NJ: Pearson Prentice Hall.

Futuyma, D.J. (2005). *Evolution* (2nd ed.). Sunderland, Massachusetts: Sinauer Associates, Inc.

Gregory, R.L. (1997). *Eye and Brain: The Psychology of Seeing* (5th ed.). Princeton, NJ: Princeton University Press.

Gould, J.L., & Gould, C.G. (1989). *Sexual Selection*. New York: Scientific American Library.

Gullan, P.J., & Cranston, P.S. (2005). *The Insects: An Outline of Entomology* (3rd ed.). Blackwell Publishing, Ltd.

Land, M.F., & Nilsson, D-E. (2002). *Animal Eyes*. Oxford, England: Oxford University Press.

Nicholls, J.G., Martin, A.R., Wallace, B.G., & Fuchs, P.A. (2007). *From Neuron to Brain* (4th ed.). Sunderland, Massachusetts: Sinauer Associates, Inc.

Parker, A. (2003). *In the Blink of an Eye: How Vision Sparked the Big Bang of Evolution*. New York: Basic Books.

Smith, C.U.M. (2000). *Biology of Sensory Systems*. West Sussex, England: John Wiley & Sons, Ltd.

Zimmer, C. (2001) *Evolution: The Triumph of an Idea*. New York: HarperCollins Publishers.

Chapter One

Del Rio-Tsonis, K., Washabaugh, C.H., and Tsonis P.A. (1995) Expression of pax-6 during urodele eye development and lens regeneration. *Proc. Natl. Acad. Sci. USA*. 92, 5092-5096.

Hamilton, E. (1998) *Mythology*. Black Bay Books.

Stone, L. S. (1967). An investigation recording all salamanders which can and cannot regenerate a lens from the dorsal iris. *Journal of Experimental Zoology*, 164, 87-104.

Chapter Two

Browne, E.J. (1996). *Charles Darwin: Voyaging*. Princeton, NJ: Princeton University Press.

Browne, E.J. (2003). *Charles Darwin: The Power of Place*. Princeton, NJ: Princeton University Press.

Dan-E. Nilsson, D-E., & Pelger, S. (1994). A Pessimistic Estimate of the Time Required for an Eye to Evolve. *Proceedings: Biological Sciences*, 256 (1345), pp. 53-58.

Darwin, C. (1993). *The Origin of Species* (6th ed.). New York: Random House, Inc.

Desmond, A., & Moore, J. (1994). *Darwin: The Life of a Tormented Evolutionist*. New York, London: W. W. Norton & Company.

Homer (1999). *The Odyssey*. (R. Fagles, Trans.). Penguin Classics.

Lyell, C (1998). *Principle of Geology*. Penguin Classics.

Chapter Three

Gregory, R.L. (1997). *Eye and Brain: The Psychology of Seeing* (5th ed.). Princeton, NJ: Princeton University Press.

Gullan, P.J., & Cranston, P.S. (2005). *The Insects: An Outline of Entomology* (3rd ed.). Blackwell Publishing, Ltd.

Osterberg, G. A. (1935). Topography of the layer of rods and cones in the human retina. *Acta Ophthalmologica*, 6 (1), 1935

Chapter Four

The breadth of research on sexual selection and stalk-eyed flies is reviewed very nicely in Freeman's *Evolutionary Analysis*.

Burkhardt, D., & de la Motte, I. (1983). How stalk-eyed flies eye stalk-eyed flies: Observations and measurements of the eyes of *Cyrtodiopsis whitei* (Dopsidae, Diptera). *Journal of Comparative Physiology*, 151, 407-421.

Emlem, D.J. (2000). Integrating Development with Evolution: A Case Study with Beetle Horns. *BioScience*, 50 (5), 403-418.

Emlem, D.J. (2001). Costs and the Diversification of Exaggerated Animal Structures. *Science*, 291, 1534-1536.

Frick, M.G., Slay, C.K., Quinn, C.A., Windham-Reid, A., Duley, P.A., Ryder, C.M., Morse, L.J. (2000). Aerial Observations of Courtship Behavior in Loggerhead Sea Turtles (*Caretta caretta*) from Southeastern Georgia and Northeastern Florida. *Journal of Herpetology*, 34 (1), 153-158.

Gerhardt, H.C., Dyson, M.L., & Tanner, S.D. (1996). Dynamic properties of the advertisement calls of gray tree frogs: Patterns of variability and female choice. *Behavioral Ecology*, 7, 7-18.

Gould, J.L., & Gould, C.G. (1989). *Sexual Selection*. New York: Scientific American Library.

Hrdy, S.B., (1977). Infanticide as a primate reproductive strategy. *American Scientist* 65 (1), 40-49.

Hrdy, S.B., (1979). Infanticide among animals: A review, classification, and examination of the implications of the reproductive strategies of females. *Ethology and Sociobiology* 1, 13-40.

Lewis, S.M., Cratsley, C.K. & Rooney, J.A. (2004). Nuptial Gifts and Sexual Selection in Photinus Fireflies. *Integr. Comp. Biol.*, 44, 234–237

Miller, G. T. & S. Pitnick (2002). Sperm-female co-evolution in *Drosophila*. *Science* 298, 1230-1233.

Rosenqvist, G. (1990). Male mate choice and female-female competition for mates in the pipefish *Nerophis ophidion. Animal Behaviour,* 39, 1110-1115.

Waage, J.K. (1984). *Sperm competition and the evolution of the Odonate mating systems*. In R.L. Smith, ed. Sperm Competition and the Evolution of Animal Mating Systems. Orlando: Academic Press, 251-290.

Waage, J.K. (1986). Evidence for the widespread sperm displacement activity among *Zygoptera* (*Odonata*) and the means for predicting its presence. *Biological Journal of the Linnean Society*, 28, 285-300.

Welch, A., Semlitsch, R.D., & Gerhardt, H.C. (1998). Call duration as an indicator of genetic quality in ale gray tree frogs. *Science,* 280, 1928-1930.

Zahavi, A. and Zahavi, A. (1997). *The handicap principle: a missing piece of Darwin's puzzle*. Oxford, England: Oxford University Press.

Chapter Five

A good deal of my education in development came from reading Sean Carrol's excellent *Endless Forms Most Beautiful* (reference below). It was there that I read of the work of Keeler and Binns with sheep and cyclopomine. I did not manage to read the primary article, but I include it below for the enterprising reader.

Carrol, S.B. (2005). *Endless Forms Most Beautiful*. New York, London: W.W. Norton & Company.

Homer (1999). *The Odyssey*. (R. Fagles, Trans.). Penguin Classics.

Jeffrey, W.R., Strickler, A.G., & Yamamota, Y. (2003). To See or Not to See: Evolution of Eye Degeneration in Mexican Blind Cavefish. *Integr, Comp. Biol.,* 43, 531–541.

Keeler, R.F. & Binns, W. (1968). Teratogenic compounds of *Veratrum californicum* (Durand). V. Comparison of cyclopian effects of steroidal alkaloids from the plant and structurally related compounds from other sources. *Teratology*, 1 (1), 5-10.

Schwarz, M., Cecconi, F., Bernier, G., Andrejewski, N., Kammandel, B., Wagner, M. & Gruss, P. (2000). Spatial specification of mammalian eye territories by reciprocal transcriptional repression of *Pax2* and *Pax6*. *Development,* 127, 4325-4334 .

Yamamoto, Y., Stock, D.W., & Jeffery, W.R. (2004). Hedgehog signaling controls eye degeneration in blind cavefish. *Nature,* 431, 844-847.

Chapter Six

Gregory, R.L. (1997). *Eye and Brain: The Psychology of Seeing* (5th ed.). Princeton, NJ: Princeton University Press.

Nicholls, J.G., Martin, A.R., Wallace, B.G., & Fuchs, P.A. (2007). *From Neuron to Brain* (4th ed.). Sunderland, Massachusetts: Sinauer Associates, Inc. (Chapter 19).

Smith, C.U.M. (2000). *Biology of Sensory Systems*. West Sussex, England: John Wiley & Sons, Ltd.

Chapter Seven

Nicholls, J.G., Martin, A.R., Wallace, B.G., & Fuchs, P.A. (2007). *From Neuron to Brain* (4th ed.). Sunderland, Massachusetts: Sinauer Associates, Inc. (Chapter 19).

Chapter Eight

Callaerts, P., Halder, G. & Gehring, W.J. (1997). Pax-6 in development and evolution. *Annu. Rev. Neurosci.* 20, 483–532.

de Oliveira, T., Pybus, O.G., Rambaut, A., Salemi, M., Cassol, S., Ciccozzi, M., Rezza, G., Gattinara, G.C., D'Arrigo, R., Amicosante, M., Perrin, Luc., Colizzi, V., Perno, C.F., & Benghazi Study Group (2006). HIV-1 and HCV sequences from Libyan outbreak. *Nature*, 444, 836-837.

Declan Butler (2007, July 26). Libyan ordeal ends: medics freed. *Nature,* 448, 398.

Halder, G.,Callaerts, P., & Gehring, W.J. (1995). Induction of Ectopic Eyes by Targeted Expression of the eyeless Gene in Drosophila. *Science*, 267, 1788-1792.

Land, M.F., & Nilsson, D-E. (2002). *Animal Eyes*. Oxford, England: Oxford University Press.

Parker, A. (2003). *In the Blink of an Eye: How Vision Sparked the Big Bang of Evolution*. New York: Basic Books.

Wadman, M. (2006, December 7). Molecular HIV evidence backs accused medics. *Nature*, 444, 658-659.

Zimmer, C. (2001). *Evolution: The Triumph of an Idea*. New York: HarperCollins Publishers.

Chapter Nine

Cina, M. (2002, June). Progress In Artificial Vision: The Dobelle Institute's Artificial Eye allows the blind to see. *Popular Mechanics*.

Wyatt, J. & Rizzo, J. (2006, June). Development of a Wireless First Generation Boston Retinal Implant Subretinal Prosthesis. *Proceedings of The Eye and the Chip - 2006 World Congress on Artificial Vision*, Detroit, MI.

Index

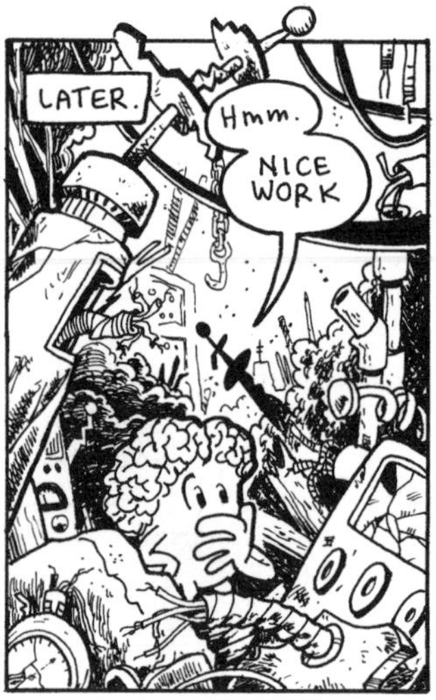
LATER.
Hmm.
NICE WORK